Grace

Grace

A China Diary, 1910–16

GRACE AND HARVEY ROYS

JUDY HOGAN, Editor

RESOURCE *Publications* · Eugene, Oregon

GRACE
A China Diary, 1910–16

Copyright © 2017 Judy Hogan. All rights reserved. Except for brief quotations in critical publications or reviews, no part of this book may be reproduced in any manner without prior written permission from the publisher. Write: Permissions, Wipf and Stock Publishers, 199 W. 8th Ave., Suite 3, Eugene, OR 97401.

Resource Publications
An Imprint of Wipf and Stock Publishers
199 W. 8th Ave., Suite 3
Eugene, OR 97401

www.wipfandstock.com

PAPERBACK ISBN: 978-1-5326-0939-8
HARDCOVER ISBN: 978-1-5326-0941-1
EBOOK ISBN: 978-1-5326-0940-4

Manufactured in the U.S.A.   FEBRUARY 8, 2017

By Permission from Simon and Schuster, Inc.: excerpts from Pearl Buck in China: Journey to the Good Earth by Hilary Spurling. Copyright by Hilary Spurling, 2010. All rights reserved.

By permission from Profile Books, London: excerpts from Burying the Bones: Pearl Buck in China (British title of Pearl Buck in China) by Hilary Spurling. World rights, excluding U.S. and Canada.

By Permission from Lensey Namioka: Excerpts from Autobiography: First 30 years, 1892–1921, Book I for Vol. 15, Chapter Six of The Complete Works of Yuen Ren Chao.

Early 20th Century Map of China, thanks to the University of Texas at Austin Library.

Photo of Judy Hogan by permission with Mary Susan Heath, photographer.

For my mother, Margaret Elizabeth Roys Stevenson [1912–2006]
whose birth is recorded in this diary,

and for my children,
Amy Fordham Cook, Timothy Michael Hogan,
and Virginia Lynn Hogan Neal

When we have passed a certain age, the soul of the child that we were and the souls of the dead from whom we spring come and bestow upon us in handfuls their treasures and their calamities, asking to be allowed to cooperate in the new sentiments which we are feeling and in which, obliterating their former image, we recast them in an original creation . . . We have to give hospitality, at a certain stage in our life, to all our relatives who have journeyed so far and gathered round us.

MARCEL PROUST, REMEMBRANCE OF THINGS PAST, MONCRIEFF TRANSLATION., VOL. II, 432

Contents

Illustrations | viii
Acknowledgments | xxxv

Introduction: Finding Grace | 1
Grace and Harvey Roys Diary: April 1910–February 1916
    1910 Diary | 17
    1911 Diary | 58
    1912 Diary | 83
    1913 Diary | 93
    1914 Diary | 107
    1915–1916 Diaries | 117
Epilogue | 122

Appendix A   The Legend of the Bleeding Heart | 131
Appendix B   Kiang Nan Government School in Nanking | 137
Appendix C   The History of Kuling, China by J. Arthur Duff and Essay by Julia Wilson | 141
Bibliography | 153
Index | 157

Map of China in the early Twentieth Century

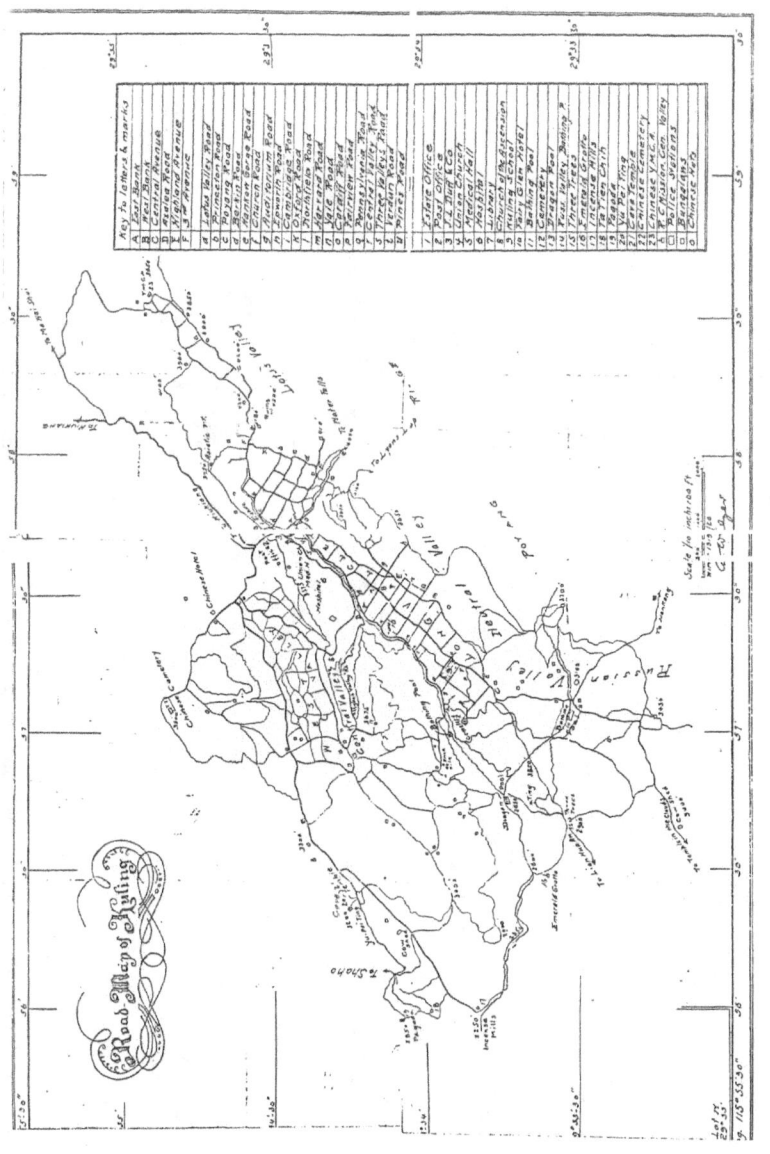

Map of Kuling Estate

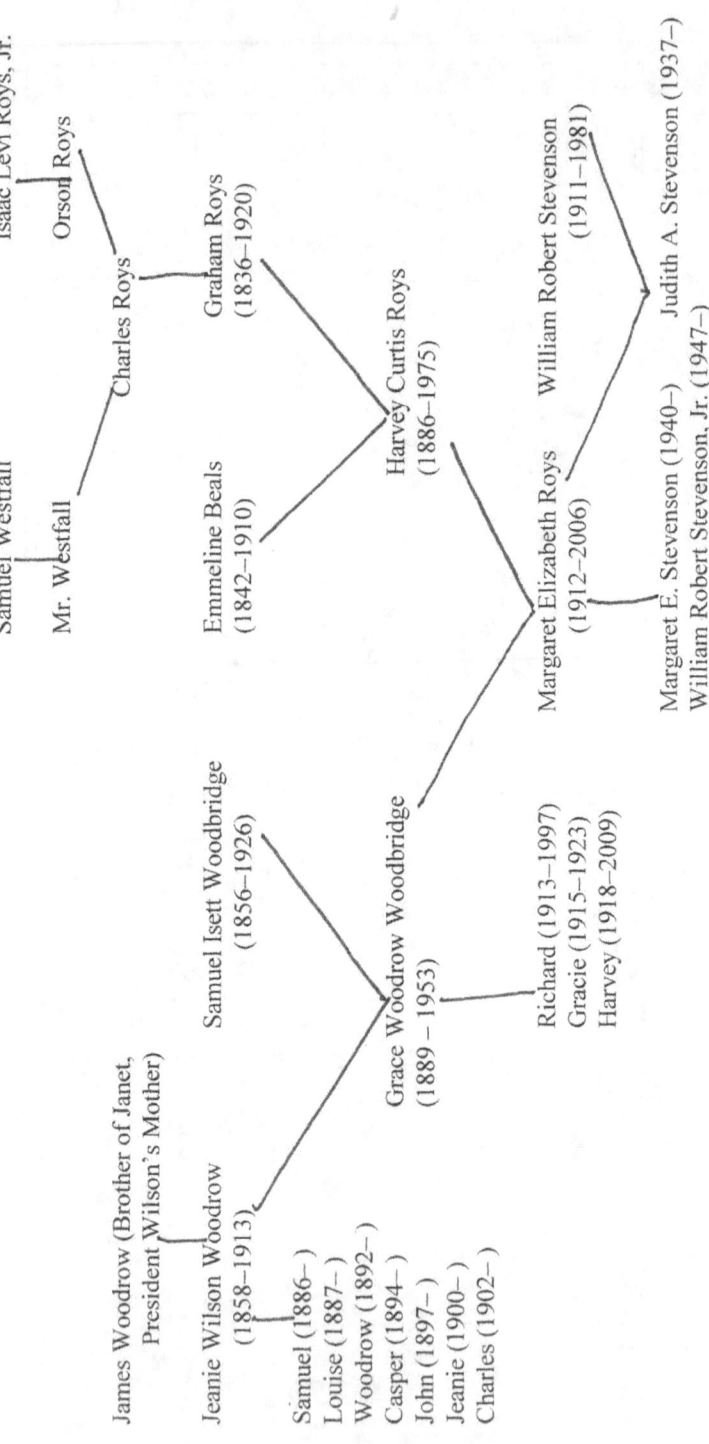

Samuel Isett Woodbridge Family, 1900, California. Grace is third from left, back row.

Grace Roys, 1911.

Harvey and Grace Roys, Kuling, 1912.

Harvey holding baby Margaret, 1912.

Baby Margaret in playpen, 1913.

Baby Margaret in Grace's sewing box, on side porch, 1913.

Baby Margaret in carriage, 1913.

Grace holding Margaret (second from left) with Mothers' group (ISC) that founded Hillcrest School. 1913.

Margaret Roys and Barbara Blackstone, summer, 1913, Kuling.

Margaret's first birthday party, July 1913, Kuling.

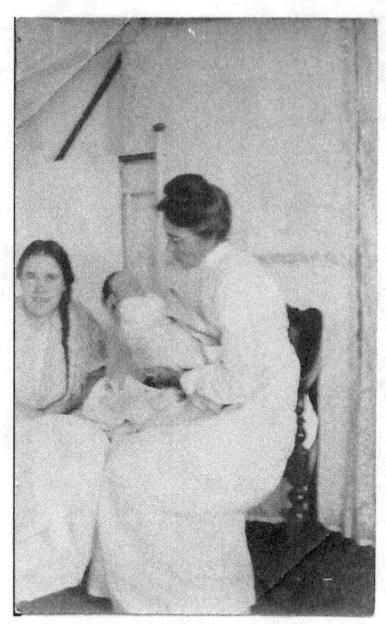

Grace with baby Dick and nurse, Nanking, 1913.

Grace and baby Dick, Nanking. 1913.

Roys baby with Chinese servant (amah)

Jeanie Woodbridge as a young teen, China, 1913.

Christmas 1913. Left to right: Grace, Jeanie, Margaret, Charlie, Samuel.
Nanking on their steps.

Grace with Dickie and Margaret, 1914.

Harvey with Dick, Grace, and Margaret, 1914.

Snow in China, February 1915. Grace probably on their steps.

Margaret, age three, Kuling, 1915

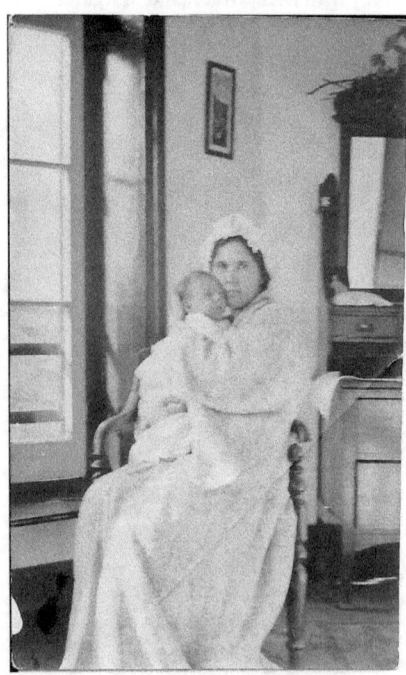

Grace with baby Gracie, September 1915.

Jeanie Woodbridge with baby Gracie, 1915.

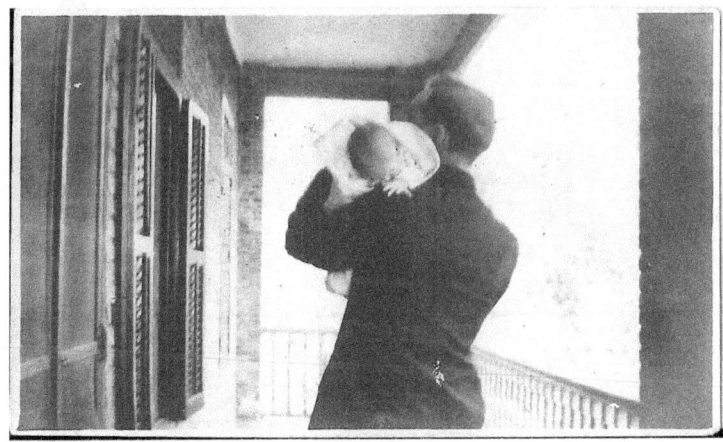

Harvey with baby Gracie, 1915.

Grace with baby Gracie, 1916.

Baby Gracie, 1916.

Dick, Gracie, and Margaret, 1917.

Grace with her daughters, Gracie and Margaret, 1917, China.

Grace with Gracie, Cedar Springs Farm, Michigan, 1917.

Graham Roys with Grace and Gracie, 1917.

Left to right: Graham Roys, Grace, Hatty holding Gracie.
front row: Dick, Margaret, 1917, furlough in Michigan.

Gracie, 1917, Michigan.

Samuel Isett Woodbridge and his second wife, Dr. Mary Newell, 1917.

Young Harvey with dog Teddy. 1919, China.

Harvey holding young Harvey, Grace holding young Gracie, Margaret and Richard, 1919.

Roys children: Dick, Gracie, Margaret, and Harvey, Christmas 1919.

Margaret and Teddy dog. 1920, China.

Margaret with two Chinese men, 1920.

Harvey with rifle and Chinese boy.

Harvey at a marketplace in China.

Harvey in China.

Grace in Norman, Oklahoma, with gladiolas, probably 1922 or 1923.

Grace and Harvey in the 1940s.

Left to right: Margaret Roys Stevenson, Grace Roys, Mrs. Mary Shannon.
Front row: Judy Stevenson, Esther Beth Shannon Rogers, Margaret Elaine Stevenson.
Norman, Oklahoma, 1944.

Grace with her granddaughter Denise, Richard's daughter, 1947.

Grace with baby Denise, 1947.

Left to right: Margaret Elaine Stevenson, David Roys, Dick Roys.
Front row: Mrs. Shannon, Judy Stevenson, Denise, Ruth Roys, Margaret Roys
Stevenson, Bill Stevenson. Norman, Oklahoma, 1952.

The house in Nanking where Grace and Harvey lived 1911–1921,
view from Hillcrest School.

Acknowledgments

I owe many people thanks for helping me with this project of editing and annotating the diary of Harvey Curtis Roys and Grace Woodrow Woodbridge Roys, missionaries in Nanking, China, who kept it 1910–1916. Edith Riggs Barakat, who was also born in China and spent some of her youth there, and her Chinese friend Ernie (Ye Gongping) helped me with information about China and the missionaries there. Emeritus Professor Lawrence Kessler, formerly of the University of North Carolina at Chapel Hill, read and commented on the manuscript twice, and Sam and Marie Hammond also read Grace and gave me good feedback. Sam also helped me with research and urged me to dig deeper and learn more about the people mentioned in the diary, and in the process of doing that, the missionary world of early twentieth century China opened up for me. Margaret Sullivan, who was also born in China, offered good feedback and suggested many books on China and the missionaries in the early 1900s. Nancy Henderson-James, whose early life was spent in Africa, with her missionary parents, understands how much those early experiences shape one's life ever after. My cousins Ruth Denise Roys Lowrie and Gini Roys Hebron helped by sharing their photographs of our family in China. Doug Williams stood by with computer help, and Anne Stone proofed the manuscript for me. I'm grateful to you all. This book would not be what it is now without your help and encouragement.

Introduction

Finding Grace

By age six one of the most important people in my life was Grace, my maternal grandmother, who, with her husband Harvey Roys, had been a missionary in China. Closely tied to Grace was another Grace, her daughter, born September 1915, who died at age eight in 1924 from heart complications following scarlet fever. Early in 1944 my mother moved my sister and me from Cameron, a small town in West Virginia, where my father, William Robert Stevenson, had been the minister of the Presbyterian Church, and where I had felt loved and protected on all sides, to Norman, Oklahoma. My father had volunteered to go into the Navy as a chaplain and was stationed in McAlister, not far from Norman, where my grandfather and grandmother Roys lived. Grandpa taught physics at the University of Oklahoma there.

Living with my grandparents at that time was also their younger son, Harvey, who was in medical school. Mother had taken a job with the YWCA on the O.U. campus. There were two naval bases in Norman, and housing was hard to find, so we lived three months in a small house with my grandparents and my uncle.

For the first time in my life I wasn't happy. My school teacher was harsh, threatening us all with being sent to the principal if we misbehaved. She was said to have a rubber hose with which she beat children. I was missing my father. Uncle Harvey, whom I at first had admired, had little sympathy for a six-year-old. My grandfather was impatient, too, when I complained about the long walk to school—about a mile. He said he'd walked farther than that when a child. Grandmother Grace startled and scared me when I encountered her as she was waking from a nap in the basement room. She told me she had dreamed she had gone to heaven to be with Gracie. She seemed sorry to have awakened.

Mother wasn't happy either. Her new-doctor brother Harvey told her she should have the lump in her breast removed immediately. Then he heard me complaining about my long school walks and how my legs ached, and he urged Mother to take me to a doctor, as I might have rheumatic fever. The diagnosis was confirmed by the local doctor. Somehow during this time, I identified myself with my mother's little sister, Grace. The family myth about Gracie was that she had been angelic. By the time she died, she had found her lord and savior. Gracie went straight to heaven. No one else could compete with her goodness, especially after she died.

By the time Mother found us a very small house to rent in May, conveniently across the street from a different and kinder elementary school, I had been diagnosed with rheumatic fever, and bed rest was ordered.

I lived in bed for a year. At first Mother arranged babysitters for me and my little sister, Margaret Elaine, so she could keep her new job, but she quit before long and stayed home with us. Gasoline was rationed, but every now and then Grace and Harvey drove across town to visit us. Grandmother gave us rabbits one Easter. For many mornings after that Mother had to chase them down, as they got out and into the neighbors' gardens. Finally one died, and she encouraged a little boy who was visiting me to take the other one home. I learned much later she was afraid to get rid of the rabbits openly because they had been her mother's gift to us. I didn't know then that Grace had bi-polar disease. This might explain why Mother didn't want to upset her mother.

During our Norman years, my ages six to nine, Grace was normal. Nor did I understand fully that, probably for everyone in the family, my illness now reminded them of their lost child and little sister, Gracie, whose death in 1924 had set off Grace's mental illness with a vengeance. Mother did tell me that she wanted to take good care of me because her little sister had died from a disease like mine. Both scarlet fever and rheumatic fever could set off heart complications.

By our adolescence both my sister and I felt hovering over us, in a half-conscious way, Mother's fear that we would become mentally ill, too. When I was fifteen and Margie twelve, Mother's other brother, Uncle Dick, took us and his family out to the Central State Mental Hospital to visit Grace. She played the piano, and he sang. She didn't seem sick to me, but she must have been to be in a mental hospital. Uncle Dick clearly loved her and treated her normally. By then we knew our mother's description of her mother by heart: "a genius, high-strung, highly sexed, artistic, and crazy."

Both Margie and I had some of these characteristics, enough so that we sensed Mother was watching for the craziness to come out. Mother always insisted that Grace's disease was schizophrenia, but her brothers, Richard and Harvey, who both became doctors, and Richard's son, David, who became a psychiatrist, have been certain it was manic-depressive or bi-polar disease. At the time of Grace's illness, in the twenties and thirties, and even in the fifties, bi-polar disease was sometimes diagnosed as schizophrenia.

The Roys family had returned from China in 1921 because Grace was not well (I have learned no details about this mental illness), but in 1926 she had to be hospitalized. My mother had to become a mother to Dick, who was only fifteen months younger, and to Harvey, nearly six years younger, when she was a young teenager.

Since 1922 they had been living in Norman, and my grandfather was teaching physics at Norman's new university. Oklahoma had only been a state since 1907, but the university had opened to students in 1892. Harvey taught there until 1957 and never had more than a Master's degree. Grace went back to school there and got a Bachelor of Arts in the late 1920s. My mother was in high school at the time. When her husband, Harvey, was teaching at O.U., Grace couldn't, as they didn't allow a husband and a wife to teach at the same time. When he taught two years in Ann Arbor, Grace did teach French at O.U.

FAMILY BACKGROUND

My exploration into Grandmother Grace's life began seriously when Mother gave me various family papers, among which was Grace and Harvey's China diary. I'm presenting it here, with my research and some information that came to me from my family about Grace. Grace Woodrow Woodbridge Roys was born in Chinkiang, a port city on the Yangtze, in China, on December 23, 1889, to Samuel Isett Woodbridge and Jeanie Wilson Woodrow, who was first cousin to the U.S. President Woodrow Wilson. Samuel and Jeanie came from Columbia, S.C. Samuel was an ordained minister and went as a Southern Presbyterian missionary to China in 1882. His fiancée followed him a year later. He met her in Yokohama, Japan, where they were married. They had eight children, my grandmother being their third child and second daughter.

Grace's mother, Jeanie, born September 8, 1858, had had a good education at Augusta Female Seminary in Virginia. She graduated there in 1879. In 1871, at age 13, she had been taken by her parents to Germany. She could speak French and German. In China Jeanie helped Samuel Isett with his missionary work, described as "evangelical and literary." They published a magazine in Chinese, which they founded in 1902, called *The Chinese Christian Intelligencer*, which became widely distributed in China. A Chinese editor, Cheng Chun-sheng, worked with the Woodbridges. Between 1882 and 1902 they lived in Chinkiang, in the same mission compound with the Sydenstrickers, also Southern Presbyterian missionaries, whose daughter Pearl (later she married Lossing Buck) was three years younger than my grandmother. Both Pearl Buck and my grandmother spoke Chinese fluently. Both were also sent back to the U.S. for their high school educations. My grandmother attended a boarding school in Fredericksburg, Virginia.

The part of the story best documented by the little five-year diary begins in April 1910, when my maternal grandfather, Harvey Curtis Roys, went out to China, as part of a YMCA program. Apparently during this period, the YMCA was recruiting students through The Student Volunteer Movement for Foreign Missions.

Their volunteers sought to "evangelize the world in one generation."[1] Between 1888 and 1919 many of the student volunteers sent overseas to China went into North American Protestant compounds. It seems likely that Harvey was one of these volunteers since he went to China under YMCA sponsorship.[2]

Harvey was born on July 5, 1886, was almost twenty-four when he left, and had a Master's degree in physics from the University of Michigan in Ann Arbor. He began the diary just before he left his home in Grand Rapids. He had been born when his mother was forty-four and his father, fifty. Harvey's mother was ill when he left, and by July 1910, she had died, apparently of cancer. He didn't learn of her death until a month later. News to China traveled slowly then, by ship across the Pacific Ocean.

The Grand Rapids house of Harvey, his father Graham, and his mother Emmeline (Beales) Roys is still standing. Harvey carved his initials in the

---

1. Hersey, *The Call*, 97.
2. Ibid., 94.

kitchen doorpost. The house was built the same year that Harvey was born. Harvey's father, Graham, owned a whip- and harness-making business in Grand Rapids. This was Graham's first marriage. He was seventy-four in 1910, born in 1836. This was Emmeline's second marriage. Harvey had a step-brother, Fred, and a step-sister, Hatty (Harriet), from Emmeline's first marriage. Emmeline Beales was born July 29, 1842, so she would have turned sixty-eight in 1910.

HARVEY ROYS ARRIVES IN CHINA

Harvey left by train from Grand Rapids on April 13, 1910, then took ship on April 19 from San Francisco, and arrived in Shanghai on May 13. He traveled by train to Nanking, where he was to teach at the Kiang Nan Provincial College run by the Chinese government. An American teaching physics in a Chinese college was a sign of the changing times in China. Missionaries, foreign businesses, and the Chinese government were all bringing new ideas, scientific methods, and inventions into China. The Nanyang Exposition in 1910 had many Western technological exhibits, including those involving electricity, still new in China.

Harvey roomed with missionary families, first at the Russells' and then at the Beebes'. He began Chinese lessons immediately, but even though in the five-year diary there are references to his study of Chinese, he was never as fluent as my grandmother. He continued to work for the YMCA until 1913, when he was named a missionary for the Board of Missions of the Methodist Episcopal (Northern) Church. Subsequently, until the family left China in 1921, he taught physics at the University of Nanking, which was run by the Presbyterians, the Methodists, both Southern and Northern, and the Disciples of Christ. In China they all worked together.

Harvey met Grace on May 24, 1910, not long after he arrived in Nanking. She was twenty and had already suffered one nervous breakdown, following her father's refusal to let her marry someone with whom she had fallen in love. As is obvious in photographs of Grace at this age, she is very beautiful, slim, with a shapely, buxom figure. In the 1940s, when she was in her fifties and plumper, she was still strikingly beautiful. She was teaching in 1910 at what became the Ginling College for Women in Nanking.[3]

---

3. The name Ginling College was adopted in 1913, when my grandmother was no longer teaching. She was teaching at a girls' school in 1910, perhaps the one run by the Methodists. When the college officially opened, it was supported by five American

INTRODUCTION

This school was eventually closely affiliated with the University of Nanking. Her parents had been living in Shanghai since 1902, and she was boarding with the Blackstone family in Nanking. She and Harvey saw each other frequently that summer when the young people within the missionary community got together to play tennis, to visit Chinese monuments, to attend the big Nanyang Exposition of 1910, or to have dinner together at one of the married families' homes. On August 27, 1910, when they were both at the resort in Kuling, they had reached "an understanding." This probably means that they had exchanged love vows but not told anyone else yet.

CHINA IN 1910

By 1902, after the Boxer Rebellion was quelled by Western powers' interference and the Empress Dowager Cixi deposed, a greater number of missionaries flooded into China than there had been before. By 1910 China had more missionaries than any other of the world's less developed countries in Asia and Africa[4], and a huge number were Protestants from the United States, both married (often newly), as well as single men and women. Many American churches had missionary societies, whose members were mainly women, which raised money for mission work abroad to supplement the funds provided by the various Protestant denominations and the Catholic Church.[5]

---

mission boards: Northern Baptist, Disciples of Christ, Northern and Southern Methodists, and Northern Presbyterians. The *University of Nanking Magazine*, May 1910, 27, reports: "In 1886 Miss Ella C. Shaw came to Nanking and the following year built the Adeline Smith Home and School. The School for Girls is now under the direction of Miss Laura M. White. Additional land and buildings have been acquired and extensive improvements are underway with the idea of developing a college for women. College work is already being done and there are at present 95 pupils of different grades in attendance. This is under the Methodist Episcopal Mission." Miss White was also Corresponding Secretary, Christian Endeavor in China, served with the Christian Literature Society, was editor, *Women's Messenger*, and worked with Women's Work. CRI, 512 (CRI, used frequently, stands for Chinese Recorder Index). There is no evidence that Grace taught anywhere after she married Harvey at the end of 1910. The Methodists also started the University of Nanking. In 1910 all the Christian boys' schools in the city were united to form the University of Nanking. See also entries for April 7, 1911; October 28, and November 27, 1913.

    4. Kessler, *Jiangyin Mission*, 43.

    5. Beaver, *American Protestant Women*, 110.

INTRODUCTION

In the early years of missionary activity in China, from the 1860s until after the Boxer Rebellion, superstitions about missionaries had run high, and they were often accused of being "foreign devils." During the Boxer Rebellion, which the Empress Cixi had instigated, many Chinese Christians were killed, though few missionaries were.[6]

Grace was eleven in 1900 during the Boxer Rebellion, and by a quirk, the missionaries in the Kiangsu province, where she and her family lived in Chinkiang, were protected by a clever administrator who received an order to *exterminate* foreigners and changed the word to *protect*. The Dowager Empress had used the secret "Boxer" society to kill off foreigners. Allied nations sent a force and took control. The Dowager fled.[7]

By 1902 the work of the missionaries in setting up schools, hospitals, and generally bringing into China more teachers of scientific information and new technologies ceased to face serious opposition from the government. The power of the Empress Dowager was gone. She had believed that the telegraph poles were built with the blood of babies and "a dead baby's tongue was required at the top of each pole to transmit the message".[8]

The early U.S. Presbyterian missionaries to China arrived in the 1850s. Rev. Elias B. Inslee had been in China under the Presbyterian Board of Foreign Missions first in 1856. After the Civil War he offered to go back as a Southern Presbyterian, the church having split, as did the Methodists, by that time. He settled with his family in Hangchow.[9] The next three Southern Presbyterian missionaries were Rev. Matthew Hale Houston, of Virginia, and Rev. Benjamin Helm[10] and Rev. John Linton Stuart,[11] both

---

6. Woodbridge, *Fifty Years*, 36.

7. Ibid., 99.

8. Ibid., 72.

9. At some point Inslee had a falling out with the Presbyterian Board of Foreign Missions and continued on his own. After the Civil War, he appealed to be taken under the care of the Executive Committee of the Southern Presbyterian Church (U.S.), and the church seemed to feel that God had thus called him to "enter that empire of darkness and sun and take an honorable position among other branches of the Christian Church in diffusing a knowledge of the gospel through the dark-minded multitudinous race." Mr. Inslee and his family were sent to China in the fall of 1866. He was in China until 1871, and in 1867 he started the station of Hangchow." From *Union Seminary Magazine*, V 67 (1866) 56. CRI, 235.

10. Helm, Benjamin, Rev., One of the first Southern Presbyterian missionaries in China, 1868–1878. Woodbridge, *Fifty Years*, 33.

11. Stuart, John Linton, Rev. Dr., was an early Southern Presbyterian missionary, 1868–1913. He was the father of Rev. Dr. John Leighton Stuart, Rev. Dr. Warren Houston

of Kentucky. Dr. James Woodrow (Jeanie's father and Grace's grandfather) was Treasurer of the Executive Committee of Foreign Missions and saw these three men off from New York in 1868. They traveled by the steamer *Alaska* to Panama, crossed the isthmus by train, boarded the *Colorado* for San Francisco, thence on the *Great Republic* to Yokohama, Japan, then the *Oregonian* to Shanghai. By this time permanent treaties between China and other countries had opened several ports along the Yangtze River to trade. Foreign merchants were allowed to reside only at these ports, but missionaries were granted the right to preach the gospel in all parts of China. Earlier the Mandarins (government officials) had "used every artifice, both open and covert, to debar the missionary."[12]

Another early missionary was the British Rev. Edward S. Little, who managed in 1897 to buy land at Kuling in the Lushan Mountains up the Yangtze River from Nanking. Such a land purchase was very difficult to arrange at the time. He then established a place where missionaries of all denominations, along with other foreigners, could retreat in the very hot summers, when malaria, bubonic plague, and other dangerous diseases were common at the lower altitudes near the coast.[13] The Duff family were the first Americans to settle there and set up a shop and hotel, where all kinds of provisions became available. They raised cattle at a time when meat and milk were not consumed in China.[14] Edward Little discovered a "strange fruit" growing in the Kuling area, the kiwi, and its propagation outside China would lead to a billion-dollar industry world-wide.[15]

The missionaries also brought the English language, and in this period, young Chinese graduates of missionary schools often went to America for further education. It was a time of great optimism among the missionaries for the "good" they could do for the Chinese. One of these optimistic missionaries, Edward Huntington Smith, who arrived in China at the end of 1901—with his new wife, Grace—wrote to his grandmother in January 1908:

> What changes in China where there was not a single Christian, and now the country is becoming studded with churches and a strong church has come into being, with preachers, pastors,

---

Stuart, and Dr. David T. Stuart. CRI, 459.
12. Woodbridge, *Fifty Years*, 36.
13. Duff, "History of Kuling," Appendix C., 145. CRI, 287.
14. Ibid., Appendix C, 150.
15. Ibid., Appendix C, 149.

schools, newspapers, and more changes than I could enumerate in a book ... I often wish I could live to see what great advances there will be at the end of this century. For you know I believe that the world will by that time begin to follow the teachings of Christ as never before. I expect to see the church doing more for the sad, weary men, women, and children than she is now. I expect to see a great Christian nation in China, in India, and Japan. Africa will be a great land. Not that I expect there will be no sorrow or evil or wickedness–but a great deal more of loving kindness and tender mercy and nations will not be the cruel tricky powers to be dreaded.[16]

REVOLUTION COMES TO CHINA

Pearl Buck, looking back, comments that her parents "reflected the spirit of their generation, which was of an America bright with the glory of a new nation, rising united from the ashes of war, and confident of power enough to save the world. Meantime they had no conception of the fact that they were in reality helping to light a revolutionary fire, the height of which we still have not seen, nor can foresee."[17]

Samuel Woodbridge quotes the Chinese editor who worked with him on *The Chinese Christian Intelligencer*, Mr. Cheng Chun-sheng:[18] "Here is a lighted lamp. The chimney, whose texture is flimsy and imperfect, is very hot, but the atmosphere of the room apparently is of even temperature and nothing happens. But suppose you suddenly throw open the window and let in a rush of cold air! The chimney will probably be smashed into pieces." Samuel adds: "Three factors contributed to the downfall of the Imperial Government of China in the year 1911: Misgovernment, unrest of the Chinese people, and the influx of new ideas."[19]

---

16. Bishop, *Family Letters*, 26. The letters of Rev. Edward Huntington Smith and his wife Grace were edited and published by their daughter, Eunice Smith Bishop. Rev. Smith was with the American Board of Commissioners for Foreign Missions. He was a missionary in Southern China from 1901. CRI, 441.

17. Buck, *Several Worlds*, 4.

18. Mr. Chen, Chuen Shang, or, according to Samuel I. Woodbridge, Cheng, Chun-sheng, was the assistant editor of the *Chinese Christian Intelligencer*, edited by Woodbridge. He is identified as a Presbyterian in *Woman's Work* v. 32 (Jan. 1917), 16. CRI, 81.

19. Woodbridge, *Fifty Years*, 79.

INTRODUCTION

Lawrence Kessler writes how the Chinese imperial state, after lasting two millennia, collapsed in 1911 because of "Western imperialism, the rising tide of new ideas, and its own anachronistic behavior." He says that for the missionaries this was a time of great promise. There were 2900 Protestant missionaries in 1915, whereas there had been 200 in 1890. Mission stations had doubled to 675, converts quadrupled; by 1915 mission stations had $25 million in property.[20]

In effect, without fully understanding what the results would be of their bringing to the Chinese quite a different way of seeing the world, the missionaries helped set off revolutions. Even before the Sun Yat-sen Revolution in 1911, there had been disaffection with the Manchu government run by the Qing line of emperors. A Christian convert, Hong Xinquan, after reading some Christian tracts, had a vision in which he saw Jesus as an elder brother. He "[persuaded] people of his spiritual powers." After studying with an American Southern Baptist teacher Isaacher Roberts, he and an early convert of his formed a Society of God Worshipers in the rugged area of eastern Guangxi province. He drew more and more supporters, rich and poor, and by 1850 had 20,000 followers. In 1851 he declared himself Heavenly King of the Taiping Tianguo (= great peace), commonly known as the Taiping. The new Taiping army fought and killed primarily Manchus. Then the Taiping ruled in Nanking until 1864 from the Old Ming dynasty imperial palace.[21]

Other disturbances and insurrections occurred, against the "foreign devils," and against the Manchus, who had defeated the Ming dynasty and had required Chinese men to wear the queue or pigtail as a sign of their subservience.[22]

In the late 1800s there were many Chinese abroad, often treated like slaves: laying railroad ties, working in guano pits, harvesting cotton and sugar, most in the U.S., South America, Cuba, the Caribbean, and other countries in Southeast Asia. Others in exile had prospered by opening small businesses.[23] Sun Yat-sen gained their support. After the railroads came through in the new century in China, wars broke out about their jurisdictions between the empire and the local provinces.[24] By the time

20. Kessler, *Jiangyin Mission*, 43–44.
21. Spence, *Modern China*, 172–5.
22. Ibid., 29.
23. Ibid., 208–14.
24. Ibid., 250–53.

Sun Yat-sen's followers started their successful revolution, there were many groups, secret societies, and provincial governments hostile to the Emperor. Although within the government there were efforts at reform, bringing in foreign science teachers, training armies and navies in the Western mode, building railroads, the reforms were not happening fast enough to satisfy all the groups hostile to their Manchu governors.[25]

Sun Yat-sen (1866–1925) was a Christian and a medical doctor, who had been educated by missionaries in Hawaii and gone to medical school in Hong Kong. The British wouldn't let him practice medicine in their domains, and the Chinese didn't take him seriously. He became focused on getting rid of the Manchu emperors and setting up a democracy. His early attempts to stage uprisings had failed. By the fall of 1911 there was enough support, money, and arms to win a revolution. Soldiers in the imperial army deserted and joined the revolutionaries. Students also participated. Many of Harvey's students left to fight. He and Grace left Nanking when the fighting came close. The final battles of this 1911 Revolution occurred in and around Nanking.[26]

Once Sun Yat-sen returned to China in December 1911, he was elected president by the assembly of sixteen provinces, but he preferred that his colleague Yuan Shika be president. When the mother of the emperor accepted a settlement from the new regime, the two-thousand-year-old empire closed. The Chinese could now govern themselves, but they had no experience in doing so. Yuan Shika lacked military power and organizing skills. China sent 100,000 Chinese to help the allies in World War I, but those countries didn't help the Chinese leaders when they were threatened by the Japanese. There followed a period of political insecurity, and by 1920 there was a nucleus for a Chinese Communist government. The new government had tried and failed to balance the central and local governments. Political power then flowed out to the elites in the provinces—both rural and urban—and hundreds of military leaders emerged as power brokers.[27]

By the mid-1920s the Communists were battling Chiang Kai-Shek for control of the government.[28] Life became much more difficult for the foreign missionaries in the 1920s and 1930s, and many left. Some did hang

25. Ibid., 226.
26. Ibid., 262–3.
27. Ibid., 267–8.
28. Ibid., 269–70

on until the Communists finally took complete control in 1949.[29] A few remained into the early 1950s, when they were forced to leave China.

MISSIONARY LIFE IN 1910.

Missionaries, for the most part, lived separately from the Chinese people. Only rarely do Grace and Harvey socialize with the Chinese, and then it is usually with other faculty at the colleges. When my mother was a child, her parents had five Chinese servants living in their basement. One of them was the children's nursemaid or *amah*. The cook was taught to prepare Western food, and the family had Chinese food only once a week. My mother, however, would go to the basement and eat Chinese food with the servants. These servants were relied on heavily and trusted implicitly. When Grace and Harvey went off on a holiday to Shanghai, they left Grace's teenage sister and brother in charge, but the servants, though not mentioned, would likely be the true caretakers. They are rarely mentioned in the diary.

The missionaries brought their culture with them and kept up its rituals. They served tea and tiffin (lunch) to each other and played tennis. In Nanking, missionary mothers started a school for their children, but all foreigners were welcome to send their children there. My mother and her brother Dick went to this Hillcrest School in the primary grades. Other schools were set up within China for foreign children of high school age.

At Shanghai American School some missionary children did their secondary school work, and in Nanking, daughters of missionaries could also go to Ginling, despite its being primarily for Chinese girls. The China Inland Mission or CIM (a non-denominational Protestant British group) also had a school, 1909–1915, in Kuling, where Grace was teaching in the summer of 1910.[30]

Grace and Harvey's social life revolved largely around the faculty at the colleges and especially the Methodist and Presbyterian missionaries in Nanking. The Nanking Association, which welcomed all foreigners in Nanking, met once a month for a meal and a program, sometimes with as many as a hundred and fifty people present.

Harvey early acquired a ricksha and the boy to pull it around. He also had a bicycle. There were few cars, but occasionally carriages were hired for traveling to and from the train station. Some mission stations on the coast

---

29. Riggs, *China Memoir*, 67.
30. *China Inland Mission, Schools*, Mundus.ac.uk.cats/4/904

INTRODUCTION

had motor boats, and the Chinese used boats with sails (junks). To reach Kuling, my grandparents took the train, then went up the Yangtze River on a boat. After staying overnight at a town by the river, they were carried up the mountain by sedan chair to this resort in the mountains for missionaries. By April 1908 there was train service between Nanking and Shanghai. This train also stopped in Soochow, not far from Shanghai, where Grace was taken during her breakdown late in 1910.

Besides setting up churches and schools, missionaries set up hospitals with highly qualified doctors. One of the ways that Western missionaries won over the Chinese was by curing their sick and helping the very poor. Samuel Isett tells this story:

> [A] woman had tried to poison herself with opium in order to come back and haunt her husband forever. Her husband got worried and called a woman missionary. A crowd followed. The missionary told the crowd to stand back, took the woman off the floor, where dying people were put so the bed wouldn't become taboo from a ghost hovering and bringing bad luck to the family. Then the missionary assessed that the wife had overdosed on opium, ordered them to give her mustard and water, take her outside, and walk her around. A new atmosphere was established. The missionary had done a "good deed." The woman lived and the report went out that the missionary had cured a case beyond the skill of a Chinese doctor.[31]

In short, when Harvey arrived in China, the missionaries were welcomed by the Chinese government, were providing church services in both Chinese and English, as well as running schools and hospitals, providing translations of the Bible into Chinese, and publishing newspapers like *The Chinese Christian Intelligencer*, which Grace's father, Samuel Isett Woodbridge, produced with his Chinese colleague.[32] The missionaries had also imported their own culture and lived in many ways like their counterparts in the United States and England.

---

31. Woodbridge, *Fifty Years*, 143–4.
32. Ibid., 205.

Grace and Harvey Roys Diary
April 1910–February 1916

1910 Diary

April 9, 1910. "As thy day, so shall thy strength be." [Deut.33:25][1] Commenced this book. Back to Ann Arbor.[2] My heart is full. Thank God for such friends. God-speeds for safe journey to China are given me on every hand. The day was beautiful.

April 10, 1910. Home[3] to Mother. Poor Mother, she has suffered much, but her faith is great. The doctor says she is better. I pray that she may live to rejoice with me in any little good thing I may do in China.[4]

April 11, 1910. Mother suffered greatly, but it was all physical pain. The doctor says he will help her. I stayed with Mother most of the day.

---

1. Deut. 33:25 reads: "As thy days, so shall thy strength be."
2. Harvey had recently graduated from the University of Michigan in Ann Arbor. His home was in Grand Rapids, where he must have been spending time. Harvey kept the diary first. See Introduction.
3. Grand Rapids.
4. Harvey's mother, Emmeline Beales Roys, was born July 29, 1842. She died apparently of cancer July 14, after Harvey left for China.

April 12, 1910. The doctor came in the morning. Mother was better today. Mother and the baby[5] took most of my time. I feel my weakness for little things seem to interfere with my "leaning on Christ."[6]

April 13, 1910. Mother slept better than usual. She bears the parting well when I leave at 1: o'clock. Greetings at Coldwater–a beautiful Christian home.

April 14, 1910. The day begins in their home with family worship. My love for Helen[7] grows. Chicago at 4 P.M. Leave at 10:45. God blesses me continually.

April 15, 1910. I can neither read nor write with any satisfaction on a train, but my thoughts run riot. The trip through Iowa and Neb. [Nebraska] is very uninteresting.

April 16, 1910. Met Cousin Abby and her mother at Cheyenne.[8] Abby is a noble girl. Wyoming is interesting. I get much comfort from a little book "With Christ."[9]

April 17, 1910. A Sunday just like other days. It's easy to forget the Sabbath when its observance is not forced upon you. Nevada is a dreary state.

April 18, 1910. Praise God for his great goodness. If we could only feel and practice the "brotherhood of men" our lives would be full of happiness. Got acquainted with some passengers today, and sorry I had not before.

April 19, 1910. Off for China on the *S.S. China*.[10] I feel now as if I was really started. I thank God continually for his wonderful care of me.

---

5. Helen Higgins-Schmidt, Harvey's older step-sister Harriet's child. Hatty was Emmeline's daughter from her previous marriage. Hatty and her husband stayed in the house with Harvey's father until he died in 1920, then continued to live there until 1954, when Mr. Higgins died.

6. This may be a reference to "Leaning on the Everlasting Arms," a hymn by Showalter published in 1887. Showalter, Wikipedia.

7. This Helen was evidently his sweetheart and lived in Coldwater, MI. From there Harvey took the train to Chicago, then on to San Francisco.

8. How exactly Cousin Abby is related to Harvey isn't clear in the genealogy after 1911 diary entries. Ella Roys Gore is Graham Roys's sister. Perhaps Abby is her daughter.

9. Probably by Andrew Murray (1828–1917), published in N.Y., 1890s.

10. The ship journey to China took three and half weeks. The *S.S. China* sailed from San Francisco. The main communication between China and the U.S. is by ship.

April 20, 1910. "Water, water everywhere"! I haven't been sick but I have not felt very good. Weather good. 336 miles at noon.[11]

April 21, 1910. When I stop and consider the vast expanse of the Pacific, my faith grows. There are some fine people aboard. Appetite good. Weather fair to cloudy. 351 miles 12 to 12 M.

April 22, 1910. Another glorious day. 360 miles at noon. I wrote a letter and read a little today.

April 23, 1910. Struck trade winds–rough. All on board felt a little off. 361 miles. Slept in my steamer chair most of the day.

April 24, 1910. A quiet Sunday. No service on board. Felt better today. Sails help out–368 miles. 304 to Honolulu.

April 25, 1910. Up at 5 A.M. Land in sight. A glorious day in Honolulu. Away to sea again at 5: PM. (Thank God for such beautiful spots.)

April 26, 1910. A beautiful day. Some very pleasant conversations. There are good people everywhere. 254 miles out of Honolulu.

April 27, 1910. Up at 4:AM to see Halley's comet. Another beautiful day. Had a good visit with a '07 M [Michigan] coed. NW 326 Miles. Saw birds, flying fish.

April 28, 1910. Another pleasant day. New acquaintances. A good sing on deck in the evening. Talk with Chinese lady. 336 miles–N–75–48' W. Very smooth. Warm and beautiful.

April 29, 1910. Reached the 180th Meridian about 1: PM. Friday until then–Sat the rest of the day. The sea is like a big

April 30, 1910. mirror and nearly as smooth. Contests on deck–turned out well. I had to run the thing but I believe they all enjoyed it. A glorious sun set. 321 miles.[12]

Telegrams and cablegrams weren't yet used in 1910. S.S. *China* was built in 1889 for the Pacific Mail Steamship Company, San Francisco-Yokohama, and Hong Kong service. S.S. *China* is in the Atlantic Transport Line.

  11. Apparently the number of miles the ship traveled from one noon to the next day's noon is information available to the passengers, and Harvey keeps track.

  12. They crossed the International Date Line, making Friday change to Saturday and

May 1, 1910. 326 miles. A pleasant Sunday–but no service on board. Most of the people gathered in the parlor to sing hymns after breakfast.

May 2, 1910. Rougher. I had to keep rather quiet. Took a nap and missed the pillow fight. 315 miles.

May 3, 1910. A pleasant day. Mrs. Dr. Kay read to me from "The Desire of the Ages" by Mrs. E.G. White.[13] 305 Miles.

May 4, 1910. The roughest we have had it. I stayed on deck but felt rather mean all day. 309 Miles.

May 5, 1910. Still very cool but not so rough. Read most of the day in "The Calling of Dan Matthews" by H.B. Wright.[14] 278 Miles.

May 6, 1910. We are all anxious to see Japan. Everybody in good spirits. 341 Miles.

May 7, 1910. Slightly foggy. Yokohama at 1:PM.[15] Went to Tokyo. Jinrikisha[16] ride to YMCA. Went to home of Mr. Clinton[17] and had a very pleasant time. Back to boat at 11 PM.

May 8, 1910. Sunday. Boat left at 10:AM. Land in sight much of the day. Before leaving, took a long ride in Yokohama. Talk with Miss Linge[18] on Religion.

April 29 to April 30. The entries are continuous.

13. Ellen Gould Harmon White, 1827–1915, was a founder of the Seventh Day Adventists.

14. Harold Bell Wright, 1872–1944. "In 1909, pastors across America were incensed by his third book, *The Calling of Dan Matthews*, which told the story of a young preacher who, like Wright, resigned from the ministry in order to retain his integrity." Article on Wright in Wikipedia.

15. The first stop is Japan. Yokohama was where Samuel Isett and Jeanie, Grace's parents, were married September 8, 1883, upon her arrival. She left China in late 1912 and died at Johns Hopkins, January 22, 1913. CRI, 529.

16. Jinricksha = ricksha. A small, oriental two-wheeled carriage drawn by one or two men.

17. This could be Jacob Mancil Clinton, who worked with YMCA in China (1904–11).

18. Miss Linge is unidentified.

May 9, 1910. Kobe. Went ashore about 11:AM. Went to Falls and park. Took several pictures. Japanese life is very interesting. First impressions (doll play) are forgotten.[19] They are workers.

May 10, 1910. Very foggy. We have to move very slowly. We have found considerable sunshine however. "Bulow"[20] passed us about 9:30. Anchored off some lighthouse point.

May 11, 1910. Nagasaki.–Temples, narrow streets, stores, parks, but the prettiest of all was the bay and hills. It was a wonderful sight to see the men, women and children coaling our boat.

May 12, 1910. No land in sight. Rain and fog all day. Anchored about 9:P.M. Spent day reading and playing games. Packed trunk. All ready to go ashore.

19. By "doll play" Harvey probably means that he had believed the Japanese to be delicate like dolls. He sees that they work hard, which breaks his stereotype.

20. This *Bulow* is a ship carrying food from U.S. for famine relief in China. This aid is another reason (besides the Opium Wars, when Britain, France, Germany had fought with China for the right to trade for opium) why the Americans were liked better than the Western European countries. Lilian C. Williams describes the Great Famine of 1911: "Relief was undertaken by the Famine Relief Committee in Shanghai and Nanking . . . .the suffering was appalling . . . The students of the University [of Nanking] gave up all their meals on Sundays to send the food to the starving . . . Doctors, teachers, students, everybody joined in a desperate fight to save the situation until the harvest . . . 40,000 live outside the city wall in small huts . . . One family, a father and mother and three small children, came boldly and built a straw hut on vacant land belonging to the University. The father was given some work to do making shoe soles and was paid enough at the end of the day to furnish the family with a good meal. The joy of that brave little family as they gathered around the little black cooking pot and ate their evening meal of coarse rice will never be forgotten by those us who witnessed it." Williams, *Yesterdays in China*, 28. She taught History to higher grades at Hillcrest in 1916. Her children attended Hillcrest, and by 1920 Walter Williams was in fifth grade, Richard was in third grade. Dorothy and Mary Williams had been in seventh-eighth grade in 1916. Hillcrest annual, 49. CRI, 519.

May 13, 1910. Jean's birthday [Added later][21] The yellow sea, the Yang-tse-kiang.[22] Letter from Mr. D.W. Lyon[23] in which I am invited to stay with him while in Shanghai. A beautiful home. Ball game with the boys.

May 14, 1910. Shopping in Shanghai, a modern city in many ways. 12:45 AM. Off for Nanking by rail. Dr. Whitmore[24] & Mr. Carver[25] met me at the train. Stayed overnight with Dr. Whitmore.

May 15, 1910. Vaccinated. Sunday breakfast at Dr. Whitmore's. Chinese Church in AM. English service at University [of Nanking] in PM.[26]

21. Jean Woodrow Woodbridge, born May 13, 1900, was the seventh Woodbridge child and Grace's younger sister, named for their mother, also Jean. She's mentioned in the Hillcrest Yearbooks for 1915-16: "Oct. 15, 1915: Jeanie and Charlie Woodbridge leave. We are all in the dumps.", 24. She married Arthur Duff in 1926.

22. The sea here looks yellow, but the Yellow Sea itself is north of Shanghai. This is the East China Sea where the Yangtze River empties into the Pacific. Shanghai is the major port for arriving and departing missionaries.

23. Dr. David Willard Lyon, M.D., a Presbyterian, was with the YMCA in Shanghai and founded the student Y there. He was in China, 1895-1930. He was on the China Continuation Committee and the Christian Endeavor in China, CRI, 299.

24. Dr. Frank Beach Whitmore was serving as General Secretary of Nanking Intercollegiate YMCA as well as carrying on daily medical clinics, teaching in the government schools, conducting a night school, teaching Bible classes, etc. *University of Nanking Magazine*, May 1910, 30.

25. David June Carver, of Nashville, TN, arrived at the Kiang Nan School to teach English a few years before Harvey, and he was very popular with the students, according to Yuen Ren Chao's *Autobiography: First 30 Years*, 424-425. An American physics teacher, Mr. Charles, left in 1910. Perhaps Harvey was his replacement. David J. Carver, B.A., Richmond College, 1905; M.A. from Richmond, 1906. He taught philosophy and psychology at Kiang Nan Provincial College in Nanking, China, for four years following his graduation from college. When he returned to the United States, he earned his doctorate in psychology from Johns Hopkins in 1920 and became an importer of Chinese art. He was also a founder of the North Baltimore YMCA. Because of his lifelong admiration for the university and his interest in both China and medicine, Dr. Carver established a scholarship fund for Asian students at the School of Medicine in 1957. There is also a professorship named for him. "David J. Carver Professorship in Medicine," on Johns Hopkins University website.

26. Both Chinese and English languages were used among the American missionaries. They all had to learn Chinese. They said prayers with servants in Chinese, and native Christians held their services in Chinese. Those who spoke English had another foreign service usually Sunday afternoon. The Bible and other religious books were being translated into Chinese by the new converts. The translation of spiritual ideas came largely from words used in Buddhist and Taoist thought. The question of the right word to use for *God* divided the missionary body for 50 years according to Samuel Isett Woodbridge. See Woodbridge, *Fifty Years*, 54.

Decide to live at Dr. Russell's[27] for two weeks. There are some fine people at Nanking.

May 16, 1910. First day at school. Only assigned lessons. I saw many interesting things during the day.

May 17, 1910. First day of teaching. I carried the day–all the praise to God. I feel my own weakness, but am looking to God for strength.

May 18, 1910. Wed. After 4 PM tennis is played considerable.[28] There are several good courts.

May 19, 1910. Took Dr. Whitmore's English class in the evening. A fine bunch of lads. The Chinese are people that one can love.

May 20, 1910. Tennis at the University. At Dr. Russell's we have family prayers after supper and the servants come in. Read from Bible in Chinese but pray in English.

---

27. Dr. Wallace B. Russell was a medical doctor and later helped with Grace's nervous breakdown. See entries for October 21, 1910 and December 13, 1910.

28. Harvey plays tennis at the University of Nanking, where he will be teaching in three more years.

May 21, 1910. Went out to Exhibition[29] grounds in the afternoon. Saw the comet [Halley's][30] after supper. A glorious evening. Ideal weather.

May 22, 1910. Sunday. Morning spent in letter writing. Dr. Whitmore's in afternoon. English class reading from the Bible. Carver and I walked across the hills to the chapel. Very pretty.

May 23, 1910. Started language study today with my teacher. It starts off easy, but wait and see. Ideal weather. A full moon and a bright comet.

---

29. Nanking was the site of a huge international exhibition called The Nanyang Industrial Exposition in 1910. The main part of it, which was near the train station at Shia Kwan, covered an area of 500 yards by 400 yards, excluding the park and the race-course. Broad, macadamized roads, artistically designed flowerbeds, with flowers of many hues and numerous ponds had been constructed. In front of the main entrance was an imposing ornamental arch of typical Chinese architecture. On either side of the principal entrance were the Education and Industrial buildings. There was a commodious Assembly Hall, in which lectures on modern subjects were given by Chinese and foreign scholars, an Administration building, and a Fine Arts building. On the east side of the oval enclosure were: Military and Public Hygiene exhibits, Chinese exhibits from foreign countries, Porcelain, Tea, Hunan, Silk, Szechuen, Provincial exhibits, and a Bazaar. On the west side were the Transportation building, Foreign exhibits, Machinery Buildings and Agricultural buildings, Restaurants, etc. Other buildings had been erected to serve as hotels for Chinese and foreigners. There were concerts and sports events. The May 1910 *University of Nanking Magazine* was devoted to this exhibition and listed favorite cultural and historical places to visit, all the educational institutions of higher learning, the various Christian missions, and contained the railroad timetable between Nanking and Shanghai, plus many photos of local monument sites and exposition buildings. The staff of the magazine were all Chinese.

30. Harvey saw this comet on shipboard on April 27, 1910.

1910 DIARY

May 24, 1910. Met Grace [added later]. Letter from Dennis.[31] Nanking Association[32] supper on the lawn at Blackstones'.[33] Lotus Lake[34] and a glorious night. If the A.A. [Ann Arbor] friends had been along, it would have been *ideal*.

May 25, 1910. Mr. Pettus arrived in Nanking and came to see me.[35] Plans for summer conference at Kuling.

May 26, 1910. Tennis at Mr. Bullock's.[36] Teaching is hard work for me, but it has been very pleasant work thus far. God blesses me daily.

May 27, 1910. I'm not a very bright student of the Chinese language and am afraid I never will be. But I intend to plug away and learn all I can. The comet was grand this night.

---

31. Dennis Egbert is Harvey's friend from Michigan, who turns up later. See Feb 24, 1915 entry. Grace and Harvey's first son Richard Dennis, born October 5, 1913, is named for him.

32. Nanking Association meets once a month and includes all foreigners in the city. See Introduction.

33. Grace had boarded with the Blackstone couple, who are fairly young (Mr. J.H. and Mrs. Barbara Treman Blackstone), Harry and Barbara. An elder Mr. Blackstone arrives later and stays with them awhile and is apparently a minister, William Eugene Blackstone and the Older Mr. Blackstone of entries March 4 and May 7, 1911. In the 1920 Hillcrest annual, 40–42, we have a fourth grade Barbara Blackstone (my mother's friend), seventh grade James Blackstone, first year of high school (ninth grade?) Eleanor Blackstone, and third year of high school (eleventh grade?) William Blackstone. Mother remembers going to their house for Christian Endeavor Sundays at 9 A.M. (similar to Sunday School). The thirteen-year-olds and up studied the *Old Testament*, the nine-thirteen-year-olds did the same but more simply, the four-nine-year-olds had *Bible* stories and illustrations. CRI, 37.

34. Lotus Lake was situated near the city wall northeast of the city. A road leads from the gate Feng Rweng Men across the lake to the five islands.

35. Mr. William Bacon Pettus, in charge of YMCA student field in China, lives in Nanking with his wife but travels widely. He was in China 1906–1940. Besides being National Student Secretary for the YMCA, he was the Director of the North China Union Language School. One of the Kiang Nan students, Yuen Ren Chao, met Mrs. Pettus in Nanking. See Appendix B. See also April 20, 1911. CRI, 381.

36. Rev. Prof. Amasa Archibald Bullock was a Northern Presbyterian missionary in Nanking. He and his wife Ruth were friends of Harvey and Grace. Anson Burlingame was born Dec. 23, 1912, same birthday as Grace's, and Frank was born, Nov. 8, 1913. She taught Sunday School at Hillcrest, *Hillcrest Annual*, 1916, 23. See also entry for November 6, 1910. CRI, 59.

May 28, 1910. "The Legend of the Bleeding Hearts."[37] Ours! The Ming Tombs. "Oh, You cute little donkeys." Miss [Grace] Woodbridge and I had a pleasant walk back to the City Gate. Supper at Drummonds'.[38]

May 29, 1910. Sunday. Taught Mr. Carver's Bible Class at Hu-be-jai.[39] Went to Dr. Whitmore's class in the P.M. Church at 4:30. Read "Legend of the Bleeding Hearts" to Carver.

May 30, 1910. A visit to the Director of my school.[40] Spent the afternoon in the laboratory. The days are getting longer and hotter.

May 31, 1910. A warm day. Missed Carver a little (Chinese eye).[41] Students show interest in work (Class E).

June 1, 1910. A warm day. Cool clothing arrived from Shanghai. 7 suits, single black coat, 3 extra duck trousers. Beautiful evening.

June 2, 1910. Another hot day. I wish I could dress like the Chinese.[42]

June 3, 1910. Carver, Gill[43] and I called on Mr. Gracey, the American Consul.[44] Spent the evening at Blackstones'. They were away, but we took possession and enjoyed their piano.[45]

---

37. For the whole legend, see Appendix A and Johnston, *Bleeding Heart*, 4021.

38. Rev. W. J. Drummond and Mrs. Frances Lane Drummond were Northern Presbyterian missionaries in Nanking. CRI, 127.

39. Hu-be-jai would be Hu Bei Zhai in modern Nanjing but location unknown.

40. The diary doesn't make clear who is the Director of the Kiang Nan School in 1910.

41. Carver had been a great help as Harvey adapted to teaching in the Chinese school. So "Chinese eye."

42. Some of the early missionaries did dress like the Chinese, even to wearing queues (the pigtails) most Chinese men wore until the Sun Yat-sen Revolution in 1911, in order not to stand out as foreigners in their "outlandish" clothes and be treated so badly. Woodbridge, *Fifty Years*, 83.

43. Rev. James Monro Banister Gill was an early friend of Harvey's in Nanking. He was with the American Episcopal Mission. See also entries for September 4, 1910 and June 18, 1911. CRI, 170.

44. American Consul Wilbur Tirrell Gracey served as Consul 1910–12 and was in charge in Nanking during Sun Yat-sen Revolution (1911).

45. Grace was no doubt present as she boarded with Rev. J.H. Blackstone (Harry) and his wife Barbara. It was likely Grace who played the piano, as she was a skilled pianist and often played the organ for church service.

June 4, 1910. Dr. Russell's left.[46] I spent the afternoon at school looking over and putting in shape some apparatus. There is considerable to be done in the laboratory before another year.

June 5, 1910. A quiet, cool Sunday. The exhibition opened, but there was no disturbance.[47] Carver and I enjoy our meals at the Beebes'.

June 6, 1910. A cool day. Tennis at the University in the afternoon. I'm a poor hand to keep a record [in a diary].

June 7, 1910. A cool day. Tennis at the University in the afternoon.

June 8, 1910. A cool day. Rain at night. Spent the afternoon at the laboratory. I wonder where the rickshaw men go on such a night.[48] 1909 Sam [Woodbridge] and Mamie married.[49] [Added later.]

June 9, 1910. A cool day. Beautiful starlight evening. Tennis at U. of N. [Nanking]. Miss G.W. [Grace] took lunch at Dr. Beebe's and played on the piano afterwards.

---

46. He moved out from Dr. Russell's after two weeks and in with Dr. and Mrs. Robert C. Beebe, Superintendent of the Philander Smith Hospital (Methodist), where his new friend Carver also boarded. Dr. Beebe was the Executive Secretary of the Chinese Medical Missionary Association, V.P. of the Hillcrest School in 1916. Harvey and Grace boarded with them after they were married. He was called Rob. He had two daughters: Margaret, who married Mr. Niles October 1914, and Josette Hilda who married Herbert E. Dennis in September 1914. CRI, 30.

47. Revolution was building, and there were disturbances regularly leading up to the actual revolution in the fall of 1911. Sun Yat-sen's Revolutionary Alliance directed or instigated a series of uprisings against the government. "Sun Yat-sen" in Wikipedia. Spence, *Modern China*, 253.

48. Generally, Harvey and Grace seem to have more empathy with the Chinese than Samuel, who respected them only when they became serious Christians. Samuel did recognize the Chinese respect for their parents and comments that of the 70 ancient civilizations, only two have survived: Jews and Chinese, and he thinks it's because of their reverence for their parents. He admits occasionally and grudgingly to admiring Confucius, e.g.: "See what a man does. It is utterly impossible for a man to conceal his true character." Woodbridge, *Fifty Years*, 138.

49. Sam Woodbridge was Grace's eldest brother, born July 16, 1886. He and Mamie later divorced and for this reason he was considered the black sheep in the family.

June 10, 1910. Warmer. No school today. The boys wanted to get ready for the Dragon Festival.[50] Tennis at Drummonds'.[51] Walked over to Gill's house after supper.

June 11, 1910. A great big glorious day filled from 10 AM to 7:30 PM by a picnic at Purple Gold Mountain.[52] Rode horseback. I taught English class after returning.

June 12, 1910. Sunday. Bright and hot, cooled off in evening with a shower. Took Carver's class. Lunch at Martins'.[53] Song service at Chapel. Sing at Martins' afterwards. Very pleasant. Miss Woodbridge, Miss Stuart, Mr. Stuart,[54] Mr. Hummel, Mr. Blackstone, Mr. Swenson,[55] Martins and self.

50. The Dragon Boat Festival (*Duanwu*) occurs on the fifth day of the fifth lunar month, near the summer solstice. It's also called the Double Fifth. Traditionally Chinese eat *zongzi* (sticky rice treats wrapped in bamboo leaves), drink realgar wine, and race dragon boats. The sun, like the Chinese dragon, traditionally represents masculine energy, whereas the phoenix, like the moon, represents feminine energy and is close to the winter solstice. "Duanwu Festival" in Wikipedia.

51. Rev. W.J. and Mrs. Emma Frances Lane Drummond. See entry of May 28, 1910.

52. Purple Mountain, or sometimes called Purple and Gold, is well-known and visible from Nanking. Many references to it are found in the Hillcrest annuals. Lilian Williams' daughter Dorothy reminisces: "Over all my childhood hovered the beautiful Tzu Ging Shan, the 'purple gold mountain' with its changing moods. I think I was always conscious of its presence in the distance and I peopled it with the folk of my imagination ... I used to wonder if God lived up there on top of the mountain." Williams, *Yesterdays in China*, 22.

53. Rev. Dr. and Mrs. Arthur Wesley Martin were Methodist Episcopal missionaries in Nanking. He was on the staff of the University of Nanking. Mrs. Martin taught the primary dept. at Hillcrest School in 1916, and four of her children were in Hillcrest: Frances, third grade, Mildred, second grade; Elizabeth and Arthur, primary (kindergarten). See also December 26, 1914. CRI, 323.

54. These young Stuarts (Mildred and George) are the children of Dr. George Stuart, MD, a Methodist, Dean of the Medical School and then President of Nanking University. He was also VP, Education Association of China, Managing Secretary of the Union Language School, Secretary, YMCA, and Editor, *Chinese Christian Advocate*. Mildred would marry Mr. Hummel. Other daughters were Alcy, Anna, Vera. Mildred was given the first diploma of the Watch Guard Society in January 1903. George Jr. debated in the Watch Guard Society in 1902. The Watch Guard Branch of the Agassiz Society for children was begun in October 1895 in Nanking. The purpose was to encourage children to observe nature carefully. The motto was: "Little by little the bird builds its nest and the child learns." Hillcrest School annual, 1916, 18–19. See also November 19, 1910. CRI, 459.

55. Hummel, Rev. Prof. William F. (1884–1976) was with the Methodist Episcopal mission and was Harvey's good friend in Nanking. See also July 3, 1910. He was on the staff of Nanking University and married Mildred Stuart in 1912. Anna May was born

June 13, 1910. Cool morning. Hot afternoon, rainy evening. *G'sein sen* [Grace]⁵⁶ read a story from the *Ladies Home Journal* to Carver and me.

June 14, 1910. A rainy day. Spent evening at Martins' playing, singing, etc. Miss G.W. and I seem to always get together.

June 15, 1910. Last day of regular school work. Sunshine after rain. Tennis at University. Went to moving picture show near Exposition grounds. Walk back as far as Martins'. Miss G.W. again.

June 16, 1910. Picnic near river in the afternoon (*Hsia gwan*)⁵⁷. Dr. Whitmore's Eng. [English] class. At Martins' afterwards. Miss G.W. and I are fast getting acquainted. It would almost appear that we had a bad case on.

June 17, 1910. First exam given. Tea at Martins'. Tennis afterwards. Miss G.W. at Dr. Beebe's for dinner. I was invited to go to the cinematograph show in the evening but decided it was time to slow up a little.

Dec. 9, 1913. CRI, 228. Rev H. Swenson is probably the son of Mrs. K. Moll Swenson, with CIM. CRI, 463.

56. Grace has told Harvey her Chinese name. He is seeing her often! In this period, when a young man and a young woman are constantly seen together, people would expect an engagement. It's probably why Harvey feels he has to "slow up a little." [June 17 entry] Or perhaps their sexual attraction was easier to handle if he saw her less often? Then there is Helen back in the U.S., to whom he may have engaged himself? And he still has exams to give at his college.

57. *Hsia gwan* is *Shia Kwan*, the railroad and dock district on the Yangtze. This gate out of the city is also referred to as the West Gate. [Harvey doesn't always spell correctly, especially Chinese names.] When Lilian and John E. Williams entered Nanking by Yangtze in 1899, "... there was a crowd of people to meet us. They were on little donkeys ... We mounted on the donkeys and rode away over the bumps which I soon learned were grave mounds. Encircling the city ran the ancient gray wall, thirty or forty feet high, twenty feet thick, twenty-four miles in length. Built in the 14th Century as a barrier of defense. We entered the city through the West Gate and I can see it again as I saw it that September morning. There was a fragrance of celery growing at the roadsides. There was yellow corn just husked and sweet potatoes newly dug. We saw the little clinging fingers of red vines and tiny wild yellow chrysanthemums, the yellow and red of dusty hedges. I saw the light on ... purple and gold mountain." Williams, *Yesterdays in China*, 10. Lilian Williams' husband, Rev. Dr. John Elias Williams, was a Northern Presbyterian missionary to China from 1899. He was with the YMCA and Vice President, Nanking University. Mrs. Williams taught history in higher grades at Hillcrest in 1916, and Dorothy and Mary Williams were in seventh-eighth grades, 9–10. By 1920 Walter Williams was in fifth grade; Richard in third grade, 5—6. CRI, 519. See also entries for November 7, 1910 and February 18, 1911.

GRACE

June 18, 1910. Getting ready for Monday's exam. Tea at Davises'. Mr. John D.[58] home from Shanghai. Supper with Gill. Tempted to go down to the Exposition but did not.

June 19, 1910. Wrote letters all the morning. A cool day (Sunday). Walked out to West Gate in PM and up on hills. Went to church at 4:30.

June 20, 1910. Exam in the morning. Tennis in the afternoon. Stayed at home and went to bed early.

June 21, 1910. Getting ready for more exams. Very hot. Took all PM trying to keep cool. Gill and friend over at 6:30. Three of us went to Expo in the evening. Chinese barber in PM.

June 22, 1910. Father's birthday–1836. Another exam over. Tennis and correcting papers filled the afternoon and evening. Not so hot as yesterday.

June 23, 1910. Gave exam for Carver. Played tennis in the afternoon. Started for Expos with Martins to see fireworks. Postponed but walked from Gu Low[59] to Martins' with Miss G.W. Full moon. A perfect night.

June 24, 1910. Exam in the AM. Planned to go on picnic in PM but got time and place wrong and did not meet party. A pleasant evening.

June 25, 1910. Hot! Well, I guess. But it rained hard before night. Work up to date. Exposition in the evening. Too late for concert but saw fireworks.

June 26, 1910. Sunday. Cool today. Last church service of the summer. Dr. Davis on Prayer.[60]

---

58. John D. is Rev. Dr. John Wright Davis, a Southern Presbyterian missionary, 1873–1917. Grace and Harvey moved into the house where he had lived in 1911. He was a friend of the Woodbridges and helpful to her parents during Grace's illness. He founded the Nanking Theological Seminary. See also entry for October 9, 1910. CRI, 115. His wife had died in 1906, Mrs. J. W. Davis (Alice I. Schmucker Davis). The daughter was Alice, the son, John. CRI, 114.

59. *Gu Lou* is the Drum Tower, which is situated on a small hill east of *Beh Gih Goh* (a hill where Taoists have a temple). It is painted red, possesses three entrances and resembles a tower over a city wall. It was built by *Tai Dzu* of the Ming Dynasty in preparation for a battle. *Tai Dzu* could view the battle from the tower, and he beat the large drum which could be heard a great distance, which served as sign for urging his soldiers to march against the enemy. From it the visitor has a good view of the city. It is about three miles from *Shia Kwan*. *University of Nanking Magazine* May 1910, 20.

60. Most of the doctors referred to are medical doctors, but there are some doctors

June 27, 1910. Rain all day. Last exam in AM. Stayed to dinner with Gill. Afternoon and evening at home.

June 28, 1910. Rain–all day. Went over to school in AM. Worked on Carver's wheel [bicycle][61] in PM. Carver and I had a little visit at Martins'. Came home in the rain.

June 29, 1910. More rain but the sun shone for a few minutes in the PM and the stars were out at night. Dr. Beebe read to us from Dwight J. Hillis's *Life Lessons from Great Books*.[62]

June 30, 1910. The days fly so fast, it is all I can do to keep up with this [the diary]. All I know is that it's still raining.

July 1, 1910. More wet. University Club [a YMCA meeting probably] at Dr. Whitmore's. Only 10 present but a distinguished gathering. Would that I could know them well.

July 2, 1910. A hard rain in the morning seemed to clear the clouds away. Contract sign [ed].[63] Exposition in PM. Plans for Kuling.

July 3, 1910. Sunday. Hummel[64] and I left for Kuling[65] about 2:30. Carriage to Shia Kwan, train to Chinkiang, boat to Kiukiang. Slept on hulk until about 1: AM.

July 4, 1910. Passed thru Nanking about 8 AM. U.S. New Orleans,[66] a British and a German cruiser all flying the U.S. flag and strings of signal flags.

---

of divinity, i.e., Dr. John W. Davis and Grace's father. All the foreigners went to the same "union" church service, often referred to as the "foreign service" and usually held Sunday afternoon about 4:30 P.M.

61. Harvey was very handy with most mechanical things. I remember he fixed household appliances and small machines when I knew him.

62. Hillis, Newel Dwight, *Great Books*.

63. Harvey must have signed a contract to teach a second year at his Kiang Nan college.

64. William F. Hummel (1884–1976) was Harvey's good friend in Nanking. See also note 55 in entry for June 12, 1910.

65. See Duff, "History of Kuling" in Appendix C for the trip to Kuling from Nanking.

66. According to Edith Riggs Barakat, also doing research on Chinese missionaries, in November 1911 the *New Orleans* cruised up to Nanking as part of the US Yangtze Patrol. This is 1910, so apparently it was cruising then, too. It came near Nanking during the period of the Sun Yat-sen Revolution in the fall of 1911 and took aboard U.S. citizens

July 5, 1910. Arrived in Kiukiang and went up to the half-way house. 24 years old today. I still feel quite young. We are traveling 1st class Chinese but get foreign meals. It's a pretty trip. Hot but a good breeze.

July 6, 1910. Not a very comfortable night. Hummel, Wharton[67] and I start up the hill at 4 AM. It took about 2 hours to reach Kuling. We took breakfast at Martins'. Spent day reading and getting settled.

July 7, 1910. A dunk in the pond at 6 AM. A swim at 4 PM. Up town and made a few purchases. Met sister of Miss G. Woodbridge in the evening.[68]

July 8, 1910. Morning dunk at 6 AM. Took tea at Stuarts'. Mrs. S., four daughters, Mr. LaQuen,[69] Hummel, and I climbed to Cradle Rock.[70]

July 9, 1910. Casper's birthday [added later, Grace's brother born in 1894]. M.D. [= Morning Dunk in Methodists' large swimming pool]. We work a little every morning. Our cook gives us good grub and the boy is doing his best. Took tea at the Stuarts' and then the crowd went to the big pool.

July 10, 1910. Sunday. M.D. Long letter home. Went to church at 10:30. Communion service afterwards. The Methodists sang on our big porch[71] in the evening.

July 11, 1910. M.D. It rained all day. Carver came about 10:30. Hummel and I went up town and bought a few things in the PM. I climbed up along the little stream but pretty wet.

July 12, 1910. M.D. Not a very bright day but no rain. Call at the Woodbridges' for tea and had a very pleasant time. Uptown in evening.

July 13, 1910. M.D. I spend a couple of hours on my Physics work for next year every morning and an hour on Chinese. Am reading *John* [Book in

---

and embassy archives. See entry for November 14, 1911.

67. Wharton is unidentified.

68. Charlotte Louise Woodbridge was the older sister of Grace, born November 30, 1887, and the second Woodbridge child. See also entries for November 13 and 19, 1910. She was a good friend to Harvey and Grace.

69. Mr. LaQuen is a friend of Harvey's in Kuling and not further identified.

70. Cradle Rock is one of the natural sights at Kuling.

71. Some families which have been in China for awhile have had houses built for them. The Kuling store sold lumber, etc. Harvey is probably staying at the hotel ("our big porch").

New Testament] now. In the PM we started for Nankang Pass (Stuarts, Langdons,[72] we'uns and LaQuen). It rained and we had a picnic supper on our porch. A pretty evening.

July 14, 1910. (Mother died peacefully and quietly early in the morn of this day). [Added later][73] M.D. I'm a poor hand to keep a diary for I don't keep it up daily but let it run for several days. Joined tennis club and played 1 set. Clouds & rain. The crowd started reading *The Girl of the Limberlost*.[74]

July 15, 1910. M.D. Went over to Russian Valley to attend convention but did not find Mr. Pettus and walked out to the big trees (5' diam.).

July 16, 1910. Sam's birthday. [Added later, Grace's eldest brother, born in 1886.] M.D. 5:30. Hummel and I took a 5-mile walk before breakfast. Saw *Po Yang Lake*.[75] Cleaned swimming pool in PM. It rained all day.

July 17, 1910. Sunday. No water in the pool. No M.D. Church twice. Crowd gathered at Stuarts' and we read in *The Girl of the Limberlost*. Crowd sang on our porch in evening.

July 18, 1910. Rain. Letter from father & diploma. [Presumably his Master's degree in Physics from the University of Michigan.] Mother's suffering is nearly over. I have thanked God daily for my parents & home but I didn't realize the blessing until I saw the loss coming.

July 19, 1910. Rain. I went to Bible study at the church in AM. The Stuart girls and we three boys ate our supper on the hill, up above Cradle Rock.

---

72. Harvey probably misspelled Longden. There is a reference to a Longden family, and a Miss Alice Longden, in Kuling, who may be the sister of Rev. W.C. Longden, Methodist Episcopalian, CRI, 293. See also entry for August 6, 1912.

73. He got word of her death in August by letter, not cablegram.

74. This novel, *A Girl of the Limberlost*, by American writer and naturalist Gene Stratton-Porter, published in August 1909, was a favorite of my mother's, often mentioned by her in my childhood. The heroine lives in the woods, has an unsympathetic mother, is poor, but knows a great deal about the moths in the woods. She is eventually able to earn money and improve her situation in life by catching rare moths for a collector.

75. *Po Yang* Lake is the largest fresh water lake in China. It's wide in the south and narrow in the north, like a huge gourd tied on the waist of the Yangtze River. It's now a national park and has rare fresh water fish and rare species of birds.

July 20, 1910. Alcy, Anna, Vera Stuart, Hummel and I climbed and took a long walk in PM. Got pretty ferns and club moss. H., C., [Hummel & Carver] and I went to the Woodbridges' in the evening.

July 21, 1910. A beautiful day. Mrs. Dexter, a widow who died of heart trouble, was buried. I was a pall bearer. I felt almost as if I was burying my own mother.[76]

July 22, 1910. A beautiful day. M.D. and long walk before breakfast. Study, tennis, a swim and a beautiful evening. I finished *The Girl of the Limberlost*.

July 23, 1910. Sunshine & rather hot. M.D. and a climb to the top. Croquet at the Woodbridges with Mr. Grant.[77] Tennis, a swim. The Stuarts' family & we'uns took supper on "top side."

July 24, 1910. Sunday. M.D. Church. George Stuart and I took a short swim afterwards. Spent afternoon reading. Sing on our porch in evening. In fooling, just before bed time, I fell on my head and God only knows why I didn't break my neck.[78]

July 25, 1910. M.D. and long tramp before breakfast with Stuart girls. Study. Swim after 5:PM. American mail. Mother is improving. Fred [Harvey's step-brother] is helping to make her comfortable.

July 26, 1910. M.D. and short tramp. Called on Bullocks in PM and stopped at Woodbridges' on way back. They wanted me to stay for supper & of course I did. A delightful evening.

July 27, 1910. M.D. A very hot day. Tennis at 5:PM–3 good sets. Wharton came up with H. [Hummel] & I. We took a swim before supper and had a pleasant evening afterwards.

---

76. Emmeline Beales Roys was buried by this time, having died July 14, 1910.

77. Dr. J.S. Grant was a Northern Baptist missionary. Harvey also sees him in Nanking before and after the Sun Yat-sen Revolution, on September 12, 1911 and December 14, 1911. CRI, 181.

78. Harvey is not above rough housing. Harvey was in his sixties when I lived with him and rather staid and serious. I find these glimpses of his youthfulness surprising but charming. He almost got into a pillow fight on shipboard, too.

1910 DIARY

July 28, 1910. Heard Dr. W.W. White in AM.[79] H. & I called at the Littles'[80] for tea and got back in time for tennis. Swim before supper.

July 29, 1910. Mother's birthday–68 years old. Two letters from Father. He says Mother cannot last long. Fred is there and doing all he can. I thank God daily for my mother & home.

July 30, 1910. It rained in the PM so that we couldn't play tennis or croquet. Went swimming at 11:AM. Did back and front flips into water. Dinner at Longdens 8 PM.

July 31, 1910. Sunday. Church. Received card from Dora Fearon.[81] Wrote to D.F. & home, then went up on ridge above us. Sunset from cradle rock. Song service on our porch.

August 1, 1910. Rain. Misses Mildred, Alcy, Anna Stuart,[82] George, Hummel, and I went to Littles' for tea. Played golf & croquet. Sing on our porch in evening with organ/dance.[83]

August 2, 1910. Tennis in AM. Hummel & I went to Woodbridges' in PM. Rained in evening. We went up to Stuarts' and played dominoes.

August 3, 1910. Rain. Tennis. The rains dry up quickly. Supper at Brockmans[84] (for Dr. White). We got away early & I went over to Woodbridges'. A beautiful home.

---

79. Rev. Dr. Wilbert Webster White also spoke later in Nanking, September 9, 1912 at the Stewarts about his work in Japan and Korea. He was with the YMCA and President, Bible Teachers Training School. CRI, 513.

80. The Littles are probably a Rev. Lacy Little and his second wife, Ella, who were Southern Presbyterian missionaries. He had been in China since 1895. Lacy Little was from N.C. Harvey seems to be in with the Southern Presbyterian crowd, Stuarts, Littles, and Woodbridges. Lawrence Kessler wrote a whole book about their mission station, Kiangyin, which is Jiangyin now. *The Jiangyin Mission*.

81. Dora Christian Fearon graduated from the University of Michigan in 1909. By 1915 she was teaching in Chiangli and before that had been teaching in Peking. She and Harvey are both listed as students in the 1905/06 University of Michigan catalog.

82. These Stuarts, Mildred, Alcy, and Anna are George Stuart's sisters. See entries June 12, 1910, November 9, 1910, and July 28, 1911.

83. At this point Harvey is not above dancing. Mother relates how, when she was in college and her mother hospitalized, Harvey took her to the Faculty Club dances until the Southern Baptists (he was their Sunday School superintendent) objected. Mother says she saw a freer, happier side of him when he danced.

84. Mr. F. S. Brockman was General YMCA Secretary for China and Korea. Harvey

August 4, 1910. The annual Methodist picnic–a supper for Dr. White. It takes most of the day getting ready on our porch. 46 sit down. I took the Woodbridge girls home.[85]

August 5, 1910. Rain all day. Wrote to Ella[86] in PM. We boys went up to Stuarts' after supper and played dominoes. I'm studying the life of Abraham now (Old Test. char.)

August 6, 1910. Rained hard in AM. Got watch and sent home to Father. Tea at Woodbridges' (42).[87] Picnic at Longdens'. Home at 10:30. I don't forget Mother and the home but I haven't mourned her death very much.

August 7, 1910. Sunday. A pretty morning. Dr. W.W. White preached a grand sermon. Rain–sunshine. Carver and I went up to Pettuses' and then to church. Mr. Chen and Dr. Fong to supper.[88] Sing.

August 8, 1910. Rain & sunshine. Carver, Hummel & I walked out toward Nankang Pass and got a lot of lilies–2 kinds. Caught a moth and formed it on a board.[89]

August 9, 1910. M.D. Sunshine. God give me strength to avoid all tricks.[90] A party at Mrs. Mendenhall's[91] in the evening. Late to bed and late to rise (12:30—7:45).

---

also sees him in Shanghai. He founded the YMCA mission in China in 1898. *University of Nanking Magazine*, May, 1910, 30. He also chaired the China Continuation Committee. CRI, 51. See also August 3, 1912.

85. Grace must be one of the Woodbridge girls here. There were only three girls of the eight children: Louise, 22, Grace, 20, and Jeanie, 10, at this time. It seems likely that Grace is at her parents' in Kuling, but Harvey doesn't seem to be seeing her much outside of her home there. Parental strictness when she was living with them? Her father isn't mentioned as being in Kuling at this time, but his rules may have been applied.

86. Ella is Harvey's father's sister.

87. 42 is a version of dominoes.

88. Chinese socializing is rare. Chen, Dr. Prof. was also in Nanking, Nov. 8, 1910. This may be the Chen who became superintendent of Harvey's Kiang Nan School in the fall of 1910. He might also be the Chen who later became President of Nanking University? CRI, 81. Dr. Fong is unidentified.

89. *Girl of the Limberlost* influenced Harvey to catch moths and preserve them.

90. Whose tricks? Female wiles? Grace's? Or other young women in Kuling?

91. Mrs. Mendenhall is only mentioned in Kuling and is unidentified.

August 10, 1910. Studied in AM. Carver and I went to Woodbridges' in the evening. "The Studies in Old Test[ament] Charac[ters]" are very interesting.

August 11, 1910. Studied in AM. Tennis in PM. Swimming. I find that I'm a poor book [diary] keeper. Still interested in moths.

August 12, 1910. Studied in AM. Tennis. Concert in evening. Very fine. Miss L.W. [Louise Woodbridge] did splendid on both piano and violin. Played on tennis courts on way home.

August 13, 1910. Rained all day from 9:AM. Studied. Went to Woodbridges' in PM. Met Miss G. on the way getting home from the Falls. She was drenched but cheerful. A plucky little maid.

August 14, 1910. Sunday. Rain continued–all day. Went to church, read. Wrote to Helen.[92] American mail. Two letters from Father. Mother died July 14 "peacefully and quietly."[93]

August 15, 1910. A bright day–thank goodness. PM walked to temple of the clouds, then to Emerald Grotto[94] with large crowd. Back at 7:45 Had a pleasant visit with Mrs. Woodbridge in even[ing].[95]

August 16, 1910. Tennis tournament at 8:30. Miss A. [Alice] Longden & I (6–2, 6–7, 6–3). Children's games in PM. Supper at Stuarts'. Serenade or ghost walk.

August 17, 1910. Breakfast at the Caves, a swim before dinner, tea at Mrs. Beebe's. Picnic supper with Y.M.C.A. people on Bull's Head.[96]

---

92. Helen was the young woman he loved when he left the U.S. He is probably writing to let her know that he now loves another–Grace. See April 14, 1910 entry.

93. It took a month to learn his mother was dead.

94. The Emerald Grotto was a favorite spot near Kuling. A natural pool was formed and made an excellent swimming hole.

95. Mrs. Woodbridge seems to be encouraging Harvey's interest in Grace. She has allowed Harvey to visit and has not kept Grace from outings with him. She must be aware of the developing love in the couple, and yet, given that Samuel Isett later disapproves, she has little power. Would Harvey have declared his intentions to Grace four days later without her encouragement?

96. Bull's Head is a mountain shaped like a bull's head at Kuling.

August 18, 1910. Spent most of the day getting ready to go to the masquerade at Miss Little's. Tea at Woodbridges'. A big evening. Home with G.W. To bed at 2:00 AM.

August 19, 1910. Mr. Fryer[97] & I walked to Nankang Pass. Nap, swim. Supper at Woodbridges'. I spent the evening with Grace. Some things are told.[98]

August 20, 1910. Started for "Water Falls"[99] at 9:AM. Arrived about 11. Swim–big lunch–swim–tea. A delightful day. God's grandeur as shown by nature is impressive at this place.

August 21, 1910. Sunday. Cool. We slept until 9. Wrote letter. Went to church in evening. A quiet day.

August 22, 1910. Waterfalls and back. 9–12:45. John W.[100] for dinner–swim. George & I to Woodbridges'. Tea, 42, croquet. Stayed to supper & went to concert with the girls. A perfect evening.

August 23, 1910. A bright day. Swim. Wrote letters, read, watched tennis at upper courts. A quiet day.

August 24, 1910. M.D. and swim at 11:30. Funeral at 9 (Mitchel Wilson–baby).[101] We were pall bearers. Tea at Longdens'. Afternoon and evening at Woodbridges'.

---

97. Dr. John Fryer was based in Shanghai, and Editor, *The School Chinese Scientific Magazine*; Editor, *Chinese Scientific and Industrial Magazine*; Founder and Acting General Secretary, Educational Association of China. Later he was head and professor of the Chinese Department, University of California. CRI, 158.

98. This is probably when Harvey told Grace of his love, and she must have given him some encouragement. He's now calling her Grace, another sign of intimacy.

99. These water falls located near Kuling were numerous in this one place and very beautiful.

100. John Woodbridge, who is thirteen.

101. Rev. Wilbur F. and Mrs. Wilson offered their home for the early years (1911–13) of Hillcrest School begun by the missionary mothers. He worked with the YMCA 1910–11. After that? In 1920 Robert was in first year of high school, Julia was in her third year of high school, Franklin was in third grade. A baby (Mitchel) died in Kuling. See also August 24, 1910 and October 29, 1913 entries. CRI, 524.

August 25, 1910. Picnic at Emerald Pool [Grotto]. Grace and I left as soon as her school[102] was out—12:15. A delightful day. We were together most of the time so I guess people know how I stand.[103]

August 26, 1910. Bible Study. John W. & I had a swim and went to the Children's Exercises at the CIM. Chinese chow at Woodbridges'. A quiet afternoon. Walk after 4. Evening at home.

August 27, 1910. All day picnic at Emerald Grotto. No one was "flip."[104] I'm bound by all the good and truth that is in me to make my life worthy of another's love. "An understanding."[105]

August 28, 1910. Sunday. Church. Letters. Church 5:30. Song service at 8:30. Walked home with Grace & Louise. Grace and I compared notes and had a good visit on the steps.

August 29, 1910. Wrote to Helen[106] and started to pack. Telegram saying school had opened.[107] Hummel & I went to Woodbridges'. Stuart girls (A. & A. [Alcy & Anna]) there for night. We left early.

August 30, 1910. All our things off for Kiukiang. With Grace from 3 to 11 PM. Alone; a pleasant walk–on the door step. Louise is in the secret.[108] Good-byes for 3 weeks.

---

102. Grace was teaching at C.I.M. [China Inland Mission], which had a school in Kuling. C.I.M. included many women and was an English mission. It was named by its founder, Hudson Taylor, who opposed opening regular mission stations at the treaty ports and preferred the inland cities, where the influence of the "wicked Europeans" was not felt. "Our mission also adopted this policy until 1883, when we occupied Chinkiang." Woodbridge, *Fifty Years*, 175–76.

103. To be with Grace so much implied a serious interest, and if Harvey were honorable, his intention must be to marry her.

104. Presumably he's thinking of the "tricks" mentioned in the entry for August 9, 1910. Grace is behaving seriously, not joking around.

105. I assume the "understanding" was that they would marry, but they hadn't yet gained her parents' permission.

106. Helen is mentioned in the April 14, 1910 entry, right before he left Michigan. He must have written to her to tell her that he was now engaged to Grace.

107. Here is a telegram within China. Telegrams haven't been mentioned before in the diary.

108. "On the doorstep" suggests a kiss goodnight. Generally, in this period, couples did not kiss until engaged. They apparently do consider themselves engaged, pending her parents' approval, and they have told Grace's sister Louise.

August 31, 1910. Up at 4:AM. Off for Kiukiang at 5:05. 1–1/2 hours to Lein Wan Dung.[109] 1 hour by carriage to Kiukiang. Everything all right. Off for Nanking. Time to think.

September 1, 1910. Arrived in Nanking safely. All well at school. Started but no complaint for us. Meals with Dr. Beebe. To bed early. Many thoughts & prayers for G.W.

September 2, 1910. School. The new superintendent [Kiang Nan School], Mr. Ching[110], is very pleasant. Things begin to straighten out. Wrote to Grace. God help me to be worthy of her.

September 3, 1910. Rain. Only two classes on Saturdays. I slept most of the afternoon. Will be glad when things are settled.[111]

September 4, 1910. Sunday. A quiet Sunday. No Church service. Wrote letters, walked over to U. of N[anking] and sat on the knoll for a time with Dr. Beebe.

September 5, 1910. A pleasant fall day. Bought Carver's rickshaw and began using it with Lao Dai.[112] American mail. Wrote to Grace. I have to study now.

September 6, 1910. School work keeps me busy. The weather is delightful, not uncomfortably hot and the nights are cool. Just a little bit lonely in Nanking now. There is enough to do that the days don't drag.

September 8, 1910. Birthday Mother Woodbridge (their wedding anniversary). [Added later]. It's getting warmer. I decide to go to Shanghai on the morrow for it's a holiday.[113]

---

109. For more information about the trip to and from Kuling, see description by Julia Wilson in Appendix C on Kuling.

110. Mr. Ching may be Dr. Chen, who became superintendent of Harvey's Kiang Nan School in the fall of 1910.

111. He probably refers to his desire to marry Grace. Her mother must suspect what's up; her father doesn't know yet; when he does, he disapproves. Or he could be referring to getting settled again in Nanking and at his college.

112. A man of prosperity; he buys his own rickshaw. The boy, Lao Dai, comes with it, and does the pulling.

113. This is the Mid-Autumn Moon festival. From Edith Riggs Barakat: "The Moon festival is important, second only to the spring festival (New Year's.) I have a mold to make moon cakes." "Mid-Autumn Festival" in *Travel China Guide*.

September 9, 1910. Up at 5:30 and off for Shanghai. Arrived at 4. Went to Evans'.[114] Up to Stuarts' in evening. Rag time music.

September 10, 1910. Lunch with Mr. Fryer. Met Mr. Woodbridge for 1st time.[115] Shopping all the AM. George and I went to ball game in PM. Supper at Stuarts'. A parlor picnic. Took train at 10 PM.

September 11, 1910. Sunday. Arrived with baggage at 6:30. Took a carriage from Shia Kwan. Letters from Grace. American mail.

September 12, 1910. Hot. No school in PM. Received a picture of Grace and her love. The picture is no compliment to her but it reminds me of her.[116]

September 13, 1910. Rain all day. We are getting settled slowly. Got some pictures of Hummel and sent two in a letter to Ella.

September 14, 1910. Rain all day. Kept close. Studying Chinese now. American mail. Fitted picture of Grace to gold frame. Letter to Father. Gill over in evening.

September 15, 1910. Clearing up. A hard day in school. Thurs. & Fri.–all are going to be. My thoughts are of Grace a good deal.

September 16, 1910. Sunshine. Tennis. I get over to the Univ. nearly every day. Grace will be here tomorrow and I'm going to make an effort to meet her.

September 17, 1910. A bright day. Off for Shia Kwan at 12:30 to meet Grace. There in time. Thank goodness. Miss Lucas,[117] Grace, and I rode

---

114. Dr. and Mrs. H.F. Evans are first mentioned as residents of Shanghai. Dr. Evans is Grace's doctor for the birth of Margaret in Kuling, and Jeanie and Charlie are sent to the Evans' home during the birth. Jean (12) and Charlie (10) were staying with Grace and Harvey in the Woodbridge cottage in Kuling that summer. In 1914 Mrs. Evans helped with the Furnishing Committee when the new Hillcrest School was built. Mary L. Evans was in fifth grade, and Philip Evans was in the Watch Guard Society, in the 1916 Hillcrest yearbook. Mrs. Evans also contributed to the Nanking cookbook. See also July 3, 1912. See also entry for December 29, 1912.

115. At this point Harvey apparently does not talk to Grace's father about his wish to marry her.

116. Grace was apparently still in Kuling. She arrives in Nanking September 17, and he meets her.

117. Miss Grace M. Lucas was a missionary in Nanking.

up in a carriage. It was a happy day and when alone I couldn't keep from singing or whistling. Thank God for Grace.

September 18, 1910. Sunday. A Chinese feast day.[118] Wrote a note to Grace and got a very sweet reply. A glimpse of her on the street. Oh, that there may be nothing in our lives to offend thee, Oh, God, and that we may not offend one another.

September 19, 1910. No school. Cloudy. Hummel and I went to the Caves[119] on horses in the PM. Letter from Grace. Answered in evening. I believe God is with us.

September 20, 1910. Gill & I called on Blackstones for tea. Grace was there. We went to Shia Kwan to meet some ladies. We had a little chance to talk it over. Grace has promised to be my wife.[120]

September 21, 1910. Dull, cloudy days without but joy and sunshine within my heart. Hummel & I called on Grace & Miss Hilster[121] in the evening.

September 22, 1910. The words of a friend M.J.: "Such a love as has come to you can transform your whole life—bring God into every part of it, and together you can climb where, if you were but one, your courage would often times fail you."[122]

September 23, 1910. Concert at the Exposition. Hummel, Grace & I came back together. Grace & I walked; Hummel rode slow using R. [rickshaw]. We had a few minutes alone at Blackstones'.

---

118. This, too, is part of the Moon Festival.

119. The caves are probably those called "Beggars Caves" and part of the remnants of the great wall around the city. Photo in *University of Nanking Magazine*, May 1910, 2–3.

120. Here Grace commits herself. She isn't waiting for her father's approval or she already knows he disapproves? The exact stages of this courtship aren't completely clear. In a letter Harvey wrote in 1936 to my father when he had engaged himself to my mother, Margaret, he said: "I assure you that I will not think of you as my father-in-law thought of me. I, too, was engaged before I had ever seen my father-in-law. He got the word before he had seen me and expressed his feelings to his daughter in no uncertain terms. He thought I was some wild, young 'upstart' that had beguiled his daughter. Well, it made lots of trouble and took me some time to change his attitude toward me."

121. Miss Hilster may have been another boarder at the Blackstones. She is unidentified.

122. M.J. is probably Hummel's friend, Mildred Stuart. See Oct. 19, 1910 entry.

September 24, 1910. To Blackstones' for supper. Just Mrs. B., Grace & I. A delightful time in the porch swing. Mr. B. is going to be a good friend of ours.

September 25, 1910. Sunday. Cool & cloudy. Wrote to Father and confided in him. Blackstones' porch–alone with Grace. Oh, these happy days. God bless us and use our lives.

September 26, 1910. Cool (cold). Reception for American Commissioners.[123] Grace looked very sweet today. She always looks sweet to me. We tell each other of our love. Walked up with Mrs. B. and Grace.

September 27, 1910. Mrs. B., Grace & I went to Shia Kwan to meet Mr. B[lackstone] but met Mr. Woodbridge instead. Supper at Blackstones' and a few minutes on the porch. Our first anniversary.[124]

September 28, 1910. The first day for a week that I did not see Grace. I tried to get a few minutes with Mr. Woodbridge but could not. Dr. Davis invited me to break [breakfast].

September 29, 1910. Breakfast at Dr. Davis's. Mr. Woodbridge and Grace there. Mr. W. & I had a long talk and I begin to see things in a new light.[125] At Blackstones' in evening. Letter to Grace.

September 30, 1910. A holiday in honor of Confucius's birthday. Studied, read, tea at Drummonds'. A rather long & dull day. I didn't see Grace.

---

123. This is no doubt the American Board of Commissioners for Foreign Missions. The board apparently has members all around Asia. Joseph Bailie and others mentioned in the diary are also noted as members of this board. See entry for May 12, 1913.

124. They reached their "understanding" on August 27.

125. This is the pivotal conversation, which may have caused Harvey to slow his courtship and seems to have contributed to Grace's mental breakdown. See also October 23, 1910 entry.

Grace

October 1, 1910. Took two of Carver's classes & my own. John W. came over at 11 AM.[126] Took tiffin with us. Exam Halls.[127] Horseback ride, supper at Blackstones'. A few minutes at the piano.[128]

October 2, 1910. Sunday. A beautiful fall day. Foreign church service. Walked to Bs with John and Grace. A few minutes together in the swing.[129]

October 3, 1910. A busy day and a happy one. There is lots to do and little time to do it in but I shall get something done all the time.

October 4, 1910. A dull and rather cool day but a busy one. Went to Blackstones' in the evening to see Grace. She was gay and happy.

October 5, 1910. A busy day. Tennis at the Univ in PM. To Blackstones' in evening with Carver to see Grace & Louise. They had gone to the Exposition so we didn't stay long.

October 6, 1910. Went to Shia Kwan to see Louise but missed her. Over to see Grace in PM. Stayed to Bs for supper. Took Grace to Univ, went to History Class at S.Y.C.[130] Home with Grace. A pleasant evening.

October 7, 1910. A hard day and long. One set of tennis at the U. of N. Didn't see Grace today. Stayed at home and went to bed early.

October 8, 1910. Preliminary Athletic Meet of the Univ. Went up to Blackstones' from there about 5:PM. Stay[ed] to supper. We three[131] had a good time until some visitors came.

---

126. John Woodbridge, Grace's younger brother, who was 13 in 1910 (born January 27, 1897) was in Nanking for schooling.

127. Harvey went to see the famous Examination Halls, constructed during the time of the Ming dynasty. They could accommodate 25,000 students, each occupying a single cell about the size of a sedan chair with movable boards as seats and desks.

128. Grace is no doubt the pianist. Harvey never played the piano. They could be alone for a few minutes.

129. Harvey and Grace snatch minutes here and there, at the piano or in the swing.

130. S.Y.C. was Student Y in China. Ryan Bean, Reference and Outreach Archivist, Kautz Family YMCA archives, University of Minnesota Libraries, confirmed this.

131. "We three" would be Mrs. Blackstone, Grace, and Harvey.

1910 DIARY

October 9, 1910. Sunday. Father's watch arrived.[132] Walked over to Blackstones' in the AM and had a little visit with Grace. Church at 4:30, to Dr. Davis's for supper. Grace there and I took her home.

October 10, 1910. A beautiful day. Tennis at the University. At home in the evening. I would like to see Grace every day but believe it best to restrain myself.[133]

October 11, 1910. A holiday. Chinese go up on a hill.[134] Last day of fall. Carver and I went to the exposition in the PM. Supper at Blackstones'.

October 12, 1910. School work kept me busy all day. Went to Prayer meeting at the Ladies'[135] in the evening. Walked home with Grace & the Blackstones but did not stop.

October 13, 1910. A busy day but bright & beautiful. Night school at Sing Djai Ko.[136] Went over to Blackstones' about 9: and saw Grace for a few minutes.

October 14, 1910. It looked like rain but turned out beautiful. Tennis at U. after 5. Evening at home. Wrote a letter to Grace.

October 15, 1910. No classes today (day held as a memorial to Djao Dzeng Wei of Class D, who died a few days ago). Tennis. Concert at Christian headquarters.[137] Everybody was abed at Bs when we got back and we had a good visit.[138]

October 16, 1910. Birthday. Father Woodbridge [added later][139]. Sunday. A beautiful day, a pleasant evening. Bible Class. Ten of the students walked

---

132. Harvey had sent his father a watch. A letter must have confirmed that it had arrived. See August 6, 1910 entry.
133. Why is he pulling back here? To manage the sexual attraction or because of what her father said? Maybe he believes this is the way to win her father's approval?
134. This is probably the Double Ninth holiday, the ninth day of the ninth lunar month celebrated with an autumn outing.
135. The Ladies Missionary Society.
136. Y.M.C.A. night school.
137. Probably this is the Christian Headquarters at the Exhibition.
138. "We" is he and Grace.
139. Samuel Isett Woodbridge was born October 16, 1856, died January 23, 1926.

out to the Foreign cemetery with Carver & I. Memorial service for Mr. Lemon.[140] Supper at Dr. Beebe's.

October 17, 1910. A busy day. Athletes & Students arrive for big meet. I went to Shia Kwan and brought Walker[141] up. A walk over the hills with Grace. Evening at Bs. Grace and I looking to God for guidance in all we do. It's a great comfort and source of strength.

October 18, 1910. Opening day of Big Meet.[142] I was at the Exposition all day. It surely was a great day. The outlook for athletes in China is good. To bed early.

October 19, 1910. No school. Spent most of the day at home. Supper at Bs. The Big Six (Mr. & Mrs. B, Hummel, Mildred, Grace, myself[143]) all went to the Expo. Got away early and spent evening at Bs.

October 20, 1910. School today. Left at 4:30 for Exposition. Supper at Bs. Went to night class but only two fellows there. Evening at Bs. Grace and I feel our need of one another. And esp. our need of God. We will look to him always in all things.

October 21, 1910. Saw Grace at Dr. Russell's for a few minutes in PM. She was all tired out but had to attend a supper that night. Was at Bs when she got back that night at 9:30.[144]

October 22, 1910. A pretty day. Went to Univ. with 4 students in PM. Did not see Grace today but wrote her a note (which was sent next morn[ing]).

---

140. Mr. Lemon is unidentified.

141. Mr. Walker might be Rev. Alfred James Walker, an Anglican missionary. He was part of the Church Missionary Society and Dean of the Shanghai Cathedral, as well as Vice Principal, Trinity College, Ningpo, CRI, 496. More than likely though he was simply an acquaintance of Harvey's.

142. Besides concerts and exhibits, the Exposition included sports events. There was a race course and a big park.

143. Mildred Stuart (1884–1972) married William F. Hummel (1884–1976) in 1912. The Hummels had children, with whom Mother remembers playing. See also note for June 12, 1910 entry.

144. Grace's fatigue here may have been one of the factors that precipitated the breakdown which occurs two days later, or a symptom of it. She may have consulted Dr. Russell about a medical problem.

October 23, 1910. Sunday. Long letter from Grace. Went over to Bs and had a long visit with her in AM. Grace went to her S.S. in PM. Nervous breakdown came that night. I was called over about 8: Stayed all night. An awful night.[145]

October 24, 1910. At Blackstones' all PM & night. Mr. & Mrs. Woodbridge arrived about 4:30 PM. Grace had a long sleep 10–2 and ate a little when she woke up. Was wild after her parents came. Father stayed up with her. She slept from 3 until about 8 AM.[146]

October 25, 1910. Went over to Bs at 10 o'clock. It was decided to take Grace to Soochow. I went down early and held a comp [train compartment] until they came. Mr. B., Dr. Shields, Dr. Snell went with Mr. & Mrs. W. & Grace.[147] She bore up well but was strange all the time. Made no fuss at depot and got off all right.

---

145. One wonders what was in these letters they exchanged, if something about the stresses in their relationship and her father's ideas about it precipitated the breakdown.

146. I have not been able to discover details of Grace's behavior in such a "breakdown," probably a psychotic and/or manic episode. She may have *talked* wildly, out of touch with reality, possibly talked about sex, because within two months of this breakdown she was married off to Harvey, perhaps with the thought that sexual gratification would relieve the mental distress? Nothing is said about sex in this diary, but I am sure that by this time in their courtship, with a significant amount of time alone, walking home, on the porch swing, etc., that they were probably sexually aroused. Her response may have been to want more but feel guilty. His may have been inclined to back off to make the situation easier to control. Being "highly sexed," as my mother described Grace, implies to me that she was perhaps ready to violate conventions more freely, less inhibited, but probably she suffered guilt for being so, especially with her stern father. I would translate "highly sexed" as "with a normal sexual appetite." In manic episodes there are often both visual and aural hallucinations. She may have told people that God or the Devil was speaking to her. She may have turned against various religious rules, as she did later, in the late 20s, 30s, when in the hospital she played cards, smoked, danced, activities she normally was against. Was she taken to Soochow because the hospital there had more medical resources or her family knew the doctors? The Southern Presbyterians had established the Elisabeth Blake Hospital there in 1901, and most of the missionaries lived together on the hospital grounds by then. Two doctors accompanied her. Dr. John A. Snell served with the Southern Methodist Episcopal mission in Soochow. CRI, 445. Grace stayed there until they let her marry Harvey. Once Grace was better, she and her mother kept house there. Note that Harvey is included in this "breakdown" as much as possible.

147. Mr. B. is Mr. Blackstone. R.T. Shields, MD is a Southern Presbyterian missionary from Mississippi, who arrived in 1904, with his wife Ella Page Shields. Later, when baby Margaret's teeth were coming in in an unusual sequence, he said, "Only freaks did that." In 1915–16 Mrs. Shields taught first and second grade at the Hillcrest School which

October 26, 1910. A bright fall day. Had a visit with Mrs. B. in PM. Dr. Shields brought good news from Soochow. Blackstones encourage me. Carver & I took dinner at Russells'.

October 27, 1910. Oh! These glorious fall days. But it's lonesome. My work keeps me from getting blue. No more news from Soochow yet. My hopes are big and God has given me strength.

October 28, 1910. Took Hong Bin[148] to see Dr. Beebe. American mail. Letter from Louise. Went horseback riding with the Blackstones. It was the first exercise this week. Heard Bishop Lewis[149] speak and went to Nanking Association at the Quakerage. It could have been a delightful evening with Grace there but it was lonesome without her. Left early.

October 29, 1910. No class but made good use of the day and got considerable work done. A talk with Dr. Shields in the afternoon. Evening at home.

October 30, 1910. Bible Class at 9:3 students present. Wrote several letters. Bishop Lewis spoke at the foreign service. Supper with the Shields and Stuarts. A note from Mrs. Bullock.

October 31, 1910. Rain. Went to Malones[150] in the evening. Made believe I had a good time but was miserable. Home at 11:30. Thoughts of Grace. I can't be bright these days.

---

my mother later attended. Their children were Evy Shields, fifth grade and Randolph Shields, Primary, in 1916 yearbook for Hillcrest, 10, 11. In Soochow Dr. James Richard Wilkinson, a medical doctor, also Southern Presbyterian, was caring for Grace. He and his wife, Annie Barr Wilkinson, had come from South Carolina in 1894. They are probably the parents of Gretchen, James, Martha, and Annie. CRI, 517.

    148. Hong, Mr. Bin is unidentified. He may have been a teacher at Harvey's school,

    149. Bishop Wilson Seeley Lewis, once ordained by the Methodist Episcopalians, was sent to China, and worked hard as an organizer and executive. He was also a close friend of Bishop Bashford. He was a man of vision and a successful educator and preacher. He is mentioned in *The Annals of Iowa* and in *The Christian Advocate*, Vol 96. CRI, 281.

    150. Possibly Rev. G. Howard and Mrs. Malone, who were with the American Advent Mission Society, CRI, 321. The women Malones (Mrs. H. W. and Mrs. G. H.) both contributed to the cookbook of American recipes with ingredients readily available in Nanking.

November 1, 1910. A long talk with Dr. Davis.[151] He had talked with Dr. Wilkinson. Grace is in a very serious and dangerous condition but not without hope. May have to send her to America yet.

November 2, 1910. A day of work. Hummel over for supper. I went over and had a little visit with Mrs. B. about 5:PM. She gave me a bunch of beautiful violets. I wish Grace could have had them. I have decided that God will straighten things out all right.

November 3, 1910. No word from or of Grace. It's a long wait but I'm leaving everything to God. I get comfort from "Job."[152] Went hunting after 4:30 with Hummel. Didn't hit anything. Supper with Mildred & H[ummel].

November 4, 1910. A long day. Went to Bs for news of Grace and stayed to supper. Home early and to bed. Hopes a little bigger. My prayer is continually for her.

November 5, 1910. A note early this morning from Dr. Davis saying Grace was all right but very weak. Later a note from Mr. Blackstone who had had a letter from Grace. Now the world is bright again for me. God has heard my prayers. A beautiful day. Went to Spirit Valley[153] and to B[lackstone]s in evening. Letter to Grace.

November 6, 1910. Sunday. Letters. Bible Study class. Walked to church with Gill, Carver, Djang Yuen Shan.[154] Supper with Mr. & Mrs. Bullock.[155] No news from Grace today.

---

151. Dr. John Davis, D.D. was a good friend of Grace's parents, which is perhaps why he is so involved here. See also note for entry June 18, 1910.

152. For Harvey to find comfort in the book of Job suggests how close he feels to despair. He keeps his life as normal as possible, revealing his essentially sturdy and common sense approach to life, which later would be very comforting to my mother. If her mother fell apart, her father didn't. Life went on as normally as possible.

153. Spirit Valley is a temple situated on the Dulong Hillock to the left of the Purple Mountain northeast of Nanking. It is renowned for its unique arch-shaped hall, which is the largest beamless hall in China.

154. Djang Yuen Shan must be Djang Yuan-shan, a student at Kiang Nan College, 1907–1911. See article in *Who's Who in China*, 3rd edition, Wikisource.org.

155. Rev. Amasa Archibald Bullock and Mrs. Ruth Bullock were friends of Harvey and Grace and Northern Presbyterian missionaries in Nanking. See entry for May 26, 1910.

November 7, 1910. Hunting at Han Si Men.[156] Supper at Mrs. Williams'.[157] Went to see Dr. Davis and got news of Grace. Still O.K. but easily excited. Could I ever forsake my dear little lady?

November 8, 1910. Hunting at Lotus Lake. Fen Ren Men.[158] Mr. Chin[159] took supper with us. Letters to Dr. Wilkinson and Dennis.[160]

November 9, 1910. At home all day except long enough to go over to Han Si Meng and say hello. Working on list of new apparatus. No news from Grace.

November 10, 1910. A good day in school. Went hunting at 4:30. Nothing doing yet. I had a good shot but nothing fell. Saw Dr. Davis a few minutes. He says, "Don't go to Soochow until Dr. Wilkinson says it is best."

November 11, 1910. Letter from Grace. It rather hurt me for it showed suffering. Also a note from Mrs. Woodbridge. She sent me Dr. Wilkinson's letter. Hunting at Han Si Meng.

November 12, 1910. A bright, beautiful day and evening. Saw Grace's letter to Blackstones. Stayed to supper with them. Letter to Grace.

---

156. Han Si Meng was part of the ruins of the Ming Dynasty, which had been centered in Nanking. In the old spelling *Xi* was *Si*. *Meng* was sometimes used for *Men* meaning gate. Han Zhong Men was built in 1931 north of the Han Xi Men, an original 14th century Ming Dynasty city gate built in 1366. The gate itself has one portal, which forms a long tunnel through the base of a high, square fortress.

157. Mrs. Williams is the Lilian Williams (Mrs. John E.) who later published *Yesterdays in China*. She and her husband were Presbyterian missionaries in Nanking from 1899. See entries for June 16, 1910 and February 18, 1911.

158. Lotus Lake was situated near the city wall north-east of the city. It is also known by the name Hswein Wu Hu. Lotus Lake may be reached by a new gate in the city wall called Feng Rweng Men. A road leads from this gate across the lake to the islands. There are five islands in the lake. The lake is filled with lotus plants which blossom beautifully in summer. Before the new gate was opened visitors went there by means of boats from Tai Ping Men. Another way is by a road leading from Tai Ping Men. On one island a temple of the Lake god had been built by Dzeng Wen Djen Gung. Several Buddhist monks live in this temple. The picking of lotus flowers by visitors is forbidden. It was about four or five miles from Shia Kwan. *The University of Nanking Magazine* May, 1910, 18–19.

159. This is probably Prof. Chen at Harvey's college. CRI, 81.

160. Dennis Egbert is Harvey's American friend for whom his first son, Richard Dennis Roys, will be named. See October 5, 1913 entry. Dennis will come to China in 1915 as a missionary.

1910 DIARY

November 13, 1910. Sunday. A bright day. Wrote letters after Bible study class until church time and all the evening. Ella, Father, Louise, Edith.[161] No word from Grace today.[162]

November 14, 1910. A busy day but not too busy to think of Grace. She is in my thoughts continually and my every prayer included her. I watch the mails close. News of Grace through Dr. Davis. She is about the same, perfectly rational but quick, nervous.

November 15, 1910. A glorious evening. Oh, if only I could be with Grace tonight. Letter to Grace.

November 16, 1910. Another beautiful day. No news from Soochow.

November 17, 1910. Letter from Mrs. Woodbridge and Louise inviting me to stay with them while in Shanghai. I decide to go and stop at Soochow on the way back.

November 18, 1910. No news from Soochow. Off for Shanghai at 1:20.[163] Arrived O.K. Slept with John. A little visit that evening with Mr. & Mrs. Woodbridge.

November 19, 1910. A busy day shopping. Louise went around with me and helped a lot. Supper & evening with Stuarts'.[164]

---

161. Charlotte Louise Woodbridge was the older sister of Grace. See entries for July 7 and November 19,1910. Edith is an American friend of Harvey's. She is not identified.

162. Letters and messages may have come by people traveling between Soochow and/or Shanghai and Nanking by train, including probably foreign mail arriving on ships that docked in Shanghai. There was a Chinese postal service, with the main station at Shia Kwan, where the Shanghai-Nanking train stopped, but Mother said that servant messengers were also used. Soochow is near Shanghai and one of the train stops between Shanghai and Nanking; another is Chinkiang, which is closer to Nanking, and where Grace was born and spent her childhood. *The University of Nanking Magazine*, May 1910, 24, gives the train schedules for the journey between Nanking and Shanghai.

163. Harvey's 1:20 p.m. express got into Shanghai at 7:35 p.m. The Woodbridges have returned to Shanghai. Mrs. Woodbridge is encouraging to Harvey. It's hard to know Mr. Woodbridge's attitude here, although he apparently stopped resisting the marriage with Harvey. Louise is also supportive.

164. These are probably the George A. Stuarts he got to know in Kuling, with daughters Alcy, Anna, Vera, and Mildred and son George. See entry for June 12, 1910.

Grace

November 20, 1910. Sunday. A beautiful day and not very cold. Two church services, a walk in the PM. A long talk with Louise and another with Dr. W. [Wilkinson]

November 21, 1910. Monday. Away at 7:45. Soochow. Grace sick again. I was with her about two hours in all. She wanted to keep me and it hurt her when I had to leave.[165]

November 22, 1910. Tuesday. To work again. A busy day. Letter to Grace in the evening. Prayers for her all day.

November 23, 1910. A bright day. Tennis in PM. No news from Soochow. Dailies from Dennis.[166] Evening at home.

November 24, 1910. Thanksgiving Day. Dinner with the Methodists at Wilsons'[167]. Letter from Mrs. Wilkinson saying Grace got worse after I left on Monday. Not slept since Saturday night. I still believe God will bring things out all right but it's certainly hard waiting.

November 25, 1910. No news. At home all day. A big supper at Blackstones' but I could not have enjoyed the fun and might have spoiled it for others. I stayed at home.

November 26, 1910. No news. Went to Bs in PM–played with the children, had tea and took a short horseback ride with Harry.[168] Evening at home. Looked all day for word telling me to come to Soochow.

November 27, 1910. Sunday. No news of Grace. Spent most of the day at home writing letters. Refused an invitation to dinner at Bullocks'. Went to church but hurried home. God's plan will work out all right in the end. Oh, for patience![169]

---

165. This suggests that she's better while Harvey is there, worse when he leaves, which is perhaps another reason they let her marry him so soon.

166. Newspapers from Harvey's American friend, Dennis Egbert.

167. For more about the Wilbur F. And Mrs. Mary Rowley Wilson, see entries for November 24, 1910 and October 29, 1913.

168. Harry must be Mr. Blackstone. Mrs. B. becomes Barbara after a certain point in their friendship, and Mr. becomes Harry.

169. Harvey loved the saying, which he often quoted to me in my late teens: "Patience is virtue, catch it if you can. Seldom found in woman. Never found in man."

November 28, 1910. Letter from Mrs. Wilkinson. Saw Dr. Davis in evening. No encouraging news as yet. Supper at Blackstones'. I'll keep hope yet awhile.

November 29, 1910. Rain. No news. The last day of the Exposition so we had no class in PM.[170] Stayed at home all day.

November 30, 1910. Louise's birthday[171] [added later] Rain. No news. I am reading Job and trying to understand it. I dream a good deal these days and feel very restless.

December 1, 1910. Letter from Miss Woodbridge [Louise] says Grace was much better. Thank God again for new hopes. Received pay. American mail.

December 2, 1910. Got ready to go to Soochow.[172] A card from Mrs. W. Grace had a good day Wednesday. It may work out all right yet. God knows best.

December 3, 1910. Left at 1:20 for Soochow. Grace was perfectly natural. Supper with Grace and Mr. [Mrs.? In December 10 entry, he mentions Mrs. Woodbridge] W. Grace and I were alone all the evening and had a very pleasant, happy time.

December 4, 1910. Sunday. Breakfast at Dr. Wilkinson's. Grace and I were together after breakfast all the AM until 2 PM when I left for Nanking. We took a walk and enjoyed the sunshine and fresh air. A happy day for both of us. God surely has blessed us.

December 5, 1910. Only one class. Memorial service for student in Class D. Letters to Father and Grace. I had time to think things over.[173] Dr. Davis is not very encouraging but I'm going to hope and be happy.

---

170. The exposition had been up since May 2010. See Entry for May 21, 1910.

171. Charlotte Louise Woodbridge, born Nov. 30, 1887, second child.

172. He had apparently been waiting for permission to go, which must have depended on Grace's improvement.

173. He is probably debating here about whether they should marry. It sounds like Dr. Davis is not optimistic about her future mental health. He's a theologian though, not a physician.

December 6, 1910. Dr. Sloan's[174] birthday. [added later in Grace's hand]. Letter from Grace written Sunday evening. The poor little lady was very lonesome but trying not to show it. God grant her strength to bear these trials.

December 7, 1910. No news from Grace. I hope and pray that she is well this week. If I could only help her in some way. I still hope for the best.

December 8, 1910. Letter from Grace written Wed. She is well and happy. Her letter made me very happy. I'm full of hope and won't be discouraged by the "few."[175]

December 9, 1910. Anna May Hummel 1913[176] [added later in a different hand] A bright day. Took class D to Electric plant.[177] Supper at Settlemeyers'.[178] A pleasant evening.

December 10, 1910. (Letter from Grace Fri night) Left for Soochow at 1:20. Grace all right. Supper with Grace and Mrs. Woodbridge. Evening with Grace. Long talk with Dr. Wilkinson.

December 11, 1910. Sunday. A bright beautiful [day]. Breakfast & dinner with Grace and mother. Grace and I were together until 2:PM. A little Bible

---

174. Dr. T.D. Sloan helped after the birth of Richard. See entry for October 5, 1913. He's a Nanking doctor who also taught Sunday School at Hillcrest in 1916. Yearbook, 15.

175. "The few" probably included Dr. Davis and Mr. Woodbridge. Possibly Dr. Wilkinson, her doctor, too?

176. Harvey's friend Hummel's first child since he and Mildred Stuart were married in 1912. Mother's childhood friend's name was June Hummel, another daughter of this family.

177. The American General Electric Company, along with other American companies, took part in the Nanyang Exposition in Nanking in 1910. "The electric-lighting facilities will be ample for the exhibition, the total capacity being more than 25,000 lights for which a British machinery plant will furnish 10,000, an American machinery plant, 8000, and a German machinery plant 10,000". U.S. Congressional Serial Set, Issue 5694. A Google book on line.

178. Mr. Charles S. Settlemeyer arrived in Nanking in 1904 as part of the Disciples of Christ mission and helped with their Christian College, as well as doing literary and evangelistic work. Later the Christian College joined with the Methodists and Presbyterians to form the University of Nanking. *University of Nanking Magazine*, May 1910, 24–25. Mrs. Settlemeyer taught piano at Hillcrest in 1916. The Hillcrest Annual for 1916, 8–9. Their sons were George Kurz and Charles William Settlemeyer.

study, a ride on the motor boat.[179] While the others went to church we took a long walk. Home again at 8 PM. I'm very thankful for God's care.

December 12, 1910. A cold day. Snow in the evening. Letter to Grace. At home all PM getting ready for an exam. At Martins'[180] in evening. Carver and I walked down and back.

December 13, 1910. No word from Grace. Dr. Russell[181] vaccinated me. Tea at Blackstones'. I'm hopeful and cheerful. God always has something for the faith-strengthened to do, or bear or suffer.

December 14, 1910. Long letter from Grace. She was well on Tuesday morning. Would that I might bear some of her suffering. Wrote to Grace and to her mother.

December 15, 1910. No word from Grace today. A good talk with Harry B.[182] in the PM. Wrote to Dr. Woodbridge.[183] Walked over to Han Si Meng. Dinner party at Dr. Russell's–a very pleasant evening. Walked home. My prayer is ever for Grace.

December 16, 1910. A bright beautiful day. Two letters from Grace at suppertime. Encouraging news. Nanking Association at Settlemeyers'. Our "octet show" proved successful. A walk home in the moonlight.

December 17, 1910. Went to Soochow on the 1:20 train. Dear Dr. Davis! Mr. Woodbridge there. Long talk with Dr. W[ilkinson]. Made up my mind.[184]

179. Motorboats were used by missionaries, e.g., at Kiangyin station. For a photo, see Kessler, *Jiangyin Mission*, 50.

180. Rev. Dr. Arthur Wesley Martin was a Methodist Episcopalian staff member of the University of Nanking. CRI, 323. See footnote for June 12, 1910.

181. Dr. Russell is the medical doctor with whom Harvey stayed two weeks upon his arrival in Nanking. Foreigners probably routinely had vaccinations for diseases rife in China; for instance, there was a plague epidemic in China and Manchuria in 1910. "Third plague pandemic," Wikipedia.

182. The J. H. Blackstones are close friends of Harvey and Grace. See also entries for May 24 and September 24, 1910.

183. Harvey's letter to Dr. Woodbridge of Dec 15, presumably asking permission to marry Grace immediately. Encouraging news of Dec. 16, receiving permission to do so? Letters could be sent by train and received fairly quickly.

184. Apparently Harvey was being advised that the mental illness might recur, to think seriously before marrying Grace. Here he seems to have decided to marry her

December 18, 1910. Sunday. This is the day the Lord hath made. Nearer my home. Who follows in His train? Holy, Holy, Holy. "Holiness to the Lord." Church [at] 4.

December 19, 1910. "Home." Early chat. Went to Shanghai for John Davis. Grace & I were married at 4:30. Had supper at the Wilkinsons and spent the night in the Haden house.

December 20, 1910. Mary Alice Sarvis 1914[185] [added later.] Off for Nanking. "Our honeymoon." Mr. & Mrs. B. [Blackstone] met us at the train. "At home" with Dr. & Mrs. Russell.[186] Wedding presents.

December 21, 1910. Back to school work again. We got settled a little and kept happy.

December 22, 1910. Happy day.

December 23, 1910. Grace's birthday. Monday, 6 AM, 1889. [Year born added later.] Grace is 21–of age but "not her own boss," as she says. I think she is boss of two.[187] Wedding & birthday presents.

December 24, 1910. A bright and beautiful day. Christmas tree at the P.S. Chapel.[188] Supper at Blackstones'.

---

as soon as possible. Dr. Davis must have become more encouraging than he had been earlier. Did the doctors finally decide that marriage would relieve the conflicts that set off her illness? Perhaps. She had still been having episodes November 21, after Harvey left. Dr. John Davis apparently married them in Soochow, where they were given a room to spend the night at Haden house in Soochow. I was surprised at how quickly after her breakdown they allowed her to marry Harvey. My best guess is that they thought it would do her good.

185. Mr. and Mrs. Guy W. Sarvis were missionaries in Nanking and visited my family in Jacksonville, Florida, about 1950. Mrs. Pearl Taylor Sarvis was one of the editors of the Nanking cookbook first produced in 1916. Their son David L. and my mother were born in 1912, and their mothers exchanged valentines for the children in 1913. The families were also in Kuling at the same time in 1912.

186. The young couple stay first with the Russells, where Harvey stayed when he first arrived in Nanking. They must have had more room than at the Beebes' where Harvey had been staying.

187. Grace will turn out to have more "will" in this marriage than Harvey, who begins immediately to adapt himself to her needs and wishes.

188. P.S. Probably Presbyterian School, where some of Grace's younger brothers attended secondary school.

December 25, 1910. Sunday. First Christmas away from home. A "green" and very beautiful Christmas Day.[189]

December 26, 1910. Last day of class work. We take long walks every day. "Plans."

December 27, 1910. Quiet and happy! Life is surely worth living. Grace & I are always going to be sweethearts.

December 28, 1910. Ann Russell Taylor's birthday, 1889.[190] [Added later] Off for Shanghai to spend a few days with Father & Mother Woodbridge. A few hours at Soochow.

December 29, 1910. Shanghai. Business and pleasure.

December 30, 1910. Shanghai. Tiffin at Stuarts'. Grace & I went shopping together.

December 31, 1910. Saturday. A long drive in the PM–Grace, Louise, John & myself. Evening at home.

[END OF 1910]

189. Harvey is used to a Michigan Christmas, not a warm one as in Nanking, where the climate is similar to that of South Carolina.

190. Anne Russell Taylor is Grace's age, a friend. Anne was born December 28, 1889, Grace, December 23, 1889. Grace visited her in Hangchow April 20, 1914. She married Richard Vipon Taylor, Jr, MD, a graduate of the University of Virginia Medical School, December 31, 1912. Anne Russell Taylor also contributed to the Nanking cookbook and was the daughter of John Russell Sampson. She attended Bryn Mawr 1907– 9.

1911 Diary

January 1, 1911. Sunday. Shanghai. A beautiful New Year's Day. Two services and communion at Union Church. Tea with Mrs. Brockman.¹ Supper with Mrs. Morgan.²

January 2, 1911. Off for Nanking. Dr. Anna, Gretchen,³ Louise met us at the train. We left presents and they gave us a fur rug. Nanking at 2:35—"Home."

January 3, 1911. First exam. Plans but rather indefinite. No place to live near the school. Bs will take us.

January 4, 1911. When a man marries, he neglects his diary. Moved to Blackstones'.⁴

January 5, 1911. I find it very hard to break my will. These are days of revelation to me–revelation of my own faults.⁵

---

1. Mrs. Mary Buford Clark Brockman is the wife of Mr. F.S. Brockman, General YMCA Secretary for China and Korea. See also entry for August 3, 1910.

2. Mrs. Ruth Bennett Morgan, MD, is the wife of Dr. Lorenzo S. Morgan. They have been Southern Presbyterian missionaries since 1904. CRI, 340.

3. Dr. Anna is possibly Dr. Anne Houston Patterson (Annie) who worked at the Suqian Ren Ji Hospital–later affiliated with the Nanking Drum Tower Hospital, and she was there in early 1911. She was associated with Dr. Sydenstricker, Pearl Buck's father. The Houstons were Southern Presbyterians. Gretchen may be Dr. Wilkinson's daughter. See footnote for December 1, 1911. If these people are meeting Grace and Harvey's train, bearing wedding gifts, they must be close friends.

4. They moved from the Russells to the Blackstones.

5. Harvey and Grace have been married only 17 days, and he begins to worry about

1911 DIARY

January 6–7, 1911. I begin to realize that there is a great deal of selfishness in my life, but by the help of God and God's gift–Grace–I will put it out of my life.

January 8–9, 1911. Scarcely a day goes by that I don't offend my sweetheart in some way, but I'm not discouraged about improvement for: "Perfect love beareth, believeth and hopeth all things."[6]

January 10, 1911. "There is no fear in love; but perfect love casteth out fear."[7]

January 11, 1911. Joy and sadness seem to go hand in hand.

January 12, 1911. Each day it seems that life is bigger, that God is nearer than the day before.

January 13, 1911. Nanking Association at Blackstones'.

January 14, 1911. Last Examination. No more school until the 1st of the 2nd moon–March 1st. Grace had a bad shock in the evening.[8]

January 15, 1911. Sunday. A quiet Sunday. Bright and beautiful. Went to Djang Tung Djai[9] with Mr. & Mrs. B. after supper. Letter to Father.

January 16, 1911. Work all over. No plans. Grace very nervous.

January 17, 1911. Decide to go to Kuling for a rest. We both feel the need.

January 18, 1911. Off for Chinkiang[10] after taking dinner at Gill's. Supper at Longdens'. Went aboard "Kingsing" about 10:30.

---

his selfishness. It sounds like Grace is not easy to live with. Mother says that in later years when Grace had breakdowns, Harvey blamed himself for not being "patient enough."

6. 1 Cor 13:7: "[Charity] beareth all things, believeth all things, hopeth all things, endureth all things."

7. 1 John 4:18a.

8. A long winter vacation–six weeks. Chinese New Year on January 30. This six-weeks winter holiday for schools is still apparently the custom in modern China.

9. Djang Tung Djai would be Zhang Dong Zhai. Edith Barakat's Nanking friend Gongping Ye, a lecturer now in art history at the School of Art and Design, Changzhou, and who had studied in Nanking earlier at the Agricultural University, doesn't know where it would be located now, a century later.

10. The journey to Kuling meant going south by rail to Chinkiang, another city on the Yangtze River, getting the boat, and then going back north through Nanking, up

January 19, 1911. On the river aboard S.S. Kingsing. Delightful. Left Nanking about 4 PM.

January 20, 1911. We live in fine style.

January 21, 1911. Arrived at Kiukiang about 1:30 AM. Breakfast at the Rowes'.[11] They urge us to stay over Sunday.

January 22, 1911. Sunday. With the Rowes'. Supper with the Kupfers'.[12] We walked around the city wall in the AM, reading our Bible and enjoying nature.

January 23, 1911. Woodrow's birthday.[13] [Added later.] Off for Kuling with a big lunch put up by Mrs. Rowe. Carriage and chairs. A pleasant trip. Home.

January 24, 1911. Charlie's birthday.[14] [Added later.] Getting settled. Sorry to say it but we fuss a little. We hope to break our wills to one another soon.[15]

---

river to Kiukiang, then up the mountain by sedan chairs to Kuling. All these places had missionary stations in 1910–11. See also Introduction and Appendix C.

11. The Rowes in Kiukiang must be Mr. and Mrs. Harry Fleming (H.F.) Rowe, who, by the fall of 1911, were living in Nanking. He stayed with Harvey at the beginning of the Sun Yat-sen Revolution. She was teaching at Hillcrest in Nanking in 1916, third and fifth grade Reading and Spelling. The Rowe children in the school in 1920: David N., who wrote the Hillcrest School song, first year of high school; Caroline, seventh grade; Harry, third grade. An older sister Louise played a piano duet and taught primary grades in 1920. Hillcrest Annuals, 1916, 8–11; 1920, 2–4, 6, 61. CRI, 414. See November 8, 1911 entry.

12. The Kupfers in Kiukiang are likely Rev. Dr. Carl Frederick and Mrs. Lydia Krill Kupfer. They were Methodists. He was President, William Nast College in Chiuchiang. CRI, 265–6.

13. Woodrow Wilson Woodbridge was Grace's younger brother, born January 23, 1892, fourth child born. He never married. President Woodrow Wilson was Grace's mother Jeanie's first cousin. Jeanie Woodbridge was the daughter of James Woodrow, whose sister Janet married Joseph Ruggles Wilson, and had Thomas Woodrow Wilson, who became U.S. President. Grace and Harvey were invited to his inauguration in 1913.

14. Charlie (Charles Jahleel) is the youngest Woodbridge, eighth child, born 1902, who will come, with his sister Jeanie, to live with Grace and Harvey after his mother dies in late 1913. He was attending Hillcrest 1914–1916 and was secretary of the Watch Guard Society. Hillcrest Annual for 1916, 19.

15. Harvey's theme of breaking his will and ridding himself of selfishness continues. He is trying hard to be sensitive to Grace, but he is so different in temperament that this eagerness to adapt is doomed to failure, given her willfulness. Later she would say that he

1911 DIARY

January 25, 1911. I find there is much selfishness in my life.

January 26, 1911. Rain. Dinner with Mrs. Barry.[16] I'm learning all the time Grace is easily hurt by my careless words.

January 27, 1911. John's [Woodbridge] birthday.[17] [Added later.] Rain. We do all our own work. I do most of the cooking so that Grace will not overwork.

January 28, 1911. Rain. Went to Estate house and to #17.[18] Got some [missing word:] Groceries?] and some wet clothes for it rained hard.

January 29, 1911. Sunday. Another day of rain but *"A perfect day."* The sweetest day of all thus far. We ask God to hear our prayer.[19]

January 30, 1911. Chinese New Year's Day. Bright and beautiful. Very quiet. Another peaceful day. We are hopeful.

January 31, 1911. Rain. Dinner at the Berkins'.[20]

February 1, 1911. We try to get out for a walk every day, rain or shine.

---

should have married someone else.

16. Mrs. Barry is likely to be Mrs. Dr. Howard G. Barrie, MD, with CIM (China Inland Mission), YMCA, Kuling 1911. CRI, 25.

17. John Sylvester Woodbridge, 14 in 1911, was born January 27,1897.

18. The estate office is shown on a map I received via Mother, and not far from it is J.L. Duff & Co., which must be the store. Also listed is: Fairy Glen Hotel. I suspect that Harvey and Grace were staying in the cottage of Grace's parents. Missionaries had been having cottages built there as leaseholds since 1897. The founder of the Kuling Estate, E.S. Little, kept a hill for himself after he bought it from the Chinese government, and then he turned the rest over to a Board of Trustees representing the major missionary societies. They had it surveyed and divided into building lots, which were sold to foreigners only (all nationalities) at a fixed price (really a leasehold). The buyers were called lease renters. The Duffs started a hotel. A hospital followed by mission subscription, a church, library, etc. By 1914 Kuling was already a thriving resort for missionaries. Some three hundred bungalows had been built; and the summer community numbered possibly fifteen hundred missionaries of many denominations. See also Duff, *History of Kuling*. Unpublished. Appendix C.

19. The prayer is probably for a baby. Grace was pregnant by the summer of 1911, but she had a miscarriage. My mother, their first child, was not born until July 17, 1912. They were also hoping for their own home, and that may have been their prayer at this time. See March 1, 1911 entry.

20. Rev. John Berkin and Mrs. Leila Doolittle Berkin, MD, were Northern Presbyterian missionaries. CRI, 33. See also entry for August 18, 1912.

February 2, 1911. A glorious winter day. Snow, wind, cold, glorious. Tea with the Misses Johnson. Dinner with the Lindsays".[21]

February 3, 1911. Most beautiful–sunshine on the snow. We prepare for callers. Grace makes her first cake–fine.[22] For tea–6.

February 4, 1911. Bright. Work, long walk. Our days seem to get more perfect all the time. God knows why.[23]

February 5, 1911. Sunday. Church service for children at C.I.M.[24] Long walk towards evening. Bible study. Letter to Father.

February 6, 1911. Baked cake (Grace) and cookies (Harvey). Mrs. Lindsay, Mrs. Elliot, Mrs. Barrie[25] for tea. Reading the rosary. Up till 1:30 AM.

February 7, 1911. Picnic at Emerald Grotto.[26] Our days are more peaceful than at first. God bless my little wife and help me to be worthy of her.

February 8, 1911. Tea at Dr. Exner's.[27] I have not yet learned to control my tongue and temper. I lost my temper today and suffered for it.

February 9, 1911. A beautiful day, cooking, cleaning, loving. I pray daily for strength to be always kind & thoughtful of Grace.

February 10, 1911. Kuling still. More love.

---

21. One of the Misses Johnson may be Miss E.C., with CIM, Shanghai. CRI, 244. Mrs. W.W. (Mabel Fishe) Lindsay was with CIM in Shanghai, and in Kuling also August 3, 1912. CRI, 286.

22. Harvey taught Grace to cook after they married. Their cooking also suggests that they're in a bungalow, not at the hotel.

23. They are so much happier in Kuling. One wonders why. Perhaps partly it is Grace's having control over her domestic arrangements. Harvey doesn't understand either.

24. China Inland Mission, which had a school in Kuling, was where Grace taught. See diary entry for August 25, 1910.

25. Mrs. Elliott may be the wife of Thomas Maxwell Elliott, who was a secretary with the YMCA 1907–1928. CRI, 137.

26. This is a natural swimming pool. If it had bats, it would be seen by the Chinese as a good omen.

27. Max Joseph Exner, MD, was with the YMCA in China 1908–12. Many Western sports and Western-style sports competitions were introduced into China by him and the YMCA, even the early organization of the Olympic movement in China. "Bios-Missionaries-China-1900–1920." CRI, 142.

February 11, 1911. Children's Day at our house—5 girls from the C.I.M. We gave them a good time and took home at 5:30.

February 12, 1911. Sunday. We stayed at home all day. It's better for children to have a little exercise even on Sunday.[28]

February 13, 1911. Bought our wood today. Up to the gap *early* and back over the hills via Hankow Gorge.[29] Went to Duffs'[30] for dinner.

February 14, 1911. A busy day. Grace did not feel very well so I baked a cake. Beginning to pack. We spend some time each day praying and reading our Bibles.

February 15, 1911. More packing. Paid a last visit to the C.I.M. & hospital late in the PM. Goodbyes. Up late–peanuts.[31]

February 16, 1911. "Finish." Left the house at 10 AM–the gap at 10:30. Chairs & rickshaws–a fine bunch. Arrived at Rowes' about 3 PM. God seems to bless us continually.

---

28. He apparently refers to himself and Grace as the children who need exercise.

29. There is a photo of Hankow Gorge at Kuling as the frontispiece of the Vol XXXIV, No. 6, June 1903 issue of *The Chinese Recorder*.

30. The Duffs ran the store and hotel in Kuling. Later Jeanie Woodbridge [born May 13, 1900], Grace's younger sister, would marry the Duffs' son, Arthur, whose essay on Kuling I have put in Appendix C. I met Jeanie in 1964 when she was living in Palo Alto in some luxury. I hadn't read the diary at that point, and I had never met her. She offered me a choice of gifts: a lovely quilted silk bathrobe made in China or a flimsy, cheap cotton one, which offered no warmth. I was a graduate student at Berkeley with two-year-old Amy, barely making it financially. I chose the Chinese warm one, and she made it clear I'd chosen the wrong one, but I didn't give it back. This gives some insight into the Woodbridge family.

31. They ate peanuts! Mrs. Williams also mentions peanuts as served to Chinese women who visited them: "As Chinese women came to my door Mrs. T. T. Lu [a neighbor, a Christian] told them they need not be afraid of me for I was really just a woman like them. So they came in, very many of them and trooped over the strange foreign house, chatting cheerfully about us. 'Her face is white because she drinks milk!' 'She nurses her baby like we do!' They thought our beds were too soft and our rooms too big, but I think they began to trust our foreign ways. And so we began to invite them into our house where Mrs. Lu could speak to them, and they liked the peanuts and cakes and tea." Williams, *Yesterdays in China*, 15.

February 17, 1911. Visited Mrs. Walley and Dr. Stone's hospital & Miss Hughes'[32] Bible school. Took the boat for home. "*Loong Wo*" is a fine boat.

February 18, 1911. Arrived in Nanking about 3:30 safe & sound. Mr. Williams[33] went up in our carriage. Home again. It certainly seems good.

February 19, 1911. Sunday. We have been married two months today and life is much more settled for us both than at first. We ask God to guide us daily.

February 20, 1911. Morning prayer –Chinese, then Grace & I studied Heb.1: Shall we go to house-keeping & where? My little girl wants a home– and so do I. "A friend."[34]

February 21, 1911. Beautiful days in Nanking.

February 22, 1911. How wonderful is love. I thank God for the love of a true, sweet girl–my wife.

February 23, 1911. We want a little home of our own.

February 24, 1911. We sustain one another and love God together.

February 25, 1911. A trip on the horses. We had a good chase after a wild pig but he gave us the slip.[35]

---

32. Mrs. John Walley was the widow of Rev. John Walley, a Methodist-Episcopal missionary (he died in 1894), CRI, 498. Dr. Stone is Dr. Mary Stone, in Kuling, a Chinese woman Shih Mei Yu who had a hospital in Kiukiang in 1911. This was not uncommon for Chinese Christians to take a Western name, especially professional people. She had received medical training under Methodist auspices at the University of Michigan. "A talented, spirited woman, she became perhaps the most widely known symbol of the goals and successes of the Methodist women's work in China." CRI, 456. See entry for July 29, 1912. She would help hire a Chinese nurse for Grace and baby Margaret; Miss Jennie Hughes worked with Dr. Stone, and is described as having a "slender body, intense and full of push," in Hunter, *Gospel of Gentility*, 74. Jennie Hughes was a Methodist Episcopal missionary who ran a Bible school in Kiukiang. CRI, 228. As her own sister lay dying in 1906, Mary Stone met Jennie Hughes." Hunter, *Gospel of Gentility*, 74.

33. This Mr. Williams is probably Lilian Williams's husband, John E. See note for June 16, 1910.

34. I puzzled over this reference to "friend," which occurs fairly often, especially in Grace's diary entries. It turns out to mean that Grace menstruated. Interesting that Harvey notes it here, but they were hoping for a child. Their wanting a child is probably another reason that Grace was restless for her own home.

35. All was not solemn for those missionaries. Horse-riding seems a favorite sport,

1911 DIARY

February 26, 1911. Sunday. "God give us strength as we need and keep our lives pure and clean." I thank God for a Christian wife.

February 27, 1911. Grace went to Shanghai. How lonesome it is. She is in my thoughts constantly and everywhere I turn, I see things to remind me of her. I miss her song, her kiss, her words of love and her bright face–yes, even her thoughts. How wonderful is love. God bless and keep my little girl.

February 28, 1911. Tuesday. Lonesome. Developed pictures.[36] Card from Grace. "Was man ever blessed as I." Prayer for Grace–7:–12:–10. [7 A.M., noon, and 10 P.M.] I [am] trusting her to God's care.

March 1, 1911. A glorious day. Received pay. Good news from Dr. Davis. It looks as though we might have a home before long.[37] God has heard [our] prayers and is abundantly blessing us. Letter from Grace. What wonderful love.

March 2, 1911. Bright & beautiful but lonely. Studied Chinese for an hour with Ding Sein Sen.[38] Then Mrs. B. and I took a long horseback ride. Class in evening. Letter from Grace (in Shanghai). Thank God for my dear little wife. I want her back badly but can wait knowing she is safe and happy.

March 3, 1911. The glorious weather continues. Fine letter from Grace and American mail. Grace says I am her personal account. I hope I will be a

---

and even chasing wild pigs. Perhaps Grace initiated Harvey here.

36. Harvey was an amateur photographer, taking and developing his own photos. Also in China at the time there were professional photographers, as I have one such photo showing Grace with her first two children, taken about 1914, when Richard was a baby. There is no mention in the diary of commercial developing options. Photographic supplies must have been available there or by ordering from overseas. By 1920 in the Hillcrest School annual for that year a Brownie Photo Company ad offers film development and prints, 86.

37. Dr. Davis has offered his house, which will be where Harvey and Grace live until 1921, when they return to the U.S. It was provided by the Mission, was quite large, and had a large yard, with a wall around it. Mother used to sit on this wall and watch what went on outside on the street. Once she saw a cart of dead (abandoned) babies go by. Many poor families killed newborn girl infants because they couldn't afford to feed them, nor would they be able to work in the fields when they were older.

38. Ding Sein Sen. Ding would be the last or family/clan name. Sein Sen means teacher. Ding, Ming-wong was Harvey's Chinese teacher in 1911. He was a professor at the Theological Seminary in Nanking and a member of the National Committee of the YMCA. CRI, 121.

good account–always in balance. When Father wrote Jan. 24th, he hadn't heard of our marriage.

March 4, 1911. Grace came home from Shanghai with Mr. B., William & Old Mr. B [Blackstone]. How glad I was to see her and how glad she was to be here again. Thank you, God, for such love.

March 5, 1911. Sunday. Rainy and quiet. We stayed at home all day long and went to bed early.

March 6, 1911. Rainy. School work is starting in nicely.

March 7, 1911. Rainy. How difficult it is to control one's desires.[39] "God give me strength for these days."

March 8, 1911. A holiday. A large crowd of us got up at 3:00 AM and went over to the Confucian Temple to see the worship and sacrifice.[40]

March 9, 1911. When we are together much we fuss a good deal. God help us to be peaceful in our home. My ideal of a home is one with children and one where father and mother never have any words. But this can't be if only one is ever willing to give up.[41] "God bless our home."

March 10, 1911. True love is of God. If we but ask God for this love, he will give it to us and by it we can conquer all things.

March 11, 1911. Thank God I've learned to give up[42] and I'm fast learning patience. If I can be as a little child in the home, I ought to be a better Christian. We walked back from Hsia [Shia] Kwan on the wall.

March 12, 1911. Sunday. Rainy.

---

39. Desires = probably sexual passion.
40. Holiday related to Confucius. The temple is five miles from Shia Kwan.
41. The fussing has returned. This ideal of never expressing anger ran in my father's family, too. The Christian ethic of the time demanded a peaceful home, one in which there were no arguments. One turned to God to work things out. My parents very much tried to live up to this ideal, too.
42. By "give up" I believe that Harvey means to "give in," i.e., not take on Grace's will in arguments. Nanking was a walled city, with the wall very thick and about twenty feet wide at the top. They always go to Shia Kwan to get the train.

March 15, 1911. Rain. Moved over to the Davis house.[43] Last meal at Blackstones'–first night in "our own home." How sweet.

March 16, 1911. Rain. First day in the home. Grace takes ahold of things *fine*.

March 17, 1911. Rain. Nanking Association.

March 18, 1911. School all the morning. We are going to have all our Saturday afternoons together.

March 19, 1911. Sunday. Neglected this book.

April 1, 1911. Sat. We went to Hsia Kwan[44] to see the U.S. Army Transport "Buford" loaded with flour for the famine sufferers.

April 2, 1911. Sunday. Letters–foreign service. Dinner at Stuarts'. We had Mr. Hummel in to supper.

April 4, 1911. Rain. No school. Tea at the "Ladies."[45] Bishops McDowell and Bashford & Mrs. McDowell spoke.[46] An inspiration received to enter mission work.

---

43. There are photos of this house, including one in the annual (23) of 1916 for Hillcrest School, a school begun by the missionary Mothers' Club in 1911. An actual school building came later (1915). Mother remembers their house as being on the outskirts of Nanking, and it is visible from the school. Once a Chinese woman came to their house because she wanted to sell Grace her baby. Instead, Grace adopted the baby and paid the mother for its care.

44. Harvey often misspells Shia Kwan, the west gate, where the railroad station is and certain ships dock.

45. Ladies = Ladies Missionary Society. Technically, Harvey wasn't a missionary in the strict sense. He was teaching in a Chinese government school under the auspices of the YMCA. Becoming a missionary with the Northern Methodist Church would keep him and Grace in China. The American Protestant missionary societies are seen by R. Pierce Beaver as the first feminist movement in North America. They began in the early 1800s with women collecting pennies for foreign missions; eventually women went with their husbands, and then, by the late 1800s, they were serving as missionaries themselves all over the world. There are many single women in China by 1910. Beaver, *American Protestant Women*, 110.

46. Bishop William Fraser McDowell (1858–1937) was elected Bishop in 1904, made an official visit to India, China, Philippines, and Japan in 1910–11. Mrs. Clotilda Lynn McDowell was President of the Woman's Foreign Missionary Society of the Methodist Episcopal Church and author of "Our Work for the World." See *History of the McDowells and Connections* by John Hugh McDowell, 499. Also CRI 307. Bishop James

April 5, 1911. Rain. School. Dr. Davis came.

April 6, 19ll. Rain. No school. Went to Consulate in P.M. with Dr. Russell and registered. Applied for passport.[47]

April 7, 1911. Rain. School all day. Evening at home. We are studying Old Testament Char[acters] now. Ladies (Miss Shaw, Miss Peters)[48] to supper.

April 8, 1911. No rain and a little sun. We walked in PM to Gu Lo, bell temple, Beh Dji Go.[49] A beautiful view from the latter place. Tea at Dr. Whitmore's. Met Dr. Machin [Macklin][50] on way back and visited his works. Took a load of vegetables home in a rickshaw.

Whitford Bashford was a Methodist Episcopal Bishop who went to China at age fifty-five at his own request in 1904. The Chinese Methodists did not elect their own bishops until 1939. Bashford led the way toward union and cooperation among Protestant forces in China, especially in educational and medical work, Bible translation, and production of a common hymnal. He was instrumental in introducing a spirit of interchurch cooperation among his fellow Methodists. He helped bring about union theological seminaries in Foochow and Nanking. He was the first president of the board of Hwa Nan Women's College, Foochow. MacInnes, "bashford-james-whitford," *Biographical Dictionary of Chinese Christianity*.

47. Harvey probably needs his passport renewed to remain another year in China. He continues to teach at the same government college.

48. Miss Ella C. Shaw, a Methodist-Episcopal missionary. came to Nanking in 1886 and built the Adeline Smith Home and School for Girls.. See also entries for December 24, 1912, October 28 and November 27, 1913, and May 23, 1914, and Introduction.

49. The bell temple (Da Djung Ting) is east of the Drum Tower [Gu Lou] and west of the hill Beh Gih Goh. The bell has been there 500 years. The keeper will strike it for 20 cents, according to the *University of Nanking Magazine* May 1910, 20.

50. Dr. W. E. Macklin (the first Disciples [of Christ] missionary in Nanking, 1886), began a dispensary and hospital work. According to Lilian Williams, he had for many years been helping the extremely poor who came to his hospital by giving work in his large vegetable garden. Out of this grew a plan, with the Dean of Agriculture and Forestry at the University of Nanking Dr. Bailie's help, to create an effective way to help famine victims. He gathered together a few hundred men who had strength enough to handle a shovel. He put them to work on clearing vacant land, planting potatoes and beans, making roads, and building small bridges. Chinese and missionary sources gave money; land eventually was secured on Purple Mountain. "By 1915 it was possible to ride far up the mountainside between long rows of thrifty fruit trees–peach, plum and pear trees, and plots of strawberries and young grape vines. Nearby were the little houses of the people who had worked the land, who had made and burned the brick, who had cleared the land and made the soil, built the houses and made the good roads. All this work was done by the famine people." Williams, *Yesterdays in China*, 30.

April 9, 1911. Letter to Dennis. A dull day. Dinner at Stuarts'. Mr. Hummel in for supper. Prayers with the servants as usual.

April 10, 1911. Clearing–a beautiful evening. Tennis in PM. We stayed all night with Mrs. B[lackstone]. Grace met me at Hu Beh Djai[51] after school and we walked home together.

April 11, 1911. A most beautiful day. Mr. Carver in for supper and we walked part way home with him.

April 12, 1911. Louise came in the afternoon. We work in our strawberry patch pulling weeds.[52] To bed early.

April 13, 1911. No school–Class C away but I worked in the lab all the AM. In PM Grace and I rode to the South Gate and walked to Han Si Men[53] on the wall. Weeding garden.

April 14, 1911. Good Friday. We all went over to Mrs. Gray's[54] in the evening for supper. Sprinkled when we left but a beautiful moon when we returned.

April 15, 1911. In the PM we all rode to the Ming Tomb gate and walked on the wall to the Tai Ping Men.[55] Very beautiful. Tea at Dr. Whitmore's.

April 16, 1911. Easter Sunday. Quiet.

51. Hu Beh Djai is Hu Bei Zhai, but Ye Gongping (Ernie) says he doesn't know where it is located now. Over 100 years many place names have changed and some have changed several times.

52. Did the Americans and/or foreigners introduce strawberries into China? Much is certainly made of the strawberries. Later in the Hillcrest School calendar they name May 19, 1916 as "Nanking Association Strawberry Festival" day, 60. Louise is still with them.

53. Han Si Men is a place to hunt, part of the ruins of the Ming Dynasty.

54. Rev. and Mrs. Alfred (Minnie Moore) Gray were Northern Presbyterian missionaries in Nanking who arrived in 1907. Mrs. Gray contributed to the Nanking cookbook. *Protestant Missionaries in China*, 1043.

55. The Ming Tomb, one of the most famous Nanking landmarks, was the tomb of Emperor Tai Dzu of the Ming Dynasty, situated outside the city wall at the foot of Purple Mountain. Before the Tai Ping rebellion in mid-1800s, there were magnificent buildings, plantings of spruces and pines, but the rebels destroyed almost the whole tomb. Several later rulers have had it repaired. In front of the main entrance are five bridges, and in front of these are stone statues and animals placed in pairs. *University of Nanking Magazine*, May 1910, 10.

April 19, 1911. Our Wedding Anniversary. We have been married four months. Gave examinations at school. Tiffin at Mrs. Settlemeyer's.

April 20, 1911. Dinner at Mrs. Pettus's. Evening class. Mr. Hummel over to tea in PM. We had a good time.

April 21, 1911. Bright. Classes in AM but none in PM because of Chinese exams.[56] We went to Blackstones' although Grace was very sick in the afternoon. Nanking Association in evening and Louise played.

April 22, 1911. Saturday. At home all day. Louise left at 12: o'clock. Father Woodbridge did not come. I corrected papers part of the day. We start sleeping in separate beds.[57] Very bright and hot.

April 23, 1911. Sunday. Warm but cloudy. We stayed at home all the AM and read and slept.

May 7, 1911. Sunday. A beautiful day. Supper at Blackstones'. We enjoy Father Blackstone very much. Mrs. Russell there. Dr. R. & Harry at Hwa Yuan. [sp?][58]

May 8, 1911. Bright and beautiful. A long day at school. Studied my Bible in evening. Getting ready for Prayer meeting.

May 10, 1911. Signed contract to stay another year with the Kiang Nan Provincial College. Led Prayer Meeting.

May 11–12, 1911. My prayer and hope for next year is that the way may open up to make my life more helpful to my boys–to reach their spiritual nature and tell them of Jesus.[59]

May 13, 1911. A big picnic at the Ming Tombs. I rode from school on a bicycle. Ice cream and cake for desert–cherries.

---

56. In Harvey's Chinese college one of the courses was in the Chinese language.

57. Grace being sick and sleeping in separate beds is probably because she is pregnant.

58. Harry is Harry Blackstone. Dr. R. is Dr. Wallace Russell, with whom Harvey stayed briefly on his arrival in Nanking a year earlier. Hwa Yuan is unidentified.

59. Harvey thinks of the next year, when he is a fully committed missionary, as his opportunity to influence his "boys," who must be his students. He had decided to become a Methodist missionary on April 4, 1911. See footnote for that entry.

1911 DIARY

May 14, 1911. Sunday. Father Blackstone[60] led the foreign service. We had supper with the Bs. Harry not back.

May 16, 1911. Dr. Davis came. Visitors. Mr. Crawford[61] stayed with us. First strawberries.

May 17, 1911. Strawberries.

May 18, 1911. Fine weather. I watch the barometer now days.

May 19, 1911. Friday. Nanking Assn. Supper on the lawn at Dr. Whitmore's. Strawberries.

May 20, 1911. Afternoon and evening at home. Some misunderstandings. "God help us to make our lives harmonious and helpful."[62]

May 21, 1911. Sunday. A beautiful [day]. Letter to father. Reading *Things Fundamental* by Dr. Jefferson.[63] Foreign service. Supper at Bs. Took some tracts to school in AM and left in Reading Room.[64]

May 22, 1911. Clear & warm. Tennis at Russells' with the Dr. Had a talk with him. Late supper. Mr. Bullock over in evening to talk wiring.[65]

---

60. Father Blackstone is probably William Eugene Blackstone (1841–1935), whose son was James Harry Blackstone (J. H.). The old Mr. B. of March 4 and May 7 entries, is someone Grace and Harvey especially enjoy. The Blackstone family seem generally a stabilizing influence in their life.

61. This is the Dr. Davis whose house they live in now–John Davis, who began the Nanking Theological Seminary and discouraged Harvey when Grace was ill. See entry for October 9, 1910. Mr. Crawford is probably Rev. Dr. Oliver C. Crawford, a Northern Presbyterian on the staff of Nanking Theological Seminary. Chairman, China Council, CRI, 103.

62. Harvey puts his prayers in quotation marks.

63. *Things Fundamental: A Course in Modern Apologetics* by Charles Edward Jefferson. New York, Thomas Y. Crowell & Co., 1903.

64. The tracts must be religious tracts left for his students. I remember when Harvey left out tracts (Southern Baptist) for me to read when I was living with him as a teenager.

65. Harvey would understand wiring with his physics degree and his practical turn of mind. How much electricity was there in China at this time? Mother told me that in their home they had no telephone and no running water. One assumes little, if any, electricity or gas. Oil stoves are mentioned and perhaps there were oil lamps. See entry for Sept. 16, 1913, when baby Margaret was taught not to touch the hot oil stove.

May 25, [1911]. Habit has a great power over a man. Should good habits be cultivated? Can bad habits be broken off?

May 26, 1911. Prof. Chin, Mr. & Mrs. Hong in for supper.[66]

May 27, 1911. Sat. Lab in AM. A few of us went to Spirit Valley in PM.[67] We left our rickshaws near the gate and walked. Grace rode a donkey back.

May 28, 1911. Sunday. Read in Corinthians and Revelations. Rain in PM and evening. We walked to church in rain. Evening at home.

June 11, 1911. Sunday. Life is a series of storms & fair weather, of clouds and sunshine, following each other in rapid succession. Letter from Dennis[68] telling that Hazel had given him her love for life.

June 17, 1911. It's a sin to waste time. Our lives are short and God wants us to use our time to the best advantage. "God help us to remember the magnitude of thy work of salvation and strive to make our minutes, our hours, and our lives all count."

June 18, [1911]. Sunday. A quiet day. Mr. Gill[69] led foreign service. Grace did not go.

June 19, 1911. We have been married 6 months today. Morning spent over at Blackstones'. Long horseback ride in PM –for swim but did not go in. A perfect day–nothing but love between Grace and me.[70]

June 25, 1911. [First Grace entry] About this time our prayer was answered, we hope.[71]

---

66. First mention of Chinese dinner guests in their new home. Grace's ease with Chinese language and culture would facilitate conversation and the social situation. Prof. Chen also taught at Kiang Nan College and may have been the Chen who became its director in 1910. Mr. and Mrs. Hong are not identified.

67. The Spirit Valley temple is situated on the Dulong hillock on the left of the Purple Mountain in the northeastern part of Nanking. PM means afternoon only in the diary, not the evening.

68. Dennis Egbert, Harvey's American friend.

69. Mr. J.M.B. Gill (James Monro Banister Gill) was an Episcopal missionary and a good friend of Harvey's. See entry for September 14, 1910.

70. Given the years and years of suffering ahead, it is good to know that some days were perfect.

71. This apparently refers to their prayer for a baby. She seems to have been pregnant

July 12, 1911. [Harvey entry] A bright day. Left Shanghai at 10:AM for Tsingtau.[72] Father Woodbridge went to the boat with us. Not rough but we got sick before night. Went to bed early and got a good sleep. Grace slept on deck.

July 13, 1911. We both felt miserable all day and kept quiet. Foggy at night so we were late in reaching port. Arrived at Tsingtau about 11:PM but did not go ashore. The noise of unloading kept us awake so we did not get much sleep.

July 14, 1911. Up early. We put our baggage on wheelbarrows and took rickshaws for the Pension Luther which we found without any trouble. Things were all ready for us. A beautiful place. Swim in the ocean in the PM. Delightful.

July 15, 1911. Bright and beautiful. I took a long walk alone. Grace felt too tired to go.

July 22, 1911. "May God thwart all our plans until His own will is clearly manifest." (From *The Tragedy of Paotingfu*.)[73]

July 23, 1911. Sunday. German Lutheran Church in AM. We went up to Mr. Scott's[74] and joined with the missionaries in an hour service at 6 o'clock.

July 25, 1911. We profit spiritually by living in the company of Father Blackstone.[75] This morning's prayer on "conversation."

---

earlier, given their sleeping separately and her feeling ill, but maybe she's more confident now. It's her first diary entry. She would have a miscarriage later this same summer.

72. Tsingtau was another place missionary families could go in the summer to get out of the heat and away from disease. I believe that this is the only time Harvey and Grace went to this beach resort, farther north along the China coast, opposite Korea. They stayed in the Pension Luther. Mother has no memory of ever going there. Perhaps getting seasick on the voyage put them off. Pension Luther offered tennis, swimming, and riding. The concession was operated by the Germans who, even before World War I began in 1914, were spying on the Chinese and the Americans in China. Downing, *Jack of Spies*.

73. Ketler, *Tragedy of Paotingfu*, 89.

74. Mr. Scott may be the Rt. Rev. Dr. Thomas Arnold Scott of the Anglican Communion in China, who became a bishop in 1921 and at this time was a missionary in the diocese of North China (1908–1921) and was later based in Shanghai. As a bishop he was Chairman of the Anglican House of Bishops and the Union Medical College. CRI, 425.

75. The elder Mr. Blackstone being there is perhaps the reason they came that year.

GRACE

July 27, 1911. A trip on a launch–big party. Very pleasant and we enjoyed it. Swim after returning. Tai Chin Gong Miao.[76]

July 28, 1911. Mr. Hummel arrived. News of Dr. Stuart's death.[77]

July 29, 1911. Sat. I fell– "failed." What a source of strength is prayer and how little we make use of it.

August 9, 1911. Delightful Days. Tennis & swimming in AM. Sleep, Tea, Tennis & Rides in PM. We also read & study a little.

August 16, 1911. Grace has been sick for two weeks today–in bed one week.[78] She has been very patient. I think our love has been strengthened.

August 27, 1911. Sunday. We remembered the day but could not do much.[79] On the boat–*Gouv. Jaeschke*–between Tsingtau & Shanghai–both of us were sick. We were happy in each other's love, however, and could look back together at the joys of a year ago.

August 28, 1911. Shanghai at 8:30 AM. Went to Evans'[80] and after resting a little spent the day shopping. A good night's sleep. Grace bought me a little book for notes–a present to remind me of August 27th.

August 29, 1911. Left for Soochow at 7:45. Walked out to the Tish-Ying-I-yueiu [sp?][81] and got wet to the skin in a driving rain. Dr. Wilkinson[82] glad to see us. We dried out with an oil stove and had a pleasant day.

---

76. Tai Chin Gong Miao is a temple. *Miao* means temple. Dr. Kessler, in an email after reading the diary, said it was probably Taoist.

77. This is probably Dr. George Stuart, whose girls Harvey had met in Kuling, while the family was living in Shanghai, though he had been Nanking University's president 1895–1908. See entry for October 19, 1910.

78. Grace is having morning sickness or a threatened miscarriage?

79. August 27, 1910 was the date of their "understanding."

80. Dr. Evans would deliver my mother in Kuling in July 1912. The family lived in Shanghai. They may have consulted the doctor about Grace's probable pregnancy. See also entry for September 9, 1910.

81. Tish-Ying-I-yueiu is unidentified.

82. Dr. Wilkinson was one of the doctors in Soochow who looked after Grace in late 1910.

August 30, 1911. Off for Nanking on the 9:39 train.[83] The cook took us to the [train] station in a motor boat. Nanking and district along the R.R. [railroad] flooded from Kiang Tse. Carriage up to hubs in water at Hsia Kwan. Home! The cook got us some supper (R.B.). Lao Dai married and sent a substitute.[84]

August 31, 1911. Beginning to get settle[d]. Note from Prof. Chin: school flooded and will not open for three weeks.[85] Showers. [rain showers][86]

September 1, 1911. Friday. Showers.

September 2, 1911. Showers.

September 3, 1911. Sunday. Clear.

September 4, 1911. Rain in afternoon and evening.

September 5, 1911. Hard rain in night and morning.

September 6, 1911. Bright and cool.

September 7, 1911. A Most Beautiful day. Fixed bicycle, developed pictures in evening. Harry [Blackstone] tried his horse on a carriage. Full moon.

September 8, 1911. Bright and warm–beautiful. Nights cool.

September 9, 1911. Rain in PM continued thru night–gentle. Went to school–received pay. Gill and Hummel to supper—dominoes.

September 10, 1911. Sunday. Rained during day and night. We stayed at home all day.

September 11, 1911. Hard rain in morning. Water higher than ever–over the road at San Sen Low. Sunshine in PM.

---

83. Shanghai fast train from Soochow at 9:39 A.M., gets into Nanking at 2:37 P.M.

84. R.B. may stand for roast beef. These cooks are a very important part of the household. Lilian Williams devotes a whole chapter to their wonderful cook, whom she taught to make their favorite Western dishes. She writes: "For his faithful service through the years [23!], I owe a debt which can never be paid. When we left Nanking that gray March day in 1927, with cherry trees just coming into bloom, my faithful cook ran beside the carriage, with his hand in mine until they made him let go." Williams, *Yesterdays in China*, 24.

85. Mr. Chen is a teacher at Harvey's college, and probably the director. See Entry for August 8, 1910.

86. The Yangtze was subject to terrible flooding, of which this is a good example.

September 12, 1911. Sunshine. Mr. Grant and Miss Swenson[87] to supper in the evening. Fixed (repaired) bicycle again.

September 24, 1911. Sunday. Very warm–water down about two feet.

September 25, 1911. Very warm, cool at night. Tennis and tea at Consul Gilbert's.[88]

September 26, 1911. Very warm.

October 9, 1911. Monday. Water down at the school grounds. School open with rather decreased attendance.

October 22, 1911. Sunday. A quiet day. Grace played the organ for three services at the chapel.[89] We all went to foreign service except Mrs. Russell, who is still in bed.

October 23, 1911. No classes today. The Unrest in China has greatly disturbed the students. Many are going home.[90]

November 5, 1911. We have been expecting Nanking to be taken by the rebels for some time now but all is quiet here as yet.

November 6, 1911. Reported this PM that the Emperor has abdicated. We all hope the trouble will soon be over.

---

87. Dr. J.S. Grant was a Northern Baptist missionary in Nanking. See entry for July 23, 1910 and for December 14, 1911. Miss Gladys Virginia Swenson was with CIM and the daughter of Mrs. K. Moll Swenson. See entry for July 15, 1913. CRI, 463.

88. Alvin W. Gilbert was Vice-Consul 1914–16 and Wilbur T. Gracey was Consul 1910–12. Both were American diplomats in Nanking. Apparently Gilbert served as Consul also in 1911. In 1916 Mrs. Gilbert was both Secretary-Treasurer and Superintendent first and second grades, and taught German and Algebra at Hillcrest School. Their children, Katherine, third grade, Alvin, second grade, Jeanette, first grade, and Edmund, seven-eighth, who was in the Watch Guard Society, are all mentioned in the Hillcrest Annual, 1916, 8–11.

89. Grace was a gifted musician and apparently played the organ as easily as the piano.

90. The first hint in the diary of political troubles. The first rumblings are felt of the Sun Yat-sen Revolution. See Introduction. Pearl Buck, in *My Several Worlds*, 9, notes about the Manchu dynasty which was to fall because of this revolution: "China conquered by letting itself be conquered and then persuading the conquerors to move into palaces and enjoy themselves." She calls the Chinese "practical and philosophical." The Manchus, when they took over in 1644, were allowed to become effete. The Chinese ran the government and waited for a revolution in the Chinese tradition.

November 8, 1911. Consul Gracey requests all ladies and children to go to consulate or leave city. Crowded. Grace decides to go to Shanghai. Went to gate in Consul's carriage with guard. Miss Swensen also. Shooting all night outside S. Gate.[91] Mr. Rowe stayed with us.

November 9, 1911. Quiet after 6 AM. Letter from Grace in PM. Fighting last night outside S. Gate. All kinds of reports abroad but you can't believe anything at one hearing. 8 PM. Moon up. Shooting begun. Ladies all out [of] the city.[92]

November 10, 1911. Quiet all day. Bright and warm. Went to Consulate in AM with letters. Catholic Priest, "Gain,"[93] came to see us in PM. HJB,[94] Brown & Drum took carriage load of cueless teachers[95] (5) from Hu Beh Djai school to Bible School compound. Report that soldiers are killing cueless gov. students. Moon rose at about 8:30.

November 11, 1911. Sat. Cloudy–a little rain about noon. Went to consulate with letters after breakfast. Gill, HJB & I rode bicycles and went from consulate down to Shia Kuan Gate which opened 10 to 11. Many went out. Home in time for dinner. No mail. Packed a trunk to send Grace or take myself. Quiet all day and evening.

November 12, 1911. Sunday. Sent trunk to Grace by Harry [Blackstone]. Went to Shia Kwan and back while gates were open. Consul received orders

---

91. S. Gate must be South Gate. Shia Kwan, near railroad and shipping dock. is the West Gate.

92. Ladies are no doubt American and other foreign women.

93. Gain may well be Theodore Gain, S.J.

94. By "HJB" Harvey may mean "JHB" for Harry Blackstone, or James Harry Blackstone. Mr. Brown may be Rev. Francis Augustus Brown, who has been in China since 1910. Drum may be Rev. W.J. Drummond.

95. As a result of the Sun Yat-sen revolution, Chinese men stopped wearing their pigtails or *queues*, which had been imposed by the Manchus 300 years earlier. The Emperor was a Manchu. Here Harvey spells *queue* as *cue*. Chinese women stopped binding their feet. Samuel Isett Woodbridge notes with glee that the Chinese women had refused to wear the drab clothes of their Tartar conquerors. They'd rather die! But the men submitted to this, too. "The Chinese even forgot that the queue was a badge of subjection, and jeered the missionaries for their queueless heads. So strange did people look with their heads unshaved that all Roman Catholic priests and many Protestant missionaries adopted the queue in order to escape peculiarity and to win the people." Woodbridge, *Fifty Years*, 83.

from Captain [of] *New Orleans*[96] to leave. Refused. Wired to Sec. of State. All quiet in city. University students went out–about 30 cueless.

November 13, 1911. Monday. Guard at Consulate withdrawn. Received mail. Rain all of PM. Gill and I went to Hwa Pai Low[97] and got wet. Harry returned from Shanghai with letter from Grace. Quiet all day in city. Plans to leave. Packed a trunk after supper. Thoughts of going to Grace.

November 14, 1911. Tuesday. Decided to go to Shanghai.[98] Took trunk, suitcase and cory.[99] At Consulate found consul removing archives and valuables to ship at Shia Kwan. Took trunk for Dr. R.[Russell] and suitcase for H.J.B. Seven foreigners besides myself. Everything went smooth. Joy at meeting Grace.

November 15, 1911. Wed. At Shanghai. Delivered letters, got trunks. Friend of Grace's came in AM and stayed all day and night (Miss Alchine).[100] Went shopping in PM.

November 16, 1911. Shopping. Rained all day. Tiffin with Louise.

November 17, 1911. Shopping in AM. Rain all day.

November 18, 1911. Sat. Rain. Called on Barbara[101] at Lincoln House.

November 20, 1911. Stuarts left for America.[102]

---

96. The *New Orleans* is an American naval vessel off the coast, at Shia Kwan. See July 4, 1910 entry.

97. Hwa Pai Low was Hua Pai Lou, which is present-day Tai Ping Lu. Apparently in 1911 it was a church compound, later destroyed by the Japanese during the Rape of Nanking. Ye Gongping (Ernie) sent additional information: the construction of Hua-Pai-Lou was intended to show the appreciation of the first Emperor to a general called Chang-Y-Chun (1330–1369) who fought bravely and played a vital role in the founding of the Ming Dynasty. The first Emperor, Zhu Yuanzhang, had granted the general the right to build a mansion in Nanking, and at the mansion gate, a special luxurious gate was built called Hua-Pai-Lou.

98. Harvey is certainly calm in this sudden Civil War crisis.

99. Cory = kori, a Japanese woven basket used to carry luggage.

100. Miss Alchine is unidentified.

101. Barbara is probably Mrs. Blackstone. Apparently her husband (Harry/JHB) had taken her and the children to Shanghai and then returned to Nanking.

102. This would be Dr. George Stuart's family, wife and daughters, because he had died. His daughter Mildred, however, stayed in Nanking.

1911 DIARY

November 22, 1911. Wed. Started studying Chinese at YMCA school. 9: to 12: and 1:30 to 3:30.

November 24, 1911. Fri. Got Yang Lein Len [probably Yan Lein Lin][103] for teacher. Promised him $15 a month.

November 28, 1911. Hanyang captured by Imperialists after 4 days of fighting. Revolutionists retreat to Wu-chang.

November 29, 1911. Went to Soochow to wedding Annie Wilkinson to Dr. Moony[104]. Very beautiful. We stayed over-night with Dr. Davis & Alice.

November 30, 1911. Thanksgiving Day at Big Pagoda & University.[105] Morning in Soochow. A big turkey dinner with Dr. & Alice Davis. "Fine." A Chinese feast at 4:30. Wilkinsons persuade us to stay over another day with them. Dr. Wilkinson with consent of his station proposes to take us into the mission.[106] Grace pleased. Hopes and plans.

December 1, 1911. Friday. Breakfast with Wilkinsons'. Gretchen, James, Martha,[107] Grace and I went to the city in Mr. Haden's[108] boat to do some shopping. Took a big lunch, bought Chinese candy. We took train for Shanghai at 2:54. (Nanking taken by Revolutionaries.)

December 2, 1911. Study. The YMCA language school is a great help to me.

103. Yang, Lein Lin was with the YMCA and the London Missionary Society and based in Nanking. He was obviously in Shanghai at this time. CRI, 537.

104. Annie Wilkinson is the daughter of the Dr. Wilkinson who treated Grace. Dr. James Potter Mooney was a Southern Presbyterian missionary with the Elizabeth Blake Hospital in Soochow. Presbyterian Heritage Center. *Biographical Index of Missionaries in China.*

105. Big Pagoda and University would be in Soochow. Thanksgiving includes the Chinese.

106. This plan, of joining the mission at Soochow, did not materialize. There was perhaps doubt when it was made that they would be able to return to Nanking, hence the plan to join the Soochow Mission? About this time Grace became pregnant with my mother, who was conceived during the Sun Yat-sen Revolution, born the following July 17. They were probably staying most of this time with Grace's parents, who welcomed the refugees from Nanking and helped them find places to stay in Shanghai. Jean Woodbridge, Grace's mother, was especially helpful to the missionary refugees. She died of cancer six months after my mother was born. One wonders if she already felt ill at this point.

107. Gretchen, James, and Martha are perhaps other Wilkinson children. See January 2, 1911 entry.

108. Robert Allen Haden (1865–1917), A Southern Presbyterian missionary in China.

December 9, 1911. Sat. Outlook rather dull. No money coming in and none saved up for a time like this. Perhaps God is trying our faith. We can't complain because we have not suffered.

December 10, 1911. Sunday. Church AM and PM. Stayed at home all the afternoon.

December 11, 1911. Monday. We decide to go to Nanking.[109]

December 12, 1911. Tues. Off for Nanking on the early train. Several of the Nanking ladies went on the same train. Home at 4 PM. Da sz fu glad to see us and gave us a good supper. To bed at 7:30.

December 13, 1911. Wed. We went over to my school and found it turned into a soldier's camp. Had been about 300 there but only 100 when we were there. My lab just as I left it.[110]

December 14, 1911. Went to Mr. Djo[111] at the University and got him to write a letter to the director for me. Grace interpreted. Got Director's address at school. Went to see Grant.[112]

December 15, 1911. Mr. Djo's brother—Djo Sien Sen–came to teach me. —Started to studying–3 hrs with teacher. 3 hrs alone.[113]

December 16, 1911. Sat. Studied in morning. Hummel and I went to the Taiping men in PM and got some relics of the battle.

December 19, 1911. Tues. Our first anniversary. Studied in morning as usual. Gave Grace a book—"Cookery Book. Just for Two."

December 23, 1911. Grace 22 and happy.[114] Day spent very much as usual. Gave Grace napkin ring. We are very happy. No days like these.

---

109. This decision to return to Nanking must have taken courage. But perhaps they were partly motivated by trying to get Harvey back on salary?

110. Harvey's lab being okay must have been a great relief.

111. Mr. Djo seems to be one of the Chinese faculty at the University of Nanking. Sein Sen means teacher. Djo would be his family or clan name.

112. Dr. J. S. Grant is a Northern Baptist missionary in Nanking. See also entries for July 23, 1910 and September 12, 1911.

113. Since Harvey can't return to his teaching yet, he is working hard on his Chinese.

114. "Grace is 22 and happy" will be echoed in following years by Grace's entries in the diary: "Grace is 23 and happy," etc.

December 24, 1911. Sunday. Foreign service at the Quakerage.[115] Miss Butler led. Psalms 19 and 91. David, a man after God's own heart. Our thoughts: "As a man thinketh so is he." Hopeful words from Mr. Bowen.[116]

December 25, 1911. Monday. A very happy Christmas. Stocking full. Hospital people in. Dinner. Tea at Blackstones'. Candy and cards to Hospital children. Christmas service at Presbyterian Chapel.[117]

December 29, 1911. Friday. Supper at Blackstones'. Cue cutting day.[118] Bright and beautiful. Meeting at Quakerage. $5000 refused because of conditions.

December 31, 1911. Sunday. Service at the Quakerage. H.J. Blackstone preached. Mr. Fen[119] and Mr. Grant came to Russells' for supper.

---

115. The Christian missionaries worshiped together in a union service. The various missions in Nanking in 1910 were: The Mission Catholique established in 1599 by the Italian Jesuit Matteo Ricci; the Disciples Mission, begun by Dr. W.E. Macklin in 1886; American Friends Mission, begun in 1890 by Miss E.H. Butler; the Methodist Episcopal Mission, begun in 1882 by Rev. Virgil C. Hart; the Presbyterian Mission, 1874; YMCA begun in Nanking in 1898 by Mr. F.S. Brockman. *University of Nanking Magazine*, May, 1910, 24.

116. The verse is from Prov 23:7. Miss Esther Butler, R.N., founded the Quaker mission in 1890. She and other women opened an orphanage and a school for women up the Yangtze, inland from Shanghai. In 1894 they established a hospital for women and children. Chinese men and women played an increasing part of the work, and by 1907 the Friends had a Chinese pastor named Gao. Both the Sichuan and Nanking Quaker missions had soon seen that "conversion" was unusual, but that their community work was effective and helpful. It also demonstrated Quaker values in a tangible way, especially when done in equal partnership with the Chinese people. quakersintheworld.org/quakers-in-action/308. CRI, 64. Mr. A.J. Bowen is President of the University of Nanking. Mrs. Bowen contributed to the Nanking cookbook.

117. Presbyterian Chapel must be part of P.S. [Presbyterian School] University of Nanking Magazine reports that Grace Memorial Chapel was added in 1895, and it seems to be near the Boys Boarding School. The Chapel, mentioned here, was also where a Christmas service was held December 24, 1910. This seems to be where the missionaries have an annual Christmas party.

118. Because of the successful revolution, all Chinese men who hadn't done so already on this day cut their queues or pigtails. The $5000 which was refused and under what conditions is unknown.

119. Rev. Courtenay H. Fenn was a Presbyterian missionary who filed a report on the Boxer rebellion and compiled the first Bible concordance in Chinese and an early Chinese-English dictionary. He was the father of William P. Fenn. Nytimes.com/1993/04/25/obituaries. CRI, 148.

End of 1911 diary entries. Under **"Memoranda."** A second entry for **December 31, 1911**. Letter from father of Nov. 20, about Dr. Roys. Wieshien. His father, Charles H. Roys was 1st cousin to Albert Geer & Lizzie Geer Roys (mother of Mabel Roys). Charles H. lived with his grandfather near Alloway, NY (Samuel Westfall). Charles H. Roys, son of Orson; Orson, son of Isaac Levi, Jr., brother of Levi & dent. Isaac–Orson–Charles H.–Dr. Charles Roys. Isaac & Levi married Curtis sisters. Harvey, son of Levi, married his cousin, Hanna Curtiss, daughter of Abijah Curtiss. Charles H. was a brilliant lawyer–killed himself. Orson died in an asylum. George, a brother of Dr. went crazy. Harvey, a brother of Orson killed himself.

Frank Roys <Ray <Gerald
    <Mable

George Roys <Norman
    <Mary
    <Bertha

Father Roys' family:

Ella Roys Gore
Graham Roys [Harvey's father] <Carrie L. Smith
Martha Roys Scott <Harry
Carrie (Louise) Roys Smith, North Brookfield, Mass. <Elizabeth Smith Varnum <Florence Louise Varnum, July 5, 1911.
Mr. & Mrs. Varnum–Elizabeth V. Is daughter of Darrel
Florence Louise Varnum, July 5, 1911. Granddaughter of Carrie Roys Smith[120]

END OF 1911 DIARY

---

120. The fascinating part about this genealogical entry is that it shows clearly that there is mental illness, quite possibly bi-polar disease, coming down through Harvey's family. I would guess that Harvey is only learning this in 1911. Did his father feel that he should warn Harvey about the mental illness in his own family when he had just married Grace, who had had a nervous breakdown? Or perhaps his father simply felt that, now that Harvey was married, he should know more about his ancestors? Harvey was very pleased, I'm sure, that one of his cousins had a little girl on his birthday, July 5. From my mother, I never heard much at all about Harvey's relatives, and nothing about any mental illness in his family. She apparently didn't read this memorandum. I broke the news to her myself when she was in her 90s.

1912 Diary

January 1, 1912. Monday. Studied. Finished Part I (10 lessons) up to the review.

March 29, 1912. [Grace entry] Grace's w.l. [waist line] 37–3/4 in.[1]

April 14, 1912. [Harvey entry] Sunday. A beautiful [day]. Grace well. W.L. 38.5. Dr. Gaynor a little better. Temp. 104.5.

April 21, 1912. [Harvey entry] Dr. Gaynor[2] died early this morning.

May 3, 1912. [Harvey entry] W.L. 40 in.

May 12, 1912. [Harvey entry] Sunday. Grace well. W.L. 40.5 (max). Taught S.S. [Sunday School] Class in AM. Nap before dinner. We looked at the baby clothes after.

May 31, 1912. [Harvey entry] Grace well. W.L. 41 in.

---

1. Grace is now pregnant with my mother, Margaret, due in July. Waist line measurements of the mother are apparently used more than her weight as a sign that the baby is growing normally.

2. Dr. Lucy Gaynor came to Nanking in 1892 as part of the Friends' mission to begin two decades of missionary work as the city's first female physician. She established a hospital and a training school for nurses. On December 6, 1911, Nanking fell to revolutionary forces; by December 10, Dr. Gaynor and her staff opened an emergency field hospital, where she contracted typhus of which she died on April 22, 1912, according to Northwestern University's Medical School: "Contribution to War Efforts." CRI, 166.

June 28, 1912. [Harvey entry] Kuling. Full moon. Love on the front porch.³ Such beautiful days in our lives. Grace well. W.L. 41.5 in.

July 3, 1912. [Harvey entry] Kuling. Bright and beautiful. Grace well. Alcohol—.50 per pt.⁴ Rec'd bed pan. Pains. Went for Dr. Evans–later for Miss Harris.⁵ Nothing doing.

July 5, 1912. [Grace entry] Harvey's birthday.⁶ Made a cap for Baby.

July 14, 1912. [Harvey entry] Sunday. Quiet, bright & warm. Waiting. Went to church in evening.

July 15, 1912. [Harvey entry] Still waiting. Played games. It rained.

July 16, 1912. [Harvey entry] Tuesday. Waiting, playing games, etc. Took a very long walk after 5 PM.⁷

July 17, 1912. [Harvey entry] Wednesday. Up at 3 AM. Regular pains and show.⁸ Dr. Evans & Nurse were called at 7. 5: Breakfast (Jean & Charlie to Evans' for breakfast). Pains worse and more frequent. A cloudy day. Grace very cheerful between hurts. Baby girl born in a thunderstorm at 2:45. Weighed 9 pounds. Grace & Harvey very happy. Grace rested but did not sleep much up to 12 o'clock at night. Baby cried a good deal before 12. I did all I could for it but it only stopped when jiggled so we let it cry and after awhile it went to sleep and slept until 6 AM. This was my first experience handling babies.⁹

---

   3. The diary entries pick up as the time of the baby's birth draws near. They've gone up to Kuling now. By "love on the front porch" Harvey probably means the exchange of loving words, maybe kisses.

   4. They probably have alcohol as part of the preparations for the birth.

   5. See entry for Dr. and Mrs. H.F. Evans on September 9, 1910. Miss Harris is Dr. Lucy E. Harris, MD. CRI, 198.

   6. Harvey is 26.

   7. Harvey and Grace both probably took this long walk. Frequently any kind of extra exertion like housecleaning or a long walk will bring on labor.

   8. Harvey knows all the obstetrical terms, e.g., show.

   9. Mother often talked about how she was born during a thunderstorm, so this became a family story. Harvey may be inexperienced, but he certainly tries his hand at everything, including a brand new baby.

July 18, 1912. [Harvey entry] Nurse–Miss Yang[10]–came early, about 6. Gave Grace a bath and cleaned her all up. Mother[11] gives lots of attention to the baby. Dr. Evans came up with his cheery way and settled a few things in our minds. It doesn't hurt a baby to cry and you can spoil them in half a day. Baby is 20 inches long without any stretching. Put the baby and basket in two chairs by Grace's bed, and I lay on the front room bed. We all went to sleep. Baby slept from before noon until after 5.

8:30 PM. Both of my girls are sleeping peacefully. They will wake up soon for refreshments but I think they are going to sleep well tonight.

July 19, 1912. [Harvey entry] Not so much sleep as I had expected. The baby had a little crying spell and Grace needed lots of attention. All went well today. We like Miss Yang very much. She left about 4 PM and returned at 8:30 to take care of Grace during the night. Mother said I might sleep on the porch and I went to bed tired out and with a headache soon after 9.

July 20, 1912. [Harvey entry] After a good night's rest I helped take care of Grace until 10 AM, when I went swimming with John[12] & Charlie. Grace is stronger and better each day.[13] Baby had her first bath today. We have decided to call her Margaret Louise.[14] Grace rested during the afternoon and evening. Sent Nurse home early for it is my night. Nursed baby every two hours today and yesterday. Milk coming today. Hard lumps in breast. Baby delights us all. We keep her awake from about 5 to 6 PM so she will sleep all night.

---

10. Yang, Miss, may be Miss Grace Yang, who was with the YWCA in Shanghai and a member of the National Committee of the YWCA, CRI, 537.

11. Mother here is Grace. We smile now at the idea that a baby could be spoiled in half a day, but even in my infancy in 1937 mothers were told to make babies wait for hours between feedings and not to pick them up. Mother tells how she yearned to pick me up! At least these parents got their reassurance that it doesn't hurt for the baby to cry. Later, when Grace was breast-feeding Margaret, she nursed her every two hours.

12. John Woodbridge is fifteen now, and Charlie is ten.

13. Women were still given long weeks of bed rest after a birth. The medical profession didn't yet understand that this slowed down the recovery.

14. She ended up Margaret Elizabeth. Grace's older sister, Louise, had been very supportive of their love. There don't seem to be any Margarets or Elizabeths in either family, but Mother used to joke that the Princesses of England, Margaret and Elizabeth, were named after her.

July 22, 1912. [Harvey entry] Decided on the name for our baby girl–Margaret Elizabeth Roys. Mother wrote nearly 100 little cards and I began tying them.

July 23, 1912. [Harvey entry] Sent about 40 little announcements to Post Office–all for Kuling people.[15]

July 25, 1912. [Harvey entry] Weighed baby after bath. 8–1/2 lbs. with cloth & band. Net wt. about 8–1/4 lbs.

July 27, 1912. [Harvey entry] Grace sat up in bed for a few minutes at two different times. She is getting stronger every day. Beautiful weather. Sent the last of the announcements out–all foreign–to M.E. Pub. Co. to be mailed in American Post Office.[16]

July 28, 1912. [Harvey entry] Sunday. Went to church and heard Mr. Gordon,[17] author of "Quiet Talks on Prayer," etc. Grace had her first visitor–Miss Hyde, and Mr. & Mrs. Duff[18] called.

July 29, 1912. [Harvey entry] Gave Dr. Mary Stone a cheque for $49[19] for nurse for three weeks. More than enough but we gave the rest as a thank offering. Mr. & Mrs. Weldon, Mildred, Barbara, Mrs. Grier, and Miss Albaugh called.[20]

July 30, 1912. [Harvey entry] Baby weighed 8 lbs. 15 oz. 22 inches long. Grace much stronger–sitting up on the edge of bed a long time. Mrs. Sarvis called for an hour.

15. This postal service must be only for Kuling. Later birth announcements were sent abroad to the U.S. in one mailing, then distributed there.

16. Probably these cards were bundled up and sent in a package with postage money via a ship from Shanghai to U.S., then mailed in U.S.

17. Gordon, Rev. Samuel Dickey, *Quiet Talks on Prayer*. This book is still in print. He also wrote *Quiet Talks on Power*, which Harvey was reading later. See note for September 15, 1912. He was also the editor of *Missionary Review of the World*.

18. Miss Hyde is unidentified. The couple would be the elder Duffs, John Duff and wife, who first settled and developed Kuling.

19. The Mexican silver dollar was the currency in China in 1912, and it was valued at $.49. One inflation calculator indicates the $.49 from 1912 would in 2016 be equal to $11.69. Multiply this by 49 to get $572.81. Service, *Golden Inches* 98. Dr. Mary Stone is a Chinese woman Shih Mei Yu. See entry for February, 17, 1911.

20. Mr. & Mrs. Weldon are unidentified. Mildred Stuart is engaged to Harvey's friend Hummel.

1912 DIARY

July 31, 1912. [Harvey entry] Wed. Made baby a baby basket 5-1/2 oz.[21] Mrs. Allison & Miss Moffet[22] called. Grace sat up in a chair with her dress on for about an hour. Our baby is beautiful.

August 1, 1912. [Harvey entry] Baby weighs (9'5"-5'1/2") = 8 lbs. 15-1/2 oz. No clothes on. Both baby & mother well. Grace sits up in a chair a little each day now.

August 2, 1912. [Harvey entry] Last night was the best night yet. Baby cried a little before 10 PM. Fed then, slept until 3 AM, another good meal, slept until 7 AM. Grace gave baby a bath for first time. Mr. Bullock called in AM. Mrs. & Miss Molland in PM. Grace sat up in a chair for a long time in PM and wrote a letter to Mrs. Bishop.[23]

August 3, 1912. [Harvey entry] Grace gave Margaret a bath after taking one herself–fine. Baby weighs 9 lbs., ½ oz. Mrs. Lindsay called and brought flowers. Mr. & Mrs. Brockman[24] called.

August 5, 1912. Grace bathed baby. Grace improved. Mr. & Mrs. McKee & brother McKee[25] [called]. Miss Yang came and stayed a long time helping us.

21. The basket weight is given because he is going to weigh the baby in the basket and then subtract it.

22. Rev. Andrew and Mrs. Ella Gates Ward Allison were Southern Presbyterian educational missionaries based in Soochow 1904-08 and in Kiangyin 1908-40, CRI, 6. Miss Carrie Lena Moffet, a Southern Presbyterian, served as educational missionary in Soochow and Kiangyin 1907-41. In Jan, 1911, she went to Kiangyin to teach in the Girls School and the Woman's Bible School, both schools being under the care of Mrs. Ella D. Little. She is probably the sister of Rev. Dr. Lacy Irvine Moffett, who had five sisters serving as missionaries in China. He was in Soochow 1908-1940. His wife was Mrs. Kate Hall Rodd Moffett. Rev. Moffett took the place of Dr. Davis in Soochow when Davis went to Nanking to serve at the Theological Seminary there. Miss Carrie Moffett, CRI, 338.

23. Professor Rev. Amasa Archibald Bullock was a Northern Presbyterian missionary based in Nanking. See entry for November 6, 1910. Mrs. Lily Webb Molland (Mrs. Charles Edwin) was a Methodist Episcopal Missionary in Shanghai, and probably the matron of the Kuling hospital. CRI 338. Miss Molland is probably her sister-in-law. Mrs. Bishop is probably Luella Bishop who lived with Harvey and Grace for awhile in 1913.

24. Mrs. W.W. Lindsay (Mabel Fishe) worked with CIM in Shanghai. See entry for February 2, 1911. CRI, 286. Mr. F.S. Brockman is General YMCA secretary for China and Korea.

25. Rev. Samuel Clark (1884-1976) and Mrs. Augusta List McKee are Northern Presbyterian missionaries. Brother McKee is unidentified, perhaps one of two other sons of W.J. McKee, Irwin William (1881-1914) or Sydney McKee (1881-1971). Rev. S. C was

August 6, 1912. [Harvey entry] Grace bathed baby. Miss Longden, Mrs. Stewart, Mr. & Mrs. DuBose[26] called.

August 7, 1912. [Harvey entry] Wednesday. Baby 3 weeks old. After bath weighed about 9 lbs. 3 oz. Grace improves every day. Walks around now without any support. Baby gives us a good night's sleep now-a-days.[27]

August 10, 1912. [Grace entry] Sunday. [If Sunday, it's actually August 11.] We read in AM. Went to church in PM. First time for me in weeks as the walk is too far and steep.

August 11, 1912. [Harvey entry] Sunday. Baby weighed 9 lbs., 8–1/2 oz.

August 14, 1912. [Harvey entry] Wed. Baby 4 weeks old. Weighs 9 lbs., 9–1/2 oz. Gained 21–1/2 oz. in 3 weeks or over 1 oz. a day.

August 17, 1912. [Harvey entry] Baby Margaret–1 month old. Weighed 9 lbs., 12–1/2 oz. Strong & well. 2 past nights were perfect. Grace stronger every day. All packed up to leave on Monday. It rained hard all day.

August 18, 1912. [Harvey entry] Sunday. Kuling. At 4:30 Margaret Elizabeth was baptized by Father (Dr. Woodbridge) in the sitting room. We invited a few of our friends. Twelve came: Mr. & Mrs. Bullock, Mr. & Mrs. Sarvis, Mr. & Mrs. Burkin, Mr. & Mrs. Brockmen [Brockman], Mr. & Mrs. Stewart, Miss Cluff & Miss King.[28] We all thought the service was beautiful.

---

the son of William James (1851–1894) and Mrs. Abby Porter Ketchum McKee, who were also Northern Presbyterian missionaries. CRI, 312.

26. Mrs. William Ramsey (Anna May White) Stewart, was with the YMCA and on the staff of the Bible Teachers Training School for Women. She was the wife of Stewart, working in China with the YMCA, 1910–1939 and the younger sister of Wilbert Webster White. Mr. Stewart was YMCA Secretary, with the Department of Missionary Training, Nanking University, and Managing Secretary of the Union Language School in Nanking, CRI, 455. Rev. Palmer Clisby DuBose is the son of the early Southern Presbyterian missionary, Rev. Hampden Coit DuBose of South Carolina, who went out in 1872 and died in 1910. CRI, 127. DuBose, also Southern Presbyterian, did missionary evangelistic work in Soochow 1906–1931. CRI, 128.

27. At three weeks Margaret allows them a good night's sleep. This is a remarkable baby.

28. Rev. and Mrs. John Berkin are Northern Presbyterian missionaries. See entry for January 31, 1911. Probably this is Miss Emma S. Clough with CIM in Shanghai. CRI, 93. Miss Margaret King was with CIM, the China Continuation Committee, the International Missionary Alliance, and based in Shanghai. CRI, 259.

Mother,[29] John, Jean & Charlie sang "There's a Song in the Air" in the other room and we came out with the baby and sat near Father by the front window. We all sang, "I Think When I Read That Sweet Story of Old,"[30] and Margaret went to sleep. Father read the 103rd Psalm, then we stood up before him while he read the Presbyterian Service. Baby only grunted a little and smiled. Father prayed a beautiful prayer; we all sang, "Gentle Jesus, Meek & Mild,"[31] and Father gave the benediction while we all stood up. I held the babe and gave her to Father when he sprinkled the water. Afterwards the friends all congratulated us and admired the baby.

September 9, 1912. [Harvey entry] Rain & cold. Tea at Stewarts' for Dr. White & party. Dr. White spoke very interestingly for a few minutes on his present trip and work in Japan & Korea. Miss Palmer said a few words. 2 Chr. 16:9.[32]

September 15, 1912. [Harvey entry] Sunday. This has been a beautiful day. I am reading "Quiet Talks on Power" by D.S. Gordon. From this book and Mr. Frank Garrett's sermon[33] on the 1st Psalm– "Habit," I have got some

29. Mother here is Grace's mother, who was ill with cancer, and in fact, left for America a few months later. She died in Johns Hopkins Hospital the following January. Perhaps Jeanie and Charlie had been staying with Grace and Harvey in Kuling that summer because she didn't feel well. My mother told me that she was born in Jeanie's cottage, so they may all have been in the same cottage. "There's a Song in the Air," which I heard in my childhood as a Christmas carol, is used at the baptism with all the Roys babies. Words: "There's a song in the air,/ there's a star in the sky,/ there's a Mother's sweet prayer,/ and a baby's low cry."

30. Words by Jemima T. Luke, 1841; music by William B. Bradbury from a Greek folk song, 1859. Called by one hymnologist in early 1930s, "best known and most widely used children's hymn."

31. Text by Charles Wesley; tune hard to guess; probably *Seymour* by Carl M. von Weber, 1826.

32. Dr. W.W. White is working as a missionary in Japan and Korea. Miss Margaret Palmer later married Rev. E.J. Cooper, CIM, CRI, 98. The passage cited is: "For the eyes of the Lord run to and fro throughout the whole earth, to shew himself strong in behalf of them whose heart is perfect toward him. Herein thou hast done foolishly in this; henceforth thou shalt have wars."

33. S.D. Gordon is the author of two books mentioned in the diary: one on prayer (See entry for July 28, 1912) and this one on power. Rev. Dr. Frank Garrett was with Christian Endeavor in China. He was also the Corresponding Secretary of the Evangelistic Association, member of Foreign Christian Mission, Associate Dean, Union Language School, Nanking University, and became President of the Hillcrest School board by 1916. Mrs. Frank Garrett (Verna) taught at Hillcrest briefly and gave $1000 for a building for the school before she died. In the 1916 annual Mardie Garrett was President of the

beautiful thoughts today and I hope some ideas that will make my life bigger.

October 31, 1912. [Grace entry] Hallowe'en party at Sarvises'. Language School[34] people with others. Masquerade. We acted very foolish.

November 15, 1912. [Grace entry] Began giving Baby one bottle feeding, 1 part milk to 2 parts water 2–1/4 mulins food & pinch of salt.[35]

November 16, 1912. [Grace entry] Went to Shanghai to see Mother off to America.[36]

November 23, 1912. [Grace entry] Mother & Father sailed for America on Str. [steamer] Korea.[37]

December 12, 1912. [Grace entry] Baby first reached for her rattle. She squeals with delight when happy and full.

School Honor System, in the ninth and tenth grade group (10), and Lawrence Garrett was in third grade (11). Mardie (Margaret) later married Lewis Smythe, was educated in the U.S. and returned to China in 1928, an M.D. She worked at the mission hospital in Nanking for the next twenty-three years. My friend and consultant Edith Riggs Barakat knew her family in Nanking later. "Oral History China Missionaries Project," "Smithe, Margaret," in Cgu.edu. See also entry for January 20, 1914.

34. The Language School was part of the University of Nanking. Missionaries arriving in China went there to learn Chinese language and culture.

35. Grace means Mellin's (not mulins) baby food, basically a malt extract but said to make cow's milk as good as breast milk and popular in U.S., made in Great Britain and U.S. The exact recipe Harvey and Grace used isn't listed, but the 2–1/4 probably refers to tablespoons. "Mellin's Food is a dry, soluble extract made from wheat and barley malt, and consists of maltose, dextrin, proteids, and salts. Mellin's Food is entirely free from unconverted starch and cane sugar." *Mellin's Food*, 22–23. All the formulas listed use water and fresh milk. Cow's milk is intended, but there were few cows in China. Kuling did have them, but in Nanking possibly they used goat milk or diluted canned milk.

36. Grace's mother, Jean Woodbridge, travels to Johns Hopkins hospital in Baltimore because she has cancer. Her aunt, President Woodrow Wilson's mother, visited her there often, and Jeanie died there some months later. My mother commented: "Both my mother's parents died when she was far away: her mother was in America while she was in China; her father was in China while she was in America."

37. The steamship *Korea* was run by the P&O, Pacific Mail Steamship Company between China, Japan, and Europe, via Honolulu and San Francisco. It was an 18,000-ton steamship with twin-screw engines. It left from Hong Kong every week and called at Shanghai. In San Francisco it was possible to get a train to anywhere in the U.S. "The Korea," Pacific Mail Steamship.

December 14, 1912. [Grace] Margaret sat up on bed alone for the first [time] today.

December 19, 1912. [Grace] Our second anniversary. Dr. Wilkinson from Soochow came up to see us on business. Miss Muir came over to supper. Candles on the cake.

December 20, 1912. [Grace] Ima Shaw's and Miss Muir's birthday.[38]

December 23, 1912. [Grace] Grace is 23 and happy. A *friend* came in the early morn to wish her "happy birthday." Went to Burlingame Bullock's birthday party.[39]

December 24, 1912. [Grace] Christmas eve. Mr. Lewis came down[40] and we hung up Baby's, the servants', and our stockings and sang "Hang up the baby's stocking." Our first Xmas as Santa Claus. Entertainment at the M.E. Girls' School.[41]

December 25, 1912. [Grace] Wednesday. A happy, happy Christmas. Baby makes life so much happier. She got 3 dolls, 3 balls, 2 sacques,[42] a dress, etc. Her little blue stocking looked so cute among the others. Went to Blackstones to dinner. Hummels over to supper. Chinese play at the University until late. "Assassination of Prince Ito."[43]

---

38. Miss G.M. Muir is a CIM missionary stationed in Shanghai. CRI, 347; Miss Ima Shaw may be related to Miss Ella C. Shaw, who built the Adeline Smith Home and School for Girls as part of the Methodist-Episcopal mission.

39. Harvey's entries for this day in 1910 and 1911 had read, "Grace is 21 and happy," etc. Grace picks up the refrain. "Friend" is her menstrual period beginning. Richard was born the following October, so this is probably the last one for awhile.

40. Mr. Lewis is the lodger at Grace and Harvey's home. Possibly he is Rev. Robert E. Lewis, who worked with the YMCA. CRI, 281.

41. M.E.= Methodist Episcopal, which is the northern branch of Methodism. They did have a girls' school in Nanking, built by Miss Ella C. Shaw, the Adeline Smith Home and School. See entry for April 7, 1911.

42. Sacques were little jackets, still being used when I was a baby in the 30s.

43. "A great man has fallen, perhaps the greatest force in the field of political action that the nineteenth century produced, the maker of Japan, the conqueror of Russia, the mighty one who first asserted Asia's superiority over Europe in Europe's own field of glory and changed in a few years the world's future." Prince Ito of Japan was assassinated in 1909. He was prime minister of Japan 1892-96, 1898, and 1900-1901 and then resident general of Korea, 1905-09, where he was shot. This is apparently a play about his death by Sri Aurobindo. Aurobindo, "Assassination."

December 26, 1912. [Grace] Went to Millward[44] baby's birthday tea. Rain. Harvey carried Baby over. She had on red Chinese dress our boarders[45] gave her and some little red lion shoes. She looked so cute but cried.

December 27, 1912. [Grace] Mildred's birthday. Went over there in A.M., then to Josette's.[46] Went to Mildred's for supper and had cold goose, etc. Had a good time. Bitterly cold.

December 28, 1912. [Grace] Sat. Went to a big Christmas party at Mr. Donovan's,[47] took Margaret. They had a big tea, then an enormous tree. Baby's first vision of Santa Claus. She was afraid of so many people. She got a Dr. Cook doll off the tree.

December 29, 1912. [Grace] Bright and cold Sunday. Killed four mice, raid in kitchen. Went to Evans'[48] in A.M. S.S. & Church in P.M. Baby is so cute. When I sing, she joins in. When I stop, she stops. She has pretty red cheeks and loves her papa & mama.

END OF 1912 DIARY

44. The Millwards' child, Mary Frances Millward, had a birthday party in December 1912. Martha Ann Millward was born Jan 11, 1915. The parents were Methodists, Mr. William Millward and Mrs. Jennie Fitzgerald Millward. See also entry for November 23, 1914.

45. Their boarders included Mr. Lewis of the December 24, 1912 entry.

46. Josette Beebe was Dr. Beebe's daughter, and one of the founders of the Watch Guard Society based in 1916 at Hillcrest School but begun in 1895. Annual, 18–19. See the note for the entry for May 19, 1914. Mildred would be Mildred Stuart Hummel.

47. Mr. Donovan is unidentified. Apparently, there were dolls based on famous people, and there was a Dr. Frederick Cook doll distributed by Strobel and Wilkin from 1909. He was one of the explorers of the North Pole. There was also an Admiral Peary doll.

48. The Dr. Evans family were in Kuling when Margaret was born July 17, 1912. See also September 9, 1910 and July 3, 1912.

1913 Diary

January 1, 1913. [Grace] Mon.[Wed?] A beautiful day. Had the Bowens, Blackstones, Josette, Rob, Alice Longden, Mr. [or Mrs.?] Rosse, & Mr. Lewis.[1] 11 folks. Potato soup. Ham & pot[ato] chips, fruit salad, goose and vegetables. Fruit gelatine. Coffee, candies, nuts, dates, figs, cakes and a good time.

January 12, 1913. [Harvey] Sunday. Baby sits up alone but upsets easily. Weighed 14-1/2 lbs. today. In 5 days she will be 6 months old. She can't draw herself up to a sitting position but will hold on tight enough to one's fingers to be drawn up. She holds out her arms to be taken. Is very happy.

January 22, 1913. [Harvey] Wed. Mother [Jeanie Woodbridge, Grace's mother] died at Johns Hopkins, Baltimore, early in the morning. Father with her.[2]

January 28, 1913. [Grace] Baby used her little chair for the first time satisfactorily. She gave me a most radiant smile and then—

---

1. If 25 Dec., 1912, was Wednesday, New Year's Day 1913, should be Wednesday, not Monday. Rev. A.J. Bowen was appointed President of the University of Nanking in 1908. See also entry for Dec. 24, 1911. Mr. Ross may be Rev. Dr. John Ross, a Northern Presbyterian stationed in Shanghai. He worked with the Anti-Opium League. CRI, 413.

2. Is this entry entered some time after they learned news? Or perhaps they received a cablegram? Chinese time is a day later than American time because of the International Date Line.

February 14, 1913. [Harvey] Margaret received two valentines today: one from Anson B. Bullock and one from David L. Sarvis, the two boys of Nanking of her age. She laughs like a grown person when I make noises with my mouth.

March 8, 1913. [Harvey] Several inches of snow which was blown into deep drifts early this morning. Margaret spends the afternoon on the porch regardless of the cold.

March 16, 1913. [Grace] Sunday. Went walking over the hills to the temple. Found crocuses just going to seed. First this year. Mr. Hanson[3] here.

March 18, 1913. [Harvey] Baby repeated bye-bye after Grace today—perfectly.

March 21, 1913. [Harvey] Baby is eight months and 4 days old. She says bye-bye and da-da. She is nearly over the measles.

March 22, 1913. [Grace] Baby learns to say "Da Da" after us and seems to know it means Harvey. Now she has two words in her vocabulary.

March 23, 1913. [Grace] Easter Sunday. Ruth B.[Bullock] sent jonquils in bloom. Baby weighs 15 lbs. 13 [oz.]. When we wag our heads she mocks us. Her first attempt to blow her nose after me.

April 7, 1913. [Grace] Baby cut her first little sharp tooth–lower right. No trouble at all. In fact she gained 11 oz. the week before it came.

April 8, 1913. [Grace] Baby's second tooth came through. Harvey had high fever in the night. Stayed home from school. Went to Meigs'[4] and Bullocks'.

April 9, 1913. [Grace] Gave Baby her first egg. Only the white with a little salt. She drank it out of a cup and enjoyed it. Harvey sick, fever. Planted seeds. Seeds. Tomato. Lettuce. Brussel sprouts. Cucumbers. Corn.

---

3. Mr. Hanson is possibly Rev. Perry O. Hanson, a Methodist Episcopal professor in Shanghai. CRI, 195.

4. Rev. F.E. Meigs, with Mrs. Meigs, was part of the Disciples Mission, arrived in 1888 and soon started a school, which grew into the Christian College. The burden of developing the school was on Meigs until Charles S. Settlemeyer arrived in 1904 and shared the work. Rev. Meigs was with the Education Association of China, the Foreign Christian Mission in Nanking, and the Department of Religion, Nanking University. CRI, 331. Mrs. Settlemeyer becomes involved in Hillcrest, the mothers' school by 1911.

April 18, 1913. [Harvey] "Some must overwork because others underwork." Verse from calendar. Bright day. Planted radish seed before break[fast].

May 4, 1913. [Harvey] Sunday. Cool and a little rain. Still wearing winter clothing. Baby can sit up alone if there is something to hold her feet down. She rolls around a great deal.

May 11, 1913. [Grace] Sunday. Children's Day. Took Margaret to church for the first time. She behaved well for a little one. She wanted us to take her when she saw me get up to sing in a quartette. She wore an embroidered (by me) dress and cap and pink ribbons and looked *beautiful*.

May 12, 1913. [Grace] First strawberries. Mr. Bailie sent us a basket. Tea to Methodists at the Heukes' [?].[5]

May 13, 1913. [Grace] Jeanie's birthday. Sent her a cake.[6] Went to Mr. Wilson's[7] birthday tennis tea. Baby can pat-a-cake and she enjoys it heartily.

May 14, 1913. [Grace] Harvey got a new tennis racquet, an early birthday gift. Have been feeding Baby with a spoon for about a week. Began yesterday to give her a little oatmeal with the gruel.

May 16, 1913. [Grace] Baby cut two upper teeth without our even knowing it. They are not in the middle! On either side. Dr. Shields said freaks did that![8]

---

5. Rev. Dr. Professor and Dean Joseph Bailie of the Agriculture Department of the University of Nanking, See entry for April 8, 1911. The Heukes may be Frederick Goodrich Henke (1876–1963) and Selma Hirsch Henke, Methodist missionaries in Nanking. He published "The Moral Development of the Chinese" in *Popular Science Monthly*, Vol. 87, July 1915.

6. Jeanie was not with them. A Jeanie Woodbridge was teaching in the girls' school at Kiangyin [Jiangyin] station, which is not far from Shanghai, in 1913. According to Lawrence Kessler in his book on the station, no one knows what became of her. This could be the 13-year old Jeanie, who later went to live with Grace and Harvey. It does seem young for her to be a teacher, but her mother had died and she must have been quite mature for her age.

7. Rev. Wilbur F. Wilson and Mrs. Mary Rowley Wilson had the Hillcrest School in their home before the building was completed–1913–14. He worked with the YMCA 1910–11. See entry for August 24, 1910.

8. This Dr. Shields doesn't seem very sensitive to a young mother's worry that her child be healthy and normal. Perhaps Shields had limited experience with babies' teeth or he was joking?

May 17, 1913. [Grace] Baby ten months old and well. 16 pounds, 13 oz. Went to meet Father. Father came from S'hai to visit us. We had strawberries for tea and while we asked the blessing baby pulled Father's plateful all over him–cream & all.

May 22, 1913. [Grace] Luella Bishop came to live with us.[9] Father left for S'hai. [Shanghai]

May 23, 1913. [Grace] Friday. Nanking Association. Harvey went alone as I was sick.

May 24, 1913. [Grace] Baby took her first crawl.

May 25, 1913. [Harvey] Sunday. Baby creeps a little and says ma-ma very distinctly.

May 26, 1913. [Grace] Baby improves in the creeping line. Rather funny because of her teeth.

May 28, 1913. [Grace] Went to Chinese restaurant (San Pai Lau) with Harvey and Dr. Tootell for dinner with Mr. Hayes.[10] Rained like forty.

May 29, 1913. [Grace] Baby has quite a cold. She enjoyed her bath *so* much. She splashes with body, arms & legs all at once and screams with delight.

May 30, 1913. [Grace] First peepaws 30 cents a basket.[11] Baby cut her upper central left tooth. Cold about well. Mighty sweet baby.

June 5, 1913. [Harvey] Margaret has six teeth. The last one just came thru.

July 3, 1913. [Grace] Baby's first bowl of soft rice, given at 10 o'clock feeding.

---

9. Luella Bishop is a new boarder, I assume.

10. Dr. G.T. Tootell, MD was a Northern Presbyterian missionary. CRI, 480. Mr. Egbert M. Hayes was born in China, the son of missionaries Rev. John Newton Hayes of the Presbyterian Church in the U.S.A. (Northern) and Mercie Briggs Hayes. The elder Hayeses arrived in China in October 1882 and spent most of their time in Soochow. Egbert worked with the YMCA in Nanking, Shanghai, Nanchang, and Peking until 1935. In Peking he was the Director of Religion and Social Work at the Peking Union Medical college. His family also originally came from Michigan. CRI, 202. "Egbert Hayes" article in *China Missionary Project*.

11. Peepaws or peebaws are loquats, not papaws. It's the fruit of a tree of the rose family (Eriobotrya japonica) native to China and Japan but grown elsewhere.

July 4, 1913. [Grace] Baby's first whole egg. Soft boiled. Agreed perfectly as far as I can see.

July 5, 1913. [Grace] Went for a picnic to Emerald Grotto, Jean, Charlie, Baby, Misses Hyde, Derry and Jordan,[12] Harvey and I. Baby's first chicken bone enjoyed. We had a *lovely* time, came home in the rain. Baby stood up in the bathtub for the first time, pulled up on side of the tub.

July 6, 1913. [Grace] Sunday. Went to Church in A.M. Father Blackstone on Babylon. Went walking in evening on Highland Ave. 10 A.M. Baby feeding: rice, cream, egg.

July 12, 1913. [Grace] Margaret really kissed her proud Mother for the first time, putting her mouth on my cheek and smacking. Tea for YWCA delegates. [Harvey] Soldier fight at Kiukiang, Shih Li Pu.[13]

July 13, 1913. [Harvey] Fighting at Shih Li Pu and Kiukiang continues. Soldiers fleeing to Kuling are disarmed. 70 or more guns and 4000 rounds of ammunition obtained in this way.

July 15, 1913. [Grace] Margaret broke the record. No wet diaper from Mon. 5 P.M.–Tues. 4 P.M. Gladys[14] came to see us. Terrible thunder and rain storm. Sent applications.[15]

July 17, 1913. [Grace] Our first birthday party. Jane Peter[16] shared honors with our little Margaret. We had two one-candle birthday cakes. Twenty-

---

12. Harvey turns 27 years old. They are in Kuling, where Emerald Grotto is. Miss Jordan may be Miss A. B., who was with the Methodist Episcopal mission. CRI, 248. Misses Derry and Hyde are unidentified.

13. This is when Nanking was attacked by army of Gen. Chang Hsuin and the "pig-tailed robbers." Many missionaries remained in the city and some who knew him personally tried to persuade him not to slaughter the innocent inhabitants, with little success. These soldiers near Kuling must be with the government (Sun Yat-sen). Apparently, the missionaries took them in but made them surrender their ammunition first. They possibly thought they might have to defend Kuling?

14. Gladys is probably Gladys Swenson, the daughter of Mrs. K. Moll Swenson. See entry for September 12, 1911.

15. The application may be to teach at the University of Nanking, where Harvey began teaching in 1913.

16. Jane Peter's parents are probably Dr. William Wesley Peter and his wife, who were in Nanking with the YMCA. He also served with the Council on Health Education, and was Secretary on the Council on Public Health. See also Feb 16 and October 26, 1914

five people came and such a good time. Margaret weighs 19 lbs., 13 oz. Chest, 22 in. Well and happy.

July 25, 1913. [Grace] Not very well. Dr. Taylor came in morning and reassured us. Must be careful and not go out much. Rather hard but worth it.[17]

July 28, 1913. [Grace] Margaret cut her seventh tooth with apparently no trouble–lower, left, central.

August 1, 1913. [Grace] Margaret gets cuter every day. Today she pulled my handkerchief out of my pocket, put it up to her nose and blew. Wasn't that cute?[18]

August 8, 1913. [Grace] Father came in the night from Shanghai. We had given him up. No one was awake when he came. Landrenters' meeting.

August 11, 1913. [Grace] Baby well. When playing with her toy dog, she said, "Dog" and "Bow-wow" after me.

August 17, 1913. [Harvey] Sunday. Margaret 13 months old; weighs 22 lbs. Fat and sweet. A little fussy this hot weather.

August 18, 1913. [Harvey] Dickie due in 6 weeks.[19] W.L. [waist line] 42.25 inches. Margaret's first step. Weak.

August 20, 1913. [Grace] Margaret stood alone for a fraction of a second.

August 21, 1913. [Grace] Cool weather again after weeks of very warm. No rain yet.

August 22, 1913. [Grace] Margaret has a new tooth–lower lateral right. She is cutting her first molars and they bother her.

---

entries. CRI, 380.

17. Grace is nearly seven months pregnant with Richard. Dr. Taylor may be Anne Russell Taylor's husband, Richard Vipon Taylor. See entry for December 28, 1910.

18. Grace keeps the diary as if she is speaking to someone and generally puts in more detail, especially domestic detail, than Harvey.

19. Of course, they don't know the baby's sex, but they apparently had a name picked out. Before Gracie was born, they were expecting a boy to be named Harvey, and he did come later, the fourth child, in 1918.

1913 DIARY

August 25, 1913. [Grace] Helen Vaughan born.[20] Harvey & I went walking on Highland Ave. in late afternoon. Margaret said "Pretty"–baby talk.

August 26, 1913. [Grace] Margaret said "hello" real plainly after me today. Picnic to No. 17.[21]

September 13, 1913. [Harvey] Returned from Kuling. Grace and Miss Hynds.[22] I got here with Dr. Sloan on Jap. boat yesterday and met Grace today at the Jardine Hulk,[23] a mile above ruined Hsia Kwan.[24]

September 16, 1913. [Harvey] Margaret says *hot* (whisper, "ha") when we light a lamp or the oil stove.[25] We taught her it was hot by letting her touch it.

September 28, 1913. [Harvey] Sunday. We are waiting for Dickie to come. It has been a long hard wait for Grace. Margaret is well and as happy a little girl as ever lived. I have had made a seat to put on the front of my bicycle

---

20. Helen Vaughan is unidentified.

21. No. 17 is often mentioned. Mother told me she thought it was where the Woodbridges normally stayed. Harvey and Grace may use the house now.

22. Miss Iva Hynds (1872–1959) was a nurse in Los Angeles before going to China in 1912 to work for Nanking's Foreign Hospital. Later she was with the University of Nanking Hospital and then stayed during the Rape of Nanking in 1937. She helped with Richard's delivery and earlier had accompanied Grace back to Nanking. At the Foreign Hospital, which was a gift from Dr. and Mrs. A.J. Bowen in memory of their son, Arthur John Bowen, and Dr. Lucy A. Gaynor, she was the Superintendent in Charge. She served with Dr. W. G. Hiltner, Dr. T. D. Sloan, and Dr. A. C. Hutcheson "who gave their lives in unstinted measure in Nanking for only a pittance." "Miss Iva Hynds" in *Woman's Missionary Friend*, a Google Book, Vol 49–50.

23. Jardine Hulk is a name given to a British ship docked at another landing place on the Yangtze, located above Shia [Hsia] Kwan.

24. During the attack of the Pig-tailed Robber (General Chang Hsuin) on Nanking, Shia Kwan had been damaged, so the ship Harvey took was different, and then to reach Nanking he apparently landed on the Yangtze a mile above the usual Shia Kwan, where the train left them. Sun Yat-sen had turned the running of the new democracy over to Li Yuan-hung, and a Parliament was set up, but those in the Parliament were not interested in or supportive of the new democracy, and the monarchic idea still prevailed even among the highest officials. General Chang had left Nanking during the revolution, but he returned in the summer of 1913 to the city to wreak vengeance on the inhabitants, and despite pleas from the missionaries in Nanking, his solders slaughtered many of the inhabitants. Woodbridge, *Fifty Years*, 187.

25. The mention of lighting a lamp or an oil stove, which baby Margaret has been taught not to touch, suggests no electricity in the home at this time.

and take her out riding frequently. She enjoys it and the Chinese all think it is "Hao Wan" [= good idea]. Margaret says, "Hei-o" for Hello and waves her hand whenever we say goodbye.

October 5, 1913. [Harvey] Sunday. Richard Dennis Roys—9 lbs.—born at 8:35 Sunday morning. Grace did not sleep much Sat. night but regular pains did not begin until 3 or 4 A.M. Time of hard labor short. "Show" Sat. 2:15 P.M. and again during the night. Doctor, T.D. Sloan; Nurse, Miss Ina [Iva] Hynds. Margaret was taken in to see her mother and new brother this afternoon. She put out a finger and touched the baby and when she saw that he was a real baby she tried to kiss him.

October 12, 1913. [Harvey] Margaret takes a few steps by herself now. When she "arrives" she is greatly pleased.

October 16, 1913. [Harvey] Birthday, Father Woodbridge. Went to Shanghai, leaving Grace in Miss Hynds' care.

October 18, 1913. [Grace] Harvey returned from Shanghai with *lots of things*, new hats, etc. Glad to see each other again. All well.

October 20, 1913. [Harvey] Miss Hynds left but spent this night with us.

October 21, 1913. [Harvey] Tuesday. Grace watched Miss Hynds bathe Richard.

October 22, 1913. [Harvey] Grace bathed Richard for the first time. Margaret took her first steps all by herself. She had walked some distance before this when we started her.

October 23, 1913. [Grace] Margaret walks better every day. She will start out for herself these days and is so proud of her achievements.

October 26, 1913. [Grace] Harvey carried me downstairs for the first time.[26] I sat on the front porch and watched Margaret and Harvey on the cement walk.

---

26. Three weeks of bed rest seems to be the norm at this time.

October 27, 1913. [Grace] Richard said "Goo" when he had just been cleaned up and was comfortable. I was afraid some would think it wasn't true, but Shoo Pau[27] heard him, too.

October 28, 1913. [Grace] Josette, Ruth B. [Bullock], and Miss White[28] came in P.M. I am feeling so much stronger.

October 29, 1913. [Grace] Margaret found the air cushion and tried to blow it up. We didn't know she had ever seen us do so. Mrs. Rowe for dinner upstairs. Mrs. Wilson[29] operated on at new Foreign Hospital.

October 30, 1913. [Grace] Dr. Sloan came over in A.M. and saw Baby's ear and sort of operated on him down below.[30] The little fellow cried but was more comfortable later.

October 31, 1913. [Grace] Baby gave me a good night. Feeding at 6 P.M., 2 A.M., 5:45. We both needed the rest. Harvey read to me in the evening. We're very happy.

November 1, 1913. [Grace] Another good night's rest. 6 P.M., 2 A.M., 5:30. Rain, much needed, came in the night.

November 2, 1913. [Grace] Sunday. Dr. Sloan came & after an exam found I would need "outside support" inside. I am trying not to be discouraged. Margaret sick with a cold. Calomel & C. Oil.[31]

November 3, 1913. [Harvey] Monday. This morning Margaret got one of my collars and put it on. She is very observing. She now gets up to a standing position in the middle of the floor. Today she picked up her little chamber [pot] and tried to sit on it. She only sat on the floor.

November 5, 1913. [Grace] Richard is one month old. He lay upon the bed and *smiled* and looked pleased so intelligently this P.M. Mrs. Westbrook

---

27. Shoo Pau must be the name of their amah or nursemaid for the children.

28. Laura M. White was the director of the Adeline Smith School for Girls. Miss White's visit to Grace suggests that they knew each other when Grace taught there. See Introduction, note for Ginling College.

29. Mrs. Wilson is the wife of Rev. W.F. Wilson. See note for August 24, 1910.

30. Circumcision, one assumes.

31. First mention of her need for uterine support. Calomel is a heavy white, tasteless compound used as purgative. C. Oil is probably castor oil, used frequently with children well into the 20th century.

and Mrs. Brown[32] came to see us. They thought R.D.R. [Richard] was *fine*. So do I!

November 6, 1913. [Grace] Margaret is cutting her lower right molar. It is almost through and the left one is coming on fast.

November 8, 1913. [Grace] Ruth Bullock's baby born.

November 11, 1913. [Harvey] While putting Richard to bed I discovered he had a hernia. Grace took him and I ran for Dr. Sloan. He came back with me and tried to reduce the hernia but did not seem to be able to. We then took the babe over to Dr. Hiltner[33] and found that the hernia had disappeared.

November 12, 1913. [Grace] Cook's baby born. We gave him a dollar from Margaret.[34] He was much pleased.

November 14, 1913. [Harvey] Bath tub with Richard in it fell off the board into the big tub. Richard was ducked in cold water but did not receive any apparent injuries. Grace had a pestery installed.[35]
 [Grace] You electrical engineer!

November 15, 1913. [Harvey] Dr. Evans came at noon and said Grace was fine (pes [pessary] & wo [womb]). Barbara [Blackstone] took her for a carriage ride in P.M. Richard's hernia came down about 6:30 and I ran for Dr. Evans after some fruitless efforts to reduce it. He returned with me on the run. And very soon reduced the hernia. We put on a "skein of yarn" truss and Richard went to sleep immediately.

---

32. Mrs. Westbrook may be Mrs. C. Hart Westbrook, a Southern Baptist missionary, stationed in Shanghai. CRI, 509. Mrs. Brown may be the wife of Francis Augustus Brown. CRI, 54.

33. Dr. Walter G. Hiltner was a Northern Presbyterian medical missionary in Nanking and worked at the Foreign Hospital. See also entry for October 28, 1914. Mrs. Carrie Hiltner contributed to the Nanking cookbook.

34. This must be their Chinese cook. $1 was obviously a lot extra. This would be the Mexican dollar currency, worth $.49 in U.S. dollars at the time. It is likely a lot above normal wages for these live-in servants.

35. Baby Richard certainly has adventures. The device is a pessary, which is worn internally to support the uterus and remedy its displacement. The pessary is still used as a nonsurgical approach to the treatment of pelvic organ prolapse. The device doesn't cure this problem, but helps to manage it and slow its progression. It adds support to the vagina and increases the tightness of the tissues and muscles of the pelvis.

1913 DIARY

November 16, 1913. [Grace] Went over to hospital to see Miss Hynds. Saw Mrs. Bullock and Frank. After all our baby is the cutest. Mrs. Gilbert, Mrs. Peters, Miss Yates[36] in. Baby is doing pretty well. 12 lbs. now. When he cries I am always afraid his hernia is down. How I wish I could bear it for him. This P.M. Margaret found her leggings and sat down on the floor and tried to put them on. She has only worn them a few times.

November 17, 1913. [Grace] Mothers' Meeting. "I.S.C."[37] met at Mildred's. Dr. Evans came over there and took my pessary out and later came over here and with the forceps even, couldn't get me right. Wait till tomorrow. Hard luck.

November 18, 1913. [Grace] Dr. Evans came in A.M. and worked over me about an hour or *more*. We were all tired out—to no effect. Too relaxed. [Uterus too relaxed?] Wait 2 weeks. Began tonic.

November 19, 1913. [Grace] This morning Margaret came in and saw me taking an extra nap. I put out my hand to her and then went off for another snooze to be awakened by the little rascal sticking my hand with a safety pin. Harvey asked her if she wanted to sit on the pot and she said "pot" pretty plainly. She had just been enthroned and told us she wanted to sit on again. We wouldn't believe her though she went to the chamber. We were rewarded by a soiled little girl. We will believe her next time!

November 27, 1913. [Grace] Thanksgiving Day. Service in A.M. led by Dr. Perkins.[38] Dinner at Miss White's. (Lest we forget for next time–*we* had 2 pheasants, 2 pumpkin pies, mashed potatoes.) We have so much to be

---

36. Mrs. Gilbert was the wife of Vice Consul Alvin W. Gilbert. Mrs. Peters is unidentified. Miss Yates may be the sister of Rev. Orville F Yates, a Southern Presbyterian missionary beginning in 1908 whose wife was Mrs. Ellen Peck Baskerville Yates, an RN. They were evangelistic missionaries in Huaian, 1909-1941. She operated the Huaian Clinic. He married her in July 1913. Woodbridge, *Fifty Years*, 227. Also "Biographical Index of Missionaries in China 1900-1920." Presbyterian Heritage Center.

37. The Mothers' group, called the I.S.C., started the Hillcrest School in Nanking for foreign children to which Margaret and Richard eventually went. These mothers were teaching their own children and decided to combine forces. The school met first in the Wilsons' home. They had a school building by 1915. I believe that I.S.C. stood for International School in China.

38. Rev. Dr. Henry P. Perkins was on the American Board of Commissioners for Foreign Missions, based in Shanghai, and with the Evangelical Association of North America. CRI, 380.

thankful for, our Dickie Boy is one precious gift during the year among others.

November 28, 1913. [Grace] Football game with Soochow.[39] Bitterly cold. Snow in night (First).

November 29, 1913. [Grace] Walked over to Mrs. Rowe's with Mildred in A.M.

November 30, 1913. [Grace] Harvey said, "Oh, shoot!" about something wrong and Margaret said, "Shoo!" Baby 8 weeks old, 12 lbs., 13 oz. Walk in A.M. Church in P.M.

December 1, 1913. [Grace] Margaret said "birdie" after me *very* plainly. Night feeding at 2:30. An unusual occurrence for us these days. Called on Hayes' and Beebes'.

December 2, 1913. [Grace] Baby well, slept from 9:30—5:30.

December 3, 1913. [Grace] Pessary put in with very little pain. It was a misfit and was changed in evening. Now it's fine. No more trouble. Reception at the Macklins' to Dr. and Mrs. Butchart.[40] Dinner in evening at the Consulate. Home late. Tired but very happy.

December 4, 1913. [Grace] Thursday. Work in A.M. about as usual. Went to Ladies' prayer meeting and was called on to lead. God helped me.

December 5, 1913. [Grace] Dinner party. Beebes', Hayes', and Dr. Sloan. Fine time. Tea in P.M. to Chinese Prof wife's. Amocat order opened.[41]

---

39. Apparently sports were encouraged at the Christian universities for the students. At the Exposition, the University of Nanking students had made a good showing. This is probably American football since the American missionaries were introducing American sports to the Chinese students, according to the *University of Nanking Magazine*, notably the article on the YMCA, May 1910, 29.

40. Dr. James Butchart MD was with the Foreign Christian Mission, the Medical Missionary Society of China, the Society for the Diffusion of Christian and General Knowledge among the Chinese. CRI, 64. The couple have children mentioned in the 1916 Hillcrest annual: Baird, fifth grade; Harvey, third grade, 8–11. She was on the board of the school, superintendent of the third and fifth grades, and taught third and fifth grades Arithmetic, Writing, nature work.

41. Amocat Trading, founded in 1891, was a business that accepted overseas orders.

December 6, 1913. Dr. Sloan's birthday. [Harvey] Grace and I went out hunting in the P.M. on the hills back of our house. I had two shots at pheasants and killed them both, one after the other. Grace deserves half the credit.

December 7, 1913. [Harvey] Margaret smells of the flowers painted on the water pitcher. She pulls Richard's stockings off and says wee-wee-wee.

December 19, 1913. [Grace] We remembered the day but did not celebrate especially except by loving.[42]

December 20, 1913. [Harvey] Richard used the chamber for both processes today for the first time.[43] Jean and Charlie came from Shanghai. I took Margaret down on the bicycle to meet them.

December 22, 1913. [Grace] Margaret was put on the chair and given the little chamber to play with! She got up off the big one, put the little chamber on the floor, sat on it and—.

December 23, 1913. [Grace] Grace is 24 and *happy*. A full day. Practice with foreign children[44] in A.M. Shopping with Barbara and children in P.M. Took M. with us & then to Bullocks' party.

December 24, 1913. [Grace] A full, busy day. Getting ready for Christmas. Harvey to S. Kwan to meet Father in P.M. H. [Harvey], J.[Jeanie], and C. [Charlie] went to Chinese play while Father and I chatted. Hung up our stockings. Father, H., and I filled them. Tired.

December 25, 1913. [Grace] Thursday. A beautiful Christmas with Father, J., and C. Stockings and tree. Lots and lots of presents. We set out bulbs. Service at church. Richard Dennis baptized by Father at beginning of service after the children sang "There's a Song in the Air."[45] Miss Preston[46] told the story of the Other Wise Man. Then the children all sang "Gentle Jesus."

---

42. They were married December 19, 1910.

43. Toilet training begins early. Richard is two and a half months old. This may be when Jean and Charlie came to live with them.

44. The "foreign children" might be the students at Hillcrest or it could be for this church service since all the Christians worshiped together in the Union service. In any case, she is helping with Christmas music.

45. See August 18, 1912 entry and Margaret's baptism.

46. Miss Preston is unidentified.

December 26, 1913. [Grace] I was getting ready to nurse R. I asked Margaret where R.'s dinner was, and she tried to open my dress and peep in! She understands quite a bit. She tries to powder Richard's legs, etc.[47]

December 28, 1913. [Grace] Margaret's right upper molar is just peeping thro'. Dr. Price[48] preached a fine sermon at foreign service. It was very helpful.

December 29, 1913. [Grace] Father left for S'hai. Dr. E [Evans] came at 4:30 and used the for. [forceps] and got the wo. [womb] in good position. I behaved abominably. Like a spoiled baby, but it wasn't very pleasant.

END OF 1913 DIARY

47. The "etc." must be his male organs.

48. The Presbyterian Dr. Philip Francis Price from Virginia had been in China since 1889. He was Director of the North China Union Language School and worked with the Union of Congregationalists and Presbyterians, was Editorial Secretary and President, Christian Endeavor in China, and President, Nanking Theological Seminary. See also January 21, 1914. CRI, 392. His son, Frank Wilson Price, born in Sinchang, China, on February 25, 1895, was principal at Hillcrest 1915–17 and taught algebra, geometry, physics, English, Latin, geography, elocution. He led students in plays and was very popular with them, according to Williams, *Yesterdays in China,* 23. A Julian Price was in the ninth-tenth grade and graduated from Hillcrest in 1916. A younger brother? 1916 Annual, 8–10. Frank Price had graduated from Davidson College in 1915 and later worked as secretary of the Nanking YMCA. He returned to the U.S. for further education, and returned to China in 1923, and stayed until he and his wife were forced to leave China in 1952. He was professor of religious education in Nanking Theological Seminary. Article on Frank Price, *Shenandoah Presbytery's Mission Heritage.*

1914 Diary

January 2, 1914. [Grace] Tailor Dong came to do some sewing in the house.

January 3, 1914. [Grace] Jean & Charlie left for S'hai.[1] Margaret's last *first molar* just peeping thro'. No trouble.

January 7, 1914. [Grace] There is still *some* selfishness left but it's in Grace.[2]

January 13, 1914. [Grace] Margaret just cut a right upper eye tooth. No trouble.

January 20, 1914. [Grace] Invited Miss Hixsom in for pot-luck. While we were eating away there was a knock at the door and the Garrets [Garretts],[3] who had been invited a week before came in. Such a bustling to open up a tin or two. We had a nice time, then went to prayer meeting.

---

1. Jeanie and Charlie left for Shanghai on January 3, but on January 21, they're back and playing jacks with Grace and Harvey. Maybe it was only decided during the Christmas visit that they would return to Nanking and go to school there. By 1914 Hillcrest was offering the first two years of high school, and Grace's younger brother and sister were enrolled there about this time.

2. Three years earlier, on January 6–7, 1911, shortly after they were married, Harvey had written: "I begin to realize that there is a great deal of selfishness in my life, but by the help of God and God's gift–Grace–I will put it out of my life."

3. Miss Hixsom is unidentified. Dr. Frank Garrett was president of the Hillcrest School board in 1916. See also entry for September 15, 1912.

January 21, 1914. [Grace] The Prices, Dr. Sloan and Mrs. Shields in to supper. We had a nice time. They left at 9 and then Jeanie, Charlie, Harvey, & I played jacks.

February 10, 1914. [Harvey] Margaret gets her hands dirty, then looks at them and says, "Dirty, ai-yah. Tch, tch, tch." She picks her nose. She pulls Richard's stockings off, catches his little toe, and says, "Wee, wee, wee."

February 14, 1914. [Harvey] Dr. Evans, Levering and I went out to the island. Left at 10:30, got there about noon, had a fine lunch and began to hunt. Dr. Evans and I each got a deer. I also got a pheasant and a duck. I knocked down 3 pheasants but 2 of them got away. We saw many deer.[4]

February 16, 1914. [Harvey] Dinner party–venison. Dr. & Mrs. Peter, Mr. & Mrs. Wilson, Mr. Rowe (Mrs. Rowe could not come). Tennis in P.M. with the Gaunts.[5] First tennis for Grace since Tsingtau.[6]

February 17, 1914. [Harvey] Margaret is 19 months old. She walked upstairs–every step–only touching the wall with one hand. She took the chamber from the table, sat on it, whistled, and pp-ed. Thunder storm. We hope the "rains" have begun. (1st thunder this year)

April 12, 1914. [Harvey] Easter Sunday. Grace put Richard in short clothes. The first thing he ever reached for to our knowledge was Margaret's toes. Grace cut her first wisdom tooth. Took Margaret to Sunday School. Collection for Children's Room, Foreign Hospital $1.50.

April 13, 1914. [Harvey] Margaret climbs in a rocking chair and says "bye-bye-baby." She took her shoe to bed and said, "Bye bye, shoe." When we put her to bed, she always calls for pillow which she calls boo-dah.

---

4. There are five islands in Lotus Lake, perhaps one of them? Levering may be Mr. Joshua, a Southern Baptist living in Shanghai, CRI, 280. The venison two evenings later no doubt comes from that hunt. Harvey would probably have done the slaughtering, perhaps with the help of their cook.

5. Dr. William Wesley Peter and his wife were in Shanghai 1911–52. See entry for July 17, 1913 and October 26, 1914. Rev and Mrs. Thomas Gaunt were with the Church Missionary Society, CRI, 165.

6. Tsingtau was the summer resort on the coast north of Nanking, where Harvey and Grace went their first summer together, 1911.

April 18, 1914. [Harvey] Grace took Richard and went to Chinkiang and Yanchow for eleven days.[7]

April 20, 1914. [Grace] Went to Yangchow. Anne Russell[8] had a boy meet me at Chinkiang. [written later?]

April 29, 1914. [Grace] Richard can roll over both ways. He is a happy baby. Came home from Yangchow.

May 5, 1914. [Grace] Richard 7 months old and his first tooth is through. [Harvey] Margaret says, "Hel' mamma" meaning "help mamma."

May 19, 1914. [Grace] Outdoor play given by the Watch Guard at Mrs. Beebe's. Margaret B.'s and Mr. Niles' engagement announced. Everyone happy.[9]

May 20, 1914. [Grace] Margaret says "Wheet Mamma." [meaning] "Sweet M." She takes her shoe and socks to and fro and says, "bye bye, shoe." She says, "Out goes you."

---

7. Chinkiang is where the parents of Pearl Buck lived (Sydenstrickers) and where Grace was born. She was three years older than Pearl Buck, and her family left Chinkiang and moved to Shanghai in 1892, the year Pearl was born.

8. Anne Russell Taylor (28 December 1889-1967 is the friend in Hangchow whom Grace is visiting. See also note on December 28,1910.

9. The Watch Guard Branch of the Agassiz Society was organized October, 1895. It originated from a little club which Josette and Margaret Beebe, Edward and Loos Williams called the "White Lily Club." It was organized to encourage its members to watch and guard–thus studying Mother Nature. Its motto, adopted in January 1903, was "Little by little the bird builds its nest and the child learns." They sponsored debates, e.g., in December 1903, "Resolved, that we learn more from observation than by books." By 1916, when they have an article in the Hillcrest yearbook, they met the first Friday of every month. 17-19. In May 1914, the play, "Sir Gareth of Orkney" was given in the beautiful garden of Dr. and Mrs. Beebe. Mrs. Beebe was one of the first teachers in the Hillcrest School, which she and other young missionary and foreign mothers had begun in the spring of 1911. At first they had only three mothers and six children and taught only the primary grades. In 1914 her daughter Margaret Beebe began teaching there at the high school level according to the 1916 yearbook. The founder of the Agassiz Society was Alexander Agassiz, 1835-1910, a U.S. zoologist. He emphasized careful observation, and in Ezra Pound's *ABC of Reading*,17, there's an anecdote about Agassiz and a postgraduate student who said, "That's only a sun fish," when Agassiz asked him to describe it. Agassiz kept sending him back to the fish until the student had learned a great deal and the fish was in a state of advanced decomposition. Grace's maternal grandfather, James Woodrow, studied at Harvard with Agassiz. Pound, *ABC of Reading*, 17-18

May 21, 1914. [Grace] Richard can pull himself along backwards a *little*. First rudiments of crawling.

May 22, 1914. [Grace] Richard cut his second tooth–lower. Nanking Assoc. at Y.M.C.A. Split because of refreshments.

May 23, 1914. [Grace] Dinner at Miss Peters'. Tea & children's supper at R. Bullocks'. Cantata "Seven Words of Christ" in evening.[10] Beautiful and impressive.

May 24, 1914. [Grace] Anniversary. We are both glad because of May 24, 1910.[11]

June 19, 1914. [Grace] Richard took his first crawl.

July 1, 1914. [Grace] Richard cut his first upper tooth left lateral. They are being cut like this.

— — —

4 3 2 1

July 4, 1914. [Grace] Richard's 2nd upper tooth broke through the skin and I can feel it.

July 10, 1914. [Grace] Richard's 3rd upper tooth arrived.

July 16, 1914. [Grace] Margaret was dry in the A.M. She waited crying for me "p.p." I want her to learn to say "Hi Hi" as the other is understood. She says "want er sit on th' pot."[12]

July 17, 1914. [Grace] M's second birthday party. On account of whooping c. I invited the mothers of M's friends.[13] We had a beautiful time. 12 came. No room to eat?

July 19, 1914. [Grace] Margaret was playing with Richard. She said, "Bore hole dere!" and punched him first, trying to "bore the hole" with her hand. Sunday, Communion service at the church, after the sermon.

---

10. This may have been "The Seven Last Words of Christ" by Theodore Dubois.
11. May 24, 1910, was the day Harvey met Grace.
12. All this care to get a two-year-old speaking the proper euphemistic language.
13. Because some child or children had whooping cough, only the mothers came.

July 20, 1914. [Grace] Richard was crying. Margaret said, "Don't cry, baby." M. had her first swim in the pool today.

July 31, 1914. [Grace] Richard's 6th tooth has come. Harvey's due in Kuling tomorrow. Three cheers!!![14]

August 1, 1914. [Grace] Harvey arrived at 9 A.M. after having spent the night at Lien Hwa Tung[15] and conducting Dr. Taft and party[16] up the hill.

August 2, 1914. [Grace] Sunday. A wonderful talk on "I sent you to reap" from Mr. Eddy.[17] "Others have labored."

August 5, 1914. [Harvey] Kuling. Went to Waterfalls, splendid trip, beautiful day.

August 6, 1914. [Harvey] Kuling. Richard pulled himself to a standing position. He is a bouncing, happy boy. Grace cut a wisdom tooth.

---

14. Grace and babies are in Kuling–she doesn't say when they arrived. Harvey's joining them only at the end of July.

15. This is the last resting place/hostel before the final sedan chair trip up to Kuling. See the entry for August 31, 1910 and Julia Wilson's essay in the Kuling Appendix C.

16. Dr. Marcus Lorenso Taft, with the Methodist Episcopal mission in Shanghai, CRI, 465, apparently brought Sherwood Eddy with him. Could Dr. Taft be related to U.S. President William Howard Taft (1909–1913), who came from Cincinnati?

17. Sherwood Eddy was at this time YMCA Executive Secretary for Asia. He had gone as a missionary to India in 1896. He became a leader in the Social Gospel school of missionary work and published nearly 40 books, including *Pilgrimage of Ideas or the Re-Education of Sherwood Eddy* in 1934, which my parents were reading in Pittsburgh, PA, in 1935 during their courtship. Eddy became a socialist by the 30s and took groups of people to Europe and Russia. My friend John Ewing's parents went with him to Germany and Russia in 1938, that very interesting pre-World War II era. The social gospel school began to influence Protestants by the late 1890s in the U.S. Between 1860 and 1890, more and more immigrants, especially Catholics and Jews, immigrated to the U.S. cities. Saloons outnumbered churches by 10 to one. Protestants no longer dominated the population. Some supported nativist movements [i.e., they were against immigrants] like the American Protestant Association, but some focused on the situation as an opportunity. "Industrialization and unrestrained capitalism had concentrated great wealth in the hands of a few. Ten percent of the nation's families had accumulated 90% of the wealth." The workers, largely immigrants, worked long hours, seven days a week, and "came home to squalid tenements afflicted with disease, drunkenness and prostitution . . . Advocates of the Social Gospel believed that the causes not merely the symptoms of urban unrest had to be addressed." *The Presbyterians*, Balmer and Fitzmier, 1994, 83–84. Within the mission community, emphasis gradually shifted from evangelism to human services like hospitals, schools, and better methods of agriculture.

August 10, 1914. [Grace] Margaret says, "Don't sha down, pease." *fall down*

August 16, 1914. [Harvey] Sunday. Margaret 34–3/4 inches high
Grace 5 ft., 2–5/8 inches high
Harvey 5 ft., 9–1/2 inches high
Richard 28–1/2 inches high

[Grace] Margaret in trying to climb in her high chair fell down. The next time she tried she said, "no fall down, please" or "no sha down pease."

September 1, 1914. [Grace] I asked Margaret where was "Pretty Papa." Then "Pretty Mama," and she pointed first to H., then to me. Then "Where's pretty baby?" She pointed to her mouth. Her mouth is an important part of her. She eats *well*.

September 2, 1914. [Grace] Harvey left for Kiukiang.[18] I walked with him until slope in the new road, about a mile or more. It was a strenuous day with packing, sending off boxes, No. 17 work, hair cut, etc. Tea at Miss Marble's [?].[19]

September 3, 1914. [Grace] Sick. Headache in evening. Went to Mildred's for supper but came home sick.

September 4, 1914. [Grace] In bed all day. Up in evening. Had a long talk with Mr. Stowe at Mrs. Johnstone's.[20] Eclipse of moon.

September 8, 1914. [Grace] Margaret saw Jean & me try some hair on her Kewpie [doll]. We must have said "cute," for a little later she got the hair, put it on the doll & said "coot."

October 5, 1914. [Grace] Richard's first birthday party. We had a lovely time on the lawn with the I.S.C. mothers and babies and a few other special friends, over thirty in all. Richard was very sweet in his little white dress that M. wore at her first birthday party.

---

18. Kiukiang is the rest house where they leave or catch the boat. See Appendix C on Kuling. Harvey is on his way back to Nanking.

19. Miss Marble is unidentified.

20. Rev. Dr. Everett M. Stowe was a Methodist Episcopal missionary, associated with Fukien Christian University. CRI, 457. Mrs. Sarah M. Black Johnston (Mrs. W. S.) was with CIM in Shanghai, CRI, 245.

October 26, 1914. [Grace] Went to a tea at Mrs. Peter's given to the I.S.C. & Fathers in honor of the Hiltners.[21] I am to have the meeting on Monday with my paper on Songs for Children.

October 27, 1914. [Grace] Took Margaret & Richard to the Peters' in A.M. to see the Hiltners. Little Walter only at home. Met the others on the st[reet] in ricksha. Rain.

October 28, 1914. [Grace] Went for a glorious (?)[22] horseback ride with Harvey. The horse was galloping and suddenly stumbled and fell, rolling over. I hit the road on my head, cut it, broke my collar bone, got a bruised hip and minor bruises. We went laboriously to Mrs. Gilbert's, Harvey riding the good horse, leading mine, while I rode in a ricksha a kind Chinese man had offered me. It was an awfully trying time, but the Lord gave us both strength. Dr. Peter[23] and Dr. Hiltner set the bone, cauterized the cut, and I came home about 10 P.M.

October 29, 1914. [Grace] Spent an awful night without being able to turn & *suffering* so. My friends are very kind. Alice M., Mrs. Evans, Mrs. Gilbert, Chinese girls and others came to see me. Notes from others. I.S.C. meeting postponed![24]

October 30, 1914. [Grace] Friday. Chinese S.S. class invited to tea but had to be put off. Still suffering but God is good and sends friends to help me bear it, better than Job's! "In all this Job sinned not, nor charged the Lord with foolishness."[25] May I follow in this example. [Job's]

October 31, 1914. [Grace] Went ahead with the H [Hallowe'en] party. Turned it over to Rachel & Margaret[26] who did beautifully without any

---

21. Dr. Walter G. Hiltner is one of the Nanking doctors. See entry for November 11, 1913.

22. Question mark is Grace's. "It had felt glorious until she fell."

23. Dr. William Wesley Peter with the YMCA is a medical doctor. See entry for July 17, 1913 and February 16, 1914.

24. Grace was to have given her paper on songs for children at the Monday, November 2, I.S.C. meeting. Alice M is Alice Macklin. Dr. Evans has been her doctor before. See entry for September 9, 1910.

25. Actual quote: "In all this Job sinned not, nor charged God foolishly." Job 1:22.

26. Margaret Beebe probably. She was a school teacher by this time. My mother may have been named after her. Rachel is unidentified.

weight on me. I went down twice for a few minutes in a dress on top of my n[ight] gown. I have to get up to rest for it hurts. Glad my legs are good.

November 1, 1914. [Grace] Sunday. Same old story. Stay in bed. Dr. & Mrs. Lasell[27] came, among others. All needed is patience. "Friend" came last eve.

November 2, 1914. [Grace] In bed still with occasional times of getting up to rest my weary bones. Pretty long tiring business. I get so cross.

November 8, 1914. [Grace] Looked in Richard's mouth and found three molars cut thro'. Poor little fellow, they did hurt him. The other is 'most through. Lower left incisor is thro', others are coming. Still in bed. Dr. Lasell doesn't want me to get up.

November 15, 1914. [Grace] Sunday. Took the law in my own hands & went to E.[Epworth] League & to church.[28] Too tired to stick it out. The 6 Evans came to see us in A.M. Still in bed.

November 16, 1914. [Grace] Dr. Lasell came to see me. "Be patient a few more days." So I'm still in bed off and on tho' I went to all three meals. Wrote to Louise & to Nat. Clock Co.

November 17, 1914. [Grace] Babies well except for colds. Dr. Hamilton[29] to dinner. Dr. Sloan and Evans boys to supper. Richard has four molars now, 4 upper incisors & 3 lower.

November 19, 1914. [Grace] Dr. Lasell came and let me out of the adhesive. It's an awful job to pull off "yards & yards" of this stuff. I look like I have small pox.

November 22, 1914. [Grace] Breakfast at Ladies' with the Hasrees' [?].[30] Visited S.S. class. Went to 10:30, 4:30 & 7:30 services. Pretty tired. Fine sermon at 4:30 on Prayer. I want my life to be more prayerful.

---

27. Dr. and Mrs. Sidney L. Lasell live in Nanking. Dr. Lasell is now taking care of Grace. Mrs. Lasell contributed to the Nanking cookbook and also helped with the new Hillcrest school building on the Furnishings Committee.

28. Here's a small sign of Grace yielding to a manic impulse after being depressed about having to stay in bed so long and finding it hard to cope.

29. Rev. Dr. Ernest A. Hamilton was with the Church Missionary Society in Shanghai. CRI, 193.

30. The Hasrees are unidentified.

1914 DIARY

November 23, 1914. [Grace] Went to L. School. In evening both of us went to the Millwards' to supper to meet Dr. & Mrs. Baldwin.[31]

November 24, 1914. [Grace] Father came to visit us. He seems to be glad Jean and C[harlie] are with us. He bro't two baskets of fruit. Generous. We all, F., J., C., H., M., and I went to little foreign school[32] after.

November 25, 1914. [Grace] Father and I went for a long walk in A.M.–my first–after the babies' baths. About 5 P.M. Harvey went hunting, and Father and I went to Williams' to the Presby. prayer meeting and Thanksgiving "lap supper." Had a fine time. It's nice to have Father here, and he seems to like our home.

November 26, 1914. [Grace] Thanksgiving Day. Went with Father at 8 A.M. to Theo[logical] Sem[inary][33] where he gave them a good address. Others went to foreign service at 10:30. Methodist dinner at Wilsons'.[34]

November 28, 1914. [Grace] Friend.

December 9, 1914. [Harvey] Margaret (almost 2–1/2 years old) undressed herself, doing nearly everything but the buttons at the back. She can untie the hard knots we put in her shoe strings. Richard has been a darling today. Grace went to Chinkiang to Anna May [Hummel]'s birthday party on the early train.[35]

---

31. Language School. Mr. William Millward and Mrs. Jennie Fitzgerald Millward were Methodists. See entry for December 26, 1912 and January 11, 1915. This visiting couple would be Rev. Dr. and Mrs. Caleb Cecil Baldwin. He was Superintendent of the Foochow Medical Mission Hospital and was also on the American Board of Commissioners for Foreign Missions. CRI, 19.

32. Little foreign school is Hillcrest, which Jeanie and Charlie are attending. Charlie belonged to the Watch Guard Society, was a secretary for it. Note Grace's use of *seems*. "He seems to be glad Jean and Charlie are with us." She wants his approval, and this suggests that it isn't easy to get.

33. This would be the Presbyterian Union Theological Seminary.

34. The Rev. and Mrs. Wilbur F. Wilson were Methodists. The dinner must be a gathering of Methodists. See entries for August 24, 1910, November 24, 1910, May 13, 1913, and October 29, 1913.

35. Anna May Hummel, born December 9, 1913. Daughter of Harvey's friend Hummel. Mother remembers playing with a June Hummel.

GRACE

December 19, 1914. [Grace] 4th anniversary. We celebrated by doing ordinary duties up to 4 P.M. Then took M. & R. for a nice ricksha ride. Harvey gave me Cashmere Bouquet soap.[36]

December 20, 1914. [Grace] Taught S.S. class in A.M. Staid home with babies in the sunshine at church time. Then after baths and nap time, H. & I took a long walk to Ching Liane Sha [?][37] & around. Saw 2 pheasants playing.

December 21, 1914. [Grace] Ordinary round of duties. Took babies to the Bullocks' to see how Burlingame was of his pneumonia. He's lots better. I think he's going to have a sister about April.

December 23, 1914. [Grace] Grace is 25 and happy. Father & the Bishops, 3+[38], came in P.M. Busy all day until 2 when all of us but Harvey drove (!) in a carriage[39] down to meet Father Christmas; decorations put up. The house is real cozy.

December 25, 1914. [Grace] Our fifth Christmas together. The tree was lovely. We all had to wait until after breakfast. Margaret folded her hands and looked at "all the pretty pretties," then she couldn't resist the kewpie [doll] lying in his little bed. This is the happiest Christmas I ever had.

December 26, 1914. [Grace] So many things to do and places to go. Christmas entertainment at Gu I Lau [?][40] supper with Father & the Bs [Blackstones] at the Martins' All tired out. To bed.

END OF 1914 DIARY

36. My grandmother always used Cashmere Bouquet bath soap and cosmetics.

37. Ching Liane Sha is most likely Qingliangshan park, a 180-acre park located in the Gulou District of Nanking (Nanjing) on Quinliang Hill, which is 100 meters high and 4 kilometers in radius. Chinese Zen Master Fayan Wenyi (885–958) and founder of the Fayan school taught at Qingliang Temple. It's now considered one of the top five parks in Nanjing.

38. This family of Bishops are unidentified.

39. Carriages are seldom hired, so it must have been a special occasion.

40. Gu I Lau is probably Gu Lou, the drum tower.

1915–1916 Diaries

January 1, 1915. [Grace] Friday. Bathed the babies as usual. Harvey had holiday. In P.M. we two went hunting in the western hills. Harvey got two pheasants.

January 2, 1915. [Grace] Went to Billy's party.[1] Harvey went hunting and killed two rabbits. His first. Went to Y.M.C.A.

January 11, 1915. [Grace] Martha Ann Millward born. I think J.W.R. began her life about this time. Later. The J.W.R. proved to be G.W.R. [Grace Woodbridge Roys, next child.][2]

January 17, 1915. [Grace] Jean cared for the babes most all day while we went to church. She said Richard took 3 steps alone. He is very sweet.

January 18, 1915. [Grace] I.S.C. meets here. Paper on songs. This A.M. Margaret cried because Shao Sao left her to pull off her own shoes. She said,

---

1. Billy McCloy, born Jan. 2, is probably the son of Charles Harold McCloy, who was with the YMCA, in the Department of Physical Education, in China from 1913 to 1921. Emma McCloy was in first grade in 1916 at Hillcrest, 11. CRI, 305.

2. Martha Ann Millward's parents were Methodists, Mr. William Millward and Mrs. Jennie Fitzgerald Millward. See entries for December 26, 1912 and November 23, 1914. Grace is now pregnant with Gracie, named Grace Woodbridge Roys, after her mother, born in September 1915 and died of heart complications following scarlet fever in 1924 at age 8, when they were back in the U.S. Their fourth child was Harvey Curtis, named for his father, and apparently, if Gracie had been a boy, she would have been J.W.R. I haven't found the name that starts with J, but W.R. is probably Woodbridge Roys. In diary entry for February 27, 1915, she calls the baby H.C., i.e., Harvey Curtis.

"I want Sha Sao to sit beside *my*."[3] Richard weighs 24 lbs., Margaret weighs 33 lbs.

February 2, 1915. [Grace] Ground Hog Day. He didn't see his shadow. I went to Chinkiang for a few days' visit with the Sydenstrickers.[4]

February 3, 1915. [Grace] Cold as everything. A cold rain and heavy wind. In the evening we went to a Chinese wedding at Methodist School. Snow. I hope my babies keep warm.

February 4, 1915. [Grace] Mildred invited me over but it was too cold and I rest well at the S's. Prayer meeting in P.M. Paxton[5] to supper.

February 5, 1915. [Grace] Came home from Chinkiang. Margaret and Richard so glad to see me. M. said, "Why, eddo, Mama. Kiss me. Your face too cold, come & get warm." She made me feel quite at home, helping me off with my wraps.[6] Richard wanted me to hold him the minute I arrived. Richard cut his first eye tooth upper left. Folks say eye teeth are hard to cut. Richard must be different for I found it by chance.

February 6, 1915. [Grace] Foreign children gave extracts from 'The Merchant of Venice.' Jean was Lorenzo and Charlie Shylock. Both were fine.[7]

---

3. I.S.C. mothers' group, which started the Hillcrest School, had scheduled Grace's paper on children's songs in the previous November, but her fall from a horse, breaking her collar bone, meant it had to be postponed. See entries for October 28 and 29, 1914. Shao Sao is the Chinese amah (nursemaid). *Sha Sao* is baby talk in Margaret.

4. Several times Grace has gone to visit the Sydenstrickers in the mission station where she grew up. This time she goes alone. She must have felt close to them. Pearl (later Buck) had been in U.S. at Randolph-Macon College from Sept 1910. She returned to China Nov 1914 to help take care of her mother, who had sprue, as yet undiagnosed. Perhaps Grace wanted to help nurse Carie and advise Pearl? Hilary Spurling, *Pearl Buck*, 79.

5. Rev. John Wardlaw Paxton and his wife, born Una Edith Hall, came to China in 1891 and 1895, respectively. They served in Chinkiang where Grace is visiting. Listed as Southern Presbyterian missionaries in Samuel Woodbridge's *Fifty Years*, 225. CRI, 377.

6. I've thought a lot about this entry, how at age 2-1/2 my mother was mothering her mother, rather than seeking mothering. A family pattern that continued of children mothering the mother.

7. This performance by foreign children is at Hillcrest. Dorothy Williams Davidson writes of it: "The little gray schoolhouse on top of 'Fifth Hill' was where we struggled through geography. There we all met in spelling and arithmetic and there I learned to read. There we were initiated into the wonders of *Hiawatha*, the *Odyssey* and the tales of the *Round Table*. Some of our happiest memories are our amateur theatricals. We went through a dramatization of *Little Women* and with our teacher, Frank Price, we went on

February 7, 1915. [Grace] Sunday. Heavy snow–the biggest I remember in China.[8] Went to foreign service in P.M. Mr. Searle[9] came home for supper with us. He is a Michigan man and he and Harvey had a delightful time. Jean & Charlie out to supper.

February 18, 1915. [Grace] Harvey came home from the hunt in the P.M. bearing his trophies–3 deer & several birds were his game. A postal from Father asking us to come to Shanghai sooner. So in evening, Harvey & Jeanie & and the servants picked and cleaned the game & we got ready to start to Shanghai in the A.M. I went to bed as I wasn't feeling "up to snuff." Harvey does everything *well*. He got the game all fixed, roasted a pheasant for our lunch on the train and got ready to leave.

February 19, 1915. [Grace] Friday. Harvey and I start off on our "second honeymoon" in the early dawn. We are as happy as two kids. The alarm goes off at five and alarms us. We hustle up, dress, get our things together and Harvey fixes a dandy lunch. That ought to be my job. We are running away and leaving our babies with Jeanie & Charlie. We didn't dare wake them to kiss them goodbye.

February 24, 1915. [Grace] Wednesday. Went to the U.Y.K. wharf at 7 A.M. to meet Hazel and Dennis Egbert.[10] Hayes[es][11] came, too. The boat got in about 10:30! Cold. Then we all went to the Hayes' to breakfast, then to Father's for tiffin, out to the Hayes' again for the afternoon & evening. The three boys went for drive over Shanghai in the P.M. while we girls rested. What a jolly time they all had talking over old times. Everyone went

---

and gave *A Midsummer Night's Dream* out under the big trees in Mrs. Meigs' garden. Oh! The frantic scrambles behind the scenes! Oh! The funny practices as we concocted medieval costumes in a Chinese city. The seriousness with which Titania and her attendants worried through their fairy dances. Many and hot were the battles we fought around the gray schoolhouse behind the bamboo trees." Dorothy Williams Davidson, Lilian Williams's daughter, in Lilian Williams' *Yesterdays in China*, 23–24.

8. This snow most likely the one with the photo of Grace on the steps. See photo on xviii.

9. Mr. Searle is unidentified.

10. Here is the arrival of Harvey's friend, Dennis, and his wife Hazel, from Michigan, a good friend he'd made at the University of Michigan in Ann Arbor. See also entry for June 11, 1911.

11. The two Hayeses apparently also went to Ann Arbor. They are Mr. Egbert M. Hayes and his wife. See also entries for May 28 and December 1, 1913.

to Mich[igan] but me, so all I had to do was sit back and listen to their reminiscences. Harvey is happy.

February 25, 1915. [Grace] Thurs. Got all packed up and then finished up our shopping. The boys went to the bank while I went and got Hazel. We met at 10 Nooseny [?] Road with Dr. & Mrs. Lacy, Bishop & Mrs. Bashford.[12] Then all went to the Hayes' for lunch and in a rush to the train. We got to the station 5 min. before train time. Had a jolly time on the way up. Arrived in Nanking in rain & came up in two dilapidated carriages. Glad to see the little babies. c t[13]

February 26, 1915. [Grace] Late breakfast. Went to the Language School and other places. Just enjoying each other. It is rainy, so we aren't very ambitious to do sightseeing. c t for G.

February 27, 1915. [Grace] Late breakfast. Bathed babies while Harvey & the others went to the school. H. is busy. There's plenty to do after a week's vacation. Dr. Sloan came over for supper and we had a pleasant evening. I'm sorry I can't be more agreeable but little H.C. wants me to remember him, so he keeps my digestion upset. c t again.

February 28, 1915. [Grace] Sunday. Dennis & Hazel with us over Sunday. Church in A.M. Hazel not well—cold.

March 9, 1915. [Grace] Richard cut his 2nd eye tooth. Both babies have had colds. They are just as sweet and interesting as they can be. Are learning to play together nicely.

April 1, 1915. [Grace] Richard cut his third eye tooth. No trouble at all.

April 9, 1915. [Grace] Richard is learning to walk. He can take quite a few steps alone if carefully balanced and started.

April 10, 1915. [Grace] Richard started alone to take a few steps. He is getting more confident every day. Big thunderstorm & rain, beginning in the P.M. and lasting until into the night. 2 Chinese reported to have been killed

12. Rev. Dr. William Henry Lacy and Mrs. Emma Nind Lacy are Methodist Episcopal missionaries in Shanghai. He was President of the China Sunday School Union, CRI, 267–8. Bishop James Whitford Bashford was the first Methodist Episcopal Church resident bishop in China. See entry for April 4, 1911.

13. Grace appears to have a code here in the next several entries. It looks like c t, with a line under t. Perhaps medicine–calomel? See entry for Nov. 2, 1913.

by lightning. I took Margaret & Richard over to the Sarvises'. Richard didn't like it a bit when I held their baby but got reconciled when I took him too and tried to kiss the baby.

April 17, 1915. [Grace] When we had prayers, Richard saw us all kneeling down to pray so he knelt down the whole time we prayed, only disturbing us by crying because Margaret teased him. We try to have only a short prayer as then babies can learn to behave easier.

May 21, 1915. [Grace] Friday. Nanking Association at the Gilberts'. Lovely time. About 150 people sat down to the table.

May 22, 1915. [Grace] Saturday. Luther[14] came for a two days' visit. Richard & I went to meet him.[15]

December 24, 1915. [Grace] A full day. Ten of us in the house. In the evening we trimmed our first real Christmas tree. No stockings this time. Everything is lovely but there's lots to do. I get pretty tired. Bed late.

February 14, 1916. [Grace] Kuling. Spent the whole day out-of-doors. Beautiful. In the evening went to supper at No. 70. Sarah, Hant, Tilly, Tom.[16]

February 16, 1916. [Grace] Gave children old Valentines from Davie[17] & Burlingame.

END OF DIARY ENTRIES.

14. Mr. Luther may be the one with CIM. CRI, 298.
15. Gracie was born in September, but she got no diary entry. Seven months went by without entries.
16. Friends in Kuling. Sarah, Hant, Tilly, and Tom are unidentified.
17. Burlingame is the son of Mr. and Mrs. (Ruth) Bullock. See entry for November 6, 1910. Davie is the son of the Sarvises. See entries for February 14, 1913 and December 20, 1914.

Epilogue

When I read Grace and Harvey's diary twelve years ago and decided to annotate it, I was focused on understanding Grace and myself better. I had nearly completed the book I intended in 2004 and laid it aside for nine years when, by one of those unlikely coincidences, I met Martha, the daughter of a Russian scholar I'd known. Martha wanted to give me her father's Russian literary tapes. She told me that her mother, Betsy Riggs Hankin, had spent much of her childhood in China, born, as were my mother and grandmother, to missionary parents there. Martha's grandfather, Charles Riggs, had even worked at the same University of Nanking, in Agriculture, where my grandfather taught physics, 1913–21. Martha didn't know a lot about the Chinese connection, but she wrote to her mother's younger sister, Edith Barakat, and introduced me by email, and Edith began writing to me. She had been collecting family history and began to share with me some things she had written, as well as many photos of her family, some scenes in China, and her mother's memoirs.

Edith read what I had written so far and made suggestions for other books to read which might help me. Three in particular, I set myself to read: Nancy Thomson Waller's *My Nanking Home: 1918–1937*; *A Daughter of Han: The Autobiography of a Chinese Working Woman* by Ida Pruitt, and the fairly recent *Pearl Buck in China: Journey to the Good Earth* by Hilary Spurling.

As I read, I realized two main things: I didn't know much about China or the Chinese people and culture. It also struck me that, since, like Pearl Buck, my grandmother had spent the first half of her life in China (1889–1921)—she was thirty-two when she left China, and she died in 1953 at

EPILOGUE

age sixty-four—Grace must have missed China. She lost a huge part of her world when she left. Pearl lived in China 1892–1934, was age forty-two when she left, and she died in 1973, at age eighty-one. Nancy Thomson Waller spent even less time in China, but she also missed it, as does Edith Barakat to this day. Pearl articulates very clearly that she had a Chinese "side" and an American "side." The two sides never quite got integrated. "For Pearl China always remained the place where she felt at home."[1]

China had been hard for me to deal with and think about because, from age seven, when I learned that the Chinese devalued baby girls and even killed them, part of me hated China. My seven-year-old distrust of the Chinese was still with me at age seventy-five when I began reading these new books. Between the correspondence with Edith and her recommended books, my view of the Chinese began to change.

In my new readings about missionaries in China I was especially caught up in the story of Pearl Buck's life. At a very young age—four years old—she had learned the harsh realities for the Chinese living outside the mission compound. She had wandered onto a nearby hillside and found the limbs of dead babies, which she buried.

> Sometimes Pearl found bones lying in the grass, fragments of limbs, mutilated hands, once a head and shoulder with parts of an arm still attached. They were so tiny she knew they belonged to dead babies, nearly always girls suffocated or strangled at birth and left out for dogs to devour . . . [She] controlled her revulsion and buried what she found according to rites of her own invention . . . Pearl made miniature grave mounds, patting down the sides and decorating them with flowers or pebbles."[2]

"She heard the crying of distraught women over the loss of their children. With her golden hair, not the black hair of her Chinese playmates, she was seen by some of the adult Chinese as 'the devil.'"[3] She went into her friends' houses and heard the women talking. She was with her mother when Chinese women came to her for help with their problems, and she had a Chinese amah who took her to town where she saw everything going on in the town.

> With her brother and Wang Amah Pearl explored streets lined with portable one-man cook shops and puppet shows, barbers, tailors,

1. Spurling, *Pearl Buck*, 14.
2. Ibid., 3.
3. Ibid., 2.

and letter writers at work in the gutter. They listened to professional storytellers and watched entertainers like the Pig Butcher in her novel, *Sons* ("if he took a pair of chopsticks he could pluck the flies out of the air as they flew, one by one he plucked them . . . and they roared with laughter to see such skill"). Even the markets were a form of street theater: "the silk shops flying brilliant banners of black and red and orange silk," the vegetable market with glittering stalls of red radish, green cabbage, and white lotus root, mounds of live yellow crabs and silver fish in the fish market, rows of shiny brown ducks turning on spits over hot coals in front of the duck shops. The children stopped to look at men measuring out grain from baskets big enough for an adult to step into and suffocate: "white rice and brown, and dark yellow wheat and pale gold wheat, and yellow soybeans and red beans and green broad beans and canary-colored millet and grey sesame." They sucked illicit unhygienic candy from paper cornets and bought paper lanterns shaped like birds, butterflies or a rabbit on wheels.[4]

Because her mother, Carie Sydenstricker, was unhappy and distracted, Pearl was less protected than Grace was. Interestingly, at age ten Pearl's parents hired Mr. Kung, a Chinese scholar, to tutor her in Mandarin Chinese. Pearl had learned the vernacular Chinese spoken by the neighbors and the servants, and this tutor had her studying the texts of Confucius and other Chinese philosophers. "[This was] a singular act of intellectual bravado on the part of her parents at a time when more conventional missionaries dismissed Chinese reverence for Confucius as rank idolatry."[5] My great-grandfather Samuel Woodbridge was quite contemptuous of all the Chinese philosophies and religions and abhorred their superstitions. He did acknowledge this about Confucius: "Confucianism teaches that government is for the benefit of the people, not of the sovereign. The only divine right of kings that the Chinese have ever known is their duty to rule well and justly. Mencius struck the democratic note still more clearly when he said that the people were of first importance, the gods second, and then the sovereign. Only Christianity teaches more clearly the value of the individual."[6]

Hence Pearl was thoroughly baptized in Chinese culture and language by the time she married Lossing Buck, and his agriculture work then took

4. Ibid., 23.
5. Ibid., 49–51.
6. Woodbridge, *Fifty Years*, 21.

her out into the rural areas where she learned what the life of a Chinese farmer was like. Out of all this soaking up of Chinese culture came, by 1931, *The Good Earth*, which shocked the missionaries and many educated Chinese alike.

Pearl told the truth about the lives of the Chinese farmers, but, as I've learned, too, people don't always want the truth. Nevertheless, *The Good Earth* became an international best seller, and is still in print. As a teenager, I was most struck by the woman who worked in the fields, stopped only long enough to give birth by herself to twins, and then went back to her field work.

I ask myself now: what was it that made these women, Pearl Buck, Nancy Waller, Edith Barakat, and probably Grace, too, long for China after years spent there?

Of course, they were all there as part of a privileged white, Western group. Their families were there to help and "save" the Chinese. In doing so, the missionaries disseminated not only Western religious thought—both Protestant and Catholic—they also brought modern medicine and modern science, as well as foreign languages, especially English. They built schools and hospitals. They educated girls and young women as well as boys and young men. Over time Chinese students went to the U.S. and other Western countries for college and graduate education. While my grandparents were in Nanking, in 1911, the Sun Yat-sen Revolution had begun the change which would culminate in the Communist takeover by 1949.

Early missionary families, after the Boxer Rebellion in 1900, when Western powers had interfered and made their place in China more secure, had plenty of servants, amahs for their children, cooks they trained to prepare Western dishes, rickshaw boys to carry them places, sedan chair men to carry them up the mountain to Kuling. When civil disturbances came or the Japanese invaded, comparatively few missionaries lost their lives, but many Chinese did.

The missionaries were exposed to the killing, even by the mother herself, of unwanted babies. They saw people, during floods and famines, dying of hunger in the streets or outside their compounds. They may not have talked about it much or written about it in their diaries, but they witnessed first-hand the constant suffering of the Chinese. The missionaries did help with famine relief when American ships arrived with grain, but the regularity of such disasters in China, as famine and floods, must have been overwhelming to the foreigners.

As is suggested about Pearl in Spurling's book, they must have distanced themselves emotionally from the tragedies they could do so little to prevent or solve. Spurling talks about how "the potent spell Pearl cast later, as a phenomenally successful writer of romantic best sellers, came in large part from this sense of a harsh hidden reality, protruding occasionally but more often invisible, present only beneath the surface of her writing as an unexamined residue of pain and fear."[7] Spurling further suggests: "[Pearl tried hard to bury] her memories of being sworn at as a foreign devil in the street, of fleeing for her life from marauding soldiers, of the young brides sold into slavery who hanged themselves at intervals in her neighbors' houses. Memories like these surface in her novels from time to time like a dismembered hand or leg. This ambivalence—the territory that lies between what is said and what can be understood—is the nub of my book."[8]

The awareness of the terrible suffering around them may have been one reason why missionaries working to improve Chinese agriculture (e.g., Lossing Buck and Edith Barakat's father, Charles Riggs) were so passionately involved in their work and tended to neglect their families. Pearl was taken for granted and ignored by Lossing soon after their marriage. Edith says she saw her parents, especially her father, very little for years at a time, because she and her siblings spent many years with their grandparents in the U.S.

I grew up in an atmosphere where serving others was a strong tradition in both my mother's and father's families. Work as a minister or missionary to help other people had more priority than one's own family life and children, though children were cherished and given a great deal of attention in my father's immediate family, maybe because three older siblings out of four of Grandpa Stevenson's had died of diphtheria when his father was a missionary in Oregon. I don't know that those missionary parents would have agreed that they neglected their families, but it is easy for children to feel that way when they are separated for years from their parents.

Grace had more domestic help in China than in the U.S. as well as a clearer sense of what she as an individual could do. What I hadn't imagined until now was that leaving China, for her, too, meant leaving the only home and culture she had known for thirty-two years—both the Chinese and the missionary culture—a blend of them. The missionaries carried on their

7. Spurling, *Pearl Buck*, 5.
8. Ibid., xii.

Western culture with their teas, dinners, church services, outings to monuments, retreat in the summer to the mountains, tennis, hunting, horseback riding. At times it is hard to believe they are in China. Yet the rickshaw boy, the cook, the amah who wants baby Margaret to do something for herself, the Chinese woman who wanted to sell Grace her baby, or the sight of a cart of dead babies going by outside their compound's wall—even if not often mentioned, these Chinese people are omni-present, with their terrible poverty and suffering, but also with their love and wisdom.

When Harvey and Grace go off to Shanghai leaving Jeanie (fourteen) and Charlie (twelve) in charge, they are trusting implicitly those servants and their faithful, dependable care. The nurse who helps Grace after Margaret's birth is Chinese. In the Spurling biography we see more clearly this world of the Chinese, its terrible suffering, but also its capacity for love, the wisdom of how to cope learned over centuries of poverty and loss, wars and revolutions.

The Americans came from a young nation, only three hundred years old at the most, when the missionary presence in China was at its greatest, in the early 1900s. The Chinese culture went back thousands of years. Over those centuries the Chinese had become a culture of acceptance, overcoming by acceptance. When the Manchus conquered China, the Chinese didn't protest. They waited and gradually regained control. "[After the defeat of the Boxer Rebellion of 1900 by the West] the defeated Chinese were acquiescent, even obsequious, and almost suspiciously eager to enlist in the ranks of a religion that had so decisively demonstrated superior supernatural strength."[9] If boy babies are more able to work and grow food, and there is never enough to eat, and the husband/father will get rid of a wife who can't produce sons, then I begin to imagine how a desperate mother would kill a baby she has just birthed to save herself and her other children.

We in the West in the latter part of the twentieth century became fascinated by the wisdom of Confucius, of Lao Tse, and other Chinese wise men, and by the Indian mystics, whose culture also knew great suffering over long centuries. Russia, too, had its centuries of wars (invaded twice in every century), and its peasants were tied like slaves to the land until the late nineteenth century. I was so moved by the kindness and the lavish hospitality of the Russian people I met, especially in Kostroma, but also by a few I became close to in Moscow and St. Petersburg.

9. Ibid., 34.

EPILOGUE

I had been afraid there, too, at times—not so much of the Communist government, still operational in 1990, but of my sense that, in times not in the distant past, there had been terror, great suffering, and unimaginable loss. They lost in the first half of the twentieth century 25,000,000 people to Stalin and 25,000,000 in World War II. Hospitality rituals were so strong because of the immense distances and because of all the loss. You might never see your friend or family member again. I received so many gifts—books, small paintings—inscribed: "For a good memory," and the feasts and events arranged for me were so intense, so crowded with good food, elaborate toasts, kindness, and soul-to-soul communication that they stuck in my memory permanently.

I believe that, in addition to Grace's personal conflicts with a father who wanted to control her love life and who was difficult to please, and some untamed willfulness in her personality, there were other factors that led to her serious breakdowns in the 1920s and 1930s, once they were back in the U.S. Her many gifts, which had some outlets in China, didn't here lend themselves to activities that would have helped her feel useful and important. Her social life in the U.S. was much reduced, and she had to cope with school-aged children and being a full-time housewife. She no longer was surrounded by the educated, passionately devoted missionaries, and those cheerful, accepting Chinese servants who had served and sustained her, even if she thought she was helping them. She didn't get love from her father. Her mother loved her, I believe, but Samuel ruled the home. I think of how happy she was in the early years of her marriage, with her babies, little jaunts with Harvey to "run away," her help to the Chinese with nursing skills, and her language dexterity. She was useful and important. Harvey's colleagues at the university often came to dinner or tea, and the active missionary social life surrounded her. In her circle there were also many professional single women, freer to do their work than in the United States. She was appreciated and valued by them. There was nothing comparable for her in Norman, Oklahoma. China *was* home.

As I learned more about the people in Grace's social circle, I realized something else. Many of these missionaries were highly educated, doctors of medicine and theology. Some had started schools or hospitals. They were intrepid. Obstacles didn't defeat them. Such intelligent and gifted people often have a call or vocation, an urgent sense that they must do something significant, achieve something important with their lives. To feel they have succeeded, they must find a way to give away their gifts so that the world is

EPILOGUE

a better place for their having lived. This means going it alone some of the time, following their inner sense of what they should do, even when others disapprove or reject them. Taking any unique path means encountering and overcoming obstacles. It means you keep on your path when others scoff, tease, dismiss. To do this requires the development of inner strength and courage and the ability to cope when you feel disappointed, frustrated, and alone against huge obstacles.

For whatever reason Grace carried that sense that she must be important to others and accomplish something unique. She was at ease in her circle, which included the American Consul and his wife, the President of the University of Nanking, founders of hospitals and schools, as well as Chinese leaders in these educational, religious, and medical institutions. Yet she didn't achieve anything comparable outside the home as most of them had. Nor had she developed that inner strength and courage. She ran her home competently in China and loved her husband and children, but Harvey and the servants did most of the work, and she hadn't much patience when she was confined to bed with a broken collar bone.

Back in the U.S., her world shrank to a more limited domestic life, with one live-in college girl to help and no opportunity to teach unless Harvey was on sabbatical and wasn't teaching at the University of Oklahoma. When her school age children got into fights, she sometimes left the house. and they didn't know when she'd come back. She'd lost the supportive world of missionary life in China, and then she lost her favorite child. She didn't cope well, and Harvey didn't know how to help her. So she "lost it."

Although my mother feared that the family mental illness might "come out" in me, it never did. I carried gifts not unlike those Grace had, and I also inherited that passion to do something unique and important. I found the inner strength and courage I needed to make my own path. I identify more with the Chinese student Harvey almost had in his physics class, Yuen Ren Chao, who decided in his teens to be a perfect man. That wasn't how I framed my own goal for myself. I sensed early, also in my teens, that I had gifts which I must use effectively. I must do something new that only I could do. These days it is easier to articulate. I want to leave behind me in my writing and my life some understanding of what it means to love and to be true to yourself, to fulfill your gifts, and give them away.

What pushes our minds over the edge into illness? It's complex, but to put it simply, the red flag is our inability to cope. If we can cope, we're okay. When we feel overwhelmed by loss or despair, then the mind lets in fantasies and nightmares and leads us astray. A gifted, sensitive mind that hadn't before had to cope with much that was difficult, especially the loss of a child, is very vulnerable. She also, in her "mentally ill" state, felt free to reject her husband and even her grown and very proper and conscientious daughter, my mother. She played cards, danced, and had love affairs, but a part of her mind felt guilty for these things. She wasn't able to forgive herself and integrate or manage her desires and frustrations.

Her loss of China, her missing it, is in none of the stories or records I have, and yet, didn't that play a huge role in how she floundered once back in the U.S.? I think so. Her supporting fabric of love and meaning was gone.

Appendix A

The Legend of the Bleeding Heart[1]

In days of old, when all things in the Wood had speech, there lived within its depths a lone Flax-spinner. She was a bent old creature, and ill to look upon, but all the tongues of all the forest leaves were ever kept a-wagging with the story of her kindly deeds. And even to this day they sometimes whisper low among themselves (because they fain would hold in mind so sweet a tale) the story of her kindness to the little orphan, Olga.

'Twas no slight task the old Flax-spinner took upon herself, the day she brought the helpless child to share the shelter of her thatch. The Oak outside her door held up his arms in solemn protest.

"Thou dost but waste thyself," he said. "Thy benefits will be forgot, thy labours unrequited. For Youth is ever but another title for Ingratitude."

"Nay, friend," the old Flax-spinner said. "My little Olga will not be ungrateful and forgetful."

All hedged about with loving care, the orphan grew to gracious maidenhood, and felt no lack of father, mother, brother or sister. In every way the old Flax-spinner took their places. But many were the sacrifices that she made to keep her fed and warmly clad, and every time she went without herself that Olga might receive a greater share, Wiseacre Oak looked down and frowned and shook his head.

---

1. Grace shared this legend with Harvey on May 28, 1910, when they were getting acquainted and called it "ours." It was published in 1907 in this version by Annie Fellows Johnston (1863–1931), who was a well-known author of children's fiction. "Annie Fellows Johnston" article in On-line Literature.

APPENDIX A: THE LEGEND OF THE BLEEDING HEART

Then would the old dame hasten to her inner room, and there she pricked herself with her spindle, until a great red drop of her heart's blood fell into her trembling hand. With witchery of words she blew upon it, and rolled it in her palm, and muttering, turned and turned and turned it. And as the spell was laid upon it, it shriveled into a tiny round ball like a seed, and she strung it on a thread where were many others like it, saying, "By this she will remember. She will not be ungrateful and forgetful."

So years went by, and Olga grew in goodness and in beauty, and helped the old Flax-spinner in her tasks as blithely and as willingly as if she were indeed her daughter. Every morning she brought water from the spring, gathered the wild fruits of the woods, and spread the linen on the grass to bleach. At such times would the bent old foster-mother hold herself erect, and call up to the Oak, "Dost see? Thou'rt wrong! Youth is not another title for Ingratitude."

"Thou hast not lived as long as I," would be the only answer.

One day as Olga was wandering by the spring, searching for watercresses, the young Prince of the castle rode by on his prancing charger. A snow-white plume waved in his hat, and a shining silver bugle hung from his shoulder, for he had been following the chase.

He was thirsty and tired, and asked for a drink, but there was no cup with which to dip the water from the spring. But Olga caught the drops as they bubbled out from the spring, holding them in the hollow of her beautiful white hands, and reaching up to where he sat, offered him the sparkling water. So gracefully was it done, that the Prince was charmed by her modest manner as well as her lovely face, and baring his head when he had slaked his thirst, he touched the white hands with his lips.

Before he rode away he asked her name and where she lived. The next day a courier in scarlet and gold stopped at the door of the cottage and invited Olga to the castle. Princesses and royal ladies from all over the realm were to be entertained there, seven days and seven nights. Every night a grand ball was to be given, and Olga was summoned to each of the balls. It was because of her pleasing manner and her great beauty that she had been bidden.

The old Flax-spinner curtsied low to the courier and promised that Olga should be at the castle without fail.

"But, good dame," cried Olga, when the courier had gone, "prithee tell me why thou didst make such a promise, knowing full well this gown of tow is all I own. Wouldst have me stand before the Prince in beggar's garb? Better to bide at home for aye than be put to shame before such guests."

APPENDIX A: THE LEGEND OF THE BLEEDING HEART

"Have done, my child!" the old dame said. "Thou shalt wear a court robe of the finest. Years have I toiled to have it ready, but that is naught. I loved thee as my own."

Then once more the old Flax-spinner went into her inner room, and pricked herself with her spindle till another great red drop of her heart's blood fell into her trembling hand. With witchery of words she blew upon it, and rolled it in her palm, and muttering, turned and turned and turned it. And as the spell was laid upon it, it shriveled into a tiny round ball like a seed, and she strung it on to a thread, where were many others like it. Seventy times seven was the number of beads on this strange rosary.

When the night of the first ball rolled around, Olga combed her long golden hair and twined it with a wreath of snowy water-lilies, and then she stood before the old dame in her dress of tow. To her wonderment and grief she saw there was no silken robe in waiting, only a string of beads to clasp around her white throat. Each bead in the necklace was like a little shriveled seed, and Olga's eyes filled with tears of disappointment.

"Obey me and all will be well," said the old woman.

"When thou reachest the castle gate clasp one bead in thy fingers and say: 'For love's sweet sake, in my hour of need, Blossom and deck me, little seed.' Straightway right royally shalt thou be clad. But remember carefully the charm. Only to the magic words, 'For love's sweet sake' will the necklace give up its treasures. If thou shouldst forget, then thou must be doomed always to wear thy gown of tow."

So Olga sped on her moon-lighted way through the forest until she came to the castle gate. There she paused, and grasping a bead of the strange necklace between her fingers, repeated the old dame's charm:

"For love's sweet sake, in my hour of need, Blossom and deck me, little seed."

Immediately the bead burst with a little puff as if a seed pod had snapped asunder. A faint perfume surrounded her, rare and subtle as if it had been blown across from some flower of Eden. Olga looked down and found herself enveloped in a robe of such delicate texture, that it seemed soft as a rose-leaf and as airy as pink clouds that sometimes float across the sunset. The water-lilies in her hair had become a coronal of opals.

When she entered the great ball-room, the Prince of the castle started up from his throne in amazement. Never before had he seen such a vision of loveliness. "Surely," said he, "some rose of Paradise hath found a soul and

APPENDIX A: THE LEGEND OF THE BLEEDING HEART

drifted earthward to blossom here." And all that night he had eyes for none but her.

The next night Olga started again to the castle in her dress of tow, and at the gate she grasped the second bead in her fingers, repeating the charm. This time the pale yellow of the daffodils seemed to have woven itself into a cloth of gold for her adorning. It was like a shimmer of moon-beams, and her hair held the diamond flashings of a hundred tiny stars.

That night the Prince paid her so many compliments and singled her out so often to bestow his favours, that Olga's head was turned. She tossed it proudly, and quite scorned the thought of the humble cottage which had given her shelter so long. The next day when she had returned to her gown of tow and was no longer a haughty court lady, but only Olga, the Flax-spinner's maiden, she repined at her lot. Frowning, she carried the water from the spring. Frowning, she gathered the cresses and plucked the woodland fruit. And then she sat all day by the spring, refusing to spread the linen on the grass to bleach.

She was discontented with the old life of toil, and pouted crossly because duties called her when she wanted to do nothing but sit idly dreaming of the gay court scenes in which she had taken a bright brief part. The old Flax-spinner's fingers trembled as she spun, when she saw the frowns, for she had given of her heart's blood to buy happiness for this maiden she loved, and well she knew there can be no happiness where frowns abide. She felt that her years of sacrifice had been in vain, but when the Oak wagged his head she called back waveringly, "My little Olga will not be ungrateful and forgetful!"

That night outside the castle gate, Olga paused. She had forgotten the charm. The day's discontent had darkened her memory as storm-clouds darken the sky. But she grasped her necklace imperiously.

"Deck me at once!" she cried in a haughty tone. "Clothe me more beautifully than mortal maid was ever clad before, so that I may find favour in the Prince's sight and become the bride of the castle! I would that I were done for ever with the spindle and the distaff!"

But the moon went under a cloud and the wind began to moan around the turrets. The black night hawks in the forest flapped their wings warningly, and the black bats flitted low around her head.

"Obey me at once!" she cried angrily, stamping her foot and jerking at the necklace. But the string broke, and the beads went rolling away in

APPENDIX A: THE LEGEND OF THE BLEEDING HEART

the darkness in every direction and were lost—all but one, which she held clasped in her hand.

Then Olga wept at the castle gate; wept outside in the night and the darkness, in her peasant's garb of tow. But after awhile through her sobbing, stole the answering sob of the night wind.

"Hush-sh!" it seemed to say. "Sh-sh! Never a heart can come to harm, if the lips but speak the old dame's charm."

The voice of the night wind sounded so much like the voice of the old Flax-spinner, that Olga was startled and looked around wonderingly. Then suddenly she seemed to see the thatched cottage and the bent form of the lonely old woman at the wheel. All the years in which the good dame had befriended her seemed to rise up in a row, and out of each one called a thousand kindnesses as with one voice: "How canst thou forget us, Olga? We were done for love's sweet sake, and that alone!"

Then was Olga sorry and ashamed that she had been so proud and forgetful, and she wept again. The tears seemed to clear her vision, for now she saw plainly that through no power of her own could she wrest strange favours from fortune. Only the power of the old charm could make them hers. She remembered it then, and holding fast the one bead in her hand, she repeated humbly:

"For love's sweet sake, in my hour of need, Blossom and deck me, little seed."

Lo, as the words left her lips, the moon shone out from behind the clouds above the dark forest. There was a fragrance of lilies all about, and a gossamer gown floated around her, whiter than the whiteness of the fairest lily. It was fine like the finest lace the frost-elves weave, and softer than the softest ermine of the snow. On her long golden hair gleamed a coronet of pearls.

So beautiful, so dazzling was she as she entered the castle door, that the Prince came down to meet her, and kneeling, kissed her hand and claimed her as his bride. Then came the bishop in his mitre, and led her to the throne, and before them all the Flax-spinner's maiden was married to the Prince, and made the Princess Olga.

Then until the seven days and seven nights were done, the revels lasted in the castle. And in the merriment the old Flax-spinner was again forgotten. Her kindness of the past, her loneliness in the present had no part in the thoughts of the Princess Olga.

All night the old Oak, tapping on the thatch, called down, "Thou'rt forgotten! Thou'rt forgotten!"

But the beads that had rolled away in the darkness, buried themselves in the earth, and took root, and sprang up, as the old woman knew they would do. There at the castle gate they bloomed, a strange, strange flower, for on every stem hung a row of little bleeding hearts.

One day the Princess Olga, seeing them from her window, went down to them in wonderment.

"What do you here?" she cried, for in her forest life she'd learned all speech of bird and beast and plant.

"We bloom for love's sweet sake," they answered. "We have sprung from the old Flax-spinner's gift—the necklace thou didst break and scatter. From her heart's best blood she gave it, and her heart still bleeds to think she is forgotten."

Then they began to tell the story of the old dame's sacrifices, all the seventy times seven that she had made for the sake of the maiden, and Olga grieved as she listened, that she could have been so ungrateful. Then she brought the Prince to hear the story of the strange, strange flowers, and when he had heard, together they went to the lowly cottage and fetched the old Flax-spinner to the castle, there to live out all her days in ease and contentment.

"See now," she whispered to the Oak at parting, but sturdily he held his ground, persisting, "Thou wouldst have been forgotten, save for that miracle of bloom."

And still the flower we call BLEEDING-HEART blooms on by cottage walls and castle gardens, to waken all the world to grateful memories. And ever it doth bring to mind the lonely hearts that bleed because they are forgotten, and all they sacrificed for love's sweet sake, to give us happiness.

Appendix B

Kiang Nan Government School in Nanking

A friend of Edith Riggs Barakat, Ernie (Ye Gongping), who has a degree in Art History, and is a postdoc student at the School of Art Studies, Southeast University, Nanjing, when he learned of my interest in the Kiang Nan government provincial school, sent me some excerpts from Yuen Ren Chao's *Autobiography: the First Thirty Years–1892–1921 (Life with Chaos)*. Chapter Six, Book One, Volume 15 of *The Complete Works of Yuen Ren Chao*. These excerpts give a good picture of what Kiang Nan School was like for a student in Nanking during the years when Harvey Curtis Roys taught there (May 1910–June 1913). I have included a few paragraphs from this autobiography, with page numbers following the excerpts.[1] Yuen Ren Chao studied at Kiang Nan School 1907–1910. He may have been there when Harvey began teaching, although he left that same spring, but he certainly knew and studied with Harvey's friend David June Carver, who was teaching at this school when Harvey arrived. Carver, as Harvey called him, was a great help to him, his "Chinese eye," as Harvey adapted to this whole new culture and his role of teaching Chinese students at what was like an American junior college.

Yuen Ren Chao was to become a Chinese-American linguist, educator, scholar, poet, and composer best known for his contributions to the modern study of Chinese phonology and grammar, especially for his Mandarin

---

1. "Yuen Ren Chao" article in Wikipedia. The book is *The Complete Works of Yuen Ren Chao,* published by the Commercial Press in Peking in 2007.

APPENDIX B: KIANG NAN GOVERNMENT SCHOOL IN NANKING

primer, one of the most widely used Mandarin Chinese textbooks in the 20th century. He lived from November 3, 1892 until February 25, 1982.

Yuen Ren Chao left his home in Changchow for the first time at age fifteen in 1907. His entrance exams qualified him for both Shang Chiang Middle School and the Kiang Nan High School, which he chose. Nanking was a hundred miles from Changchow, but to get there before the railroad between Shanghai and Nanking was finished in the spring of 1908, he had to take a river steamer east to Soochow, change to a steamer bound for Shanghai, stay overnight in a hotel, and then change to a large Yangtze River steamship. This meant traveling for five days and three hundred miles. By rail in 1908 it would take less than four hours.

> The grounds of the [Kiang Nan] High School were quite spacious, with dormitories for nearly 300 students, packed six in a room, plus large classrooms, a gymnasium, a large drill ground or playground, and a pond. As usual, the subjects covered in the curriculum of a high school were about the same as in the grammar school, only a little more advanced. The following translation of my diary . . . will give some idea of a typical day in 1907, when I first entered the school:
>
> Wednesday March 20th. First hour, English Dictation. Teacher explained new lesson and had us read it. When it came to my turn I read it rather fast. Teacher Chao said, 'When you come to a fool-stop [sic], you mustn't continue without a pause.' Each of us was given a notebook. Second hour, mathematics, had three exercises, one in geometry, one in algebra, and one in arithmetic. I did the first part. Each of us was given a big volume of mathematics [I might add that since the Chinese text was in vertical columns and the algebraic formulae had to be horizontal, we would sometimes find a whole page with a line or two of text, then a formula occupying a great width of the page, followed by words vertically again.] and a ruled notebook. The third class was history, for which Teacher Ting had not yet arrived from Changshu and [distant] cousin Great Uncle [Ting] Meng-Yu was his substitute. Each of us got an eight-volume set of history textbooks. He did not start it. After lunch went with Shih-Ch'un and other classmates to Yuch'ang Hsiang Tailors to have measurement made for our uniforms. There was no class for physical exercise. For the fifth hour went to the library for drawing class. Each of us was given a volume of model pictures to use, compiled by Teacher Miao, and a drawing pen. Today we were taught to make points. Mine was passable. Class in Chinese to the end of lesson 1.

APPENDIX B: KIANG NAN GOVERNMENT SCHOOL IN NANKING

As some of us had been toying with the idea of going abroad to study in America, we were greatly excited when an American teacher arrived to teach us English. His name was David John Carver, of Nashville, Tennessee. This was my first American teacher, and he was very popular with the students. He was careful to talk slowly to us, unlike Teacher Shen of the Ch'i Shan School in Changchow. Our pronunciation was very much improved by his training, although to be sure we picked up a few Southern traits such as *dzero* for zero and *li'amp* for lamp, which I took for standard General American until much later. But anyway I was soon corrected of all Chinese features in my use of English. At one of the informal evening meetings where there was a program of songs and recitations, I recited a poem called "Clear and Cool."[2] Toward the end I got nervous and hesitated quite a while before I could continue and finish the recitation, after which Mr. Carver advised me that I'd better have something short and know it well rather than something long and be too slow with it. I did find it as much fun to play with the English language as with Chinese, such as asking my schoolmates what was meant by 'O I C, U R A B.'

Another American teacher was Mr. Charles, who taught us physics. He was extremely shy and nervous and his language was hard to understand. I do not remember who taught us the biological sciences, but it was quite a big occasion when the whole school, the High School proper as well as the prep classes, met in a big auditorium to watch a demonstration of the dissection of a dead dog in great detail. Toward the end of my stay in Nanking I took a class in German, which I later found useful as second foreign language at the examination for studying abroad. Finally, physical education in the form of calisthenics was taught in combination with military drill, for which real rifles were used toward the end.

With a real speaker of English, Mr. D. J. Carver, to teach us, we were all glad to do more study than required in class. I borrowed his *World's Work* to read. I read a biography of Abraham Lincoln.[3] For new words, I bought a copy of Webster's *Collegiate Dictionary*[4] for $5.00, of which I still have a (different) copy on my desk now. My favorite book was Franklin's *Autobiography*, after reading which I resolved to be a perfect man. I do not remember whether it was a textbook or as outside reading that I had Philip Van Ness Myers'

---

2. Kingsley, "The Lido River."

3. Possibly (unless he means an independent biography of Lincoln) Aubere, "A Reminiscence of Abraham Lincoln," *World's Work* 13 *(1907)* 8528-30.

4. First ed: 1898; second ed. 1910.

General History.⁵ I was greatly attracted by its idea of a world state and decided right away to join it as world citizen.

Teacher Carver was especially good to me and to my classmate Y.S. Djang. When he returned to Nanking after having gone back to America to get married, we were often invited to the house for dinners and sometimes private Sunday services, at which Mrs. Carver would play the organ, or later the piano, which was the first time I ever saw a piano. On weekdays we were introduced to such songs as 'Home Sweet Home' and 'Auld Lang Syne.' It was at the Carvers that I met Mrs. W.B. Pettus, though it was some years later that I first met Mr. Pettus, head of the North China Language School. It was at the Kiang Nan High School that Mr. C.H. Robertson⁶. of the Tientsin Y.M.C.A. came to give lectures, once in March and again in October of 1909. I was much impressed with his pure Mandarin, with a slight Tientsin accent, but no trace of any American accent.

We students of the high school were rather more unruly than those at the Ch'i Shan School. We often made trouble in the dining hall. When the food was bad, we would beat the bowls with our chopsticks to get the waiter to change dishes. Sometimes the kitchen refused and then the whole body of students would rise and disperse until a new dinner was served. This happened three times in the three years I was there.

. . . As before, most students of our age were revolution-minded and took for granted that the Manchu dynasty's days were numbered. In November 1908 Emperor Kuang Hsu and Empress Dowager Tz'u Hsi died in quick succession. We were required to kowtow prostate to their spirits and when the M.C. announced, 'Commence lamentations!' we all laughed aloud and nobody could tell laughing from crying when we did in it chorus, with our faces down.⁷

---

5. Philip Van Ness Myers (1846–1937). *A General History for Colleges and High Schools*. Boston; London: Ginn & co. 1897 [c 1889].

6. Clarence H. Robertson (1871–1960). Purdue University has his papers. He was in China 1902–1932 as Director of Education for the YMCA. He taught millions to read and write.

7. Chao, Autobiography, Chapter Six, Book One, Volume 15, 422–428.

Appendix C

The History of Kuling, China

by J. Arthur Duff[1]

The Reverend E.S. Little was founder of the Kuling Estate in the Lushan Mountains of Kiangsi, China in 1897. Ninety years ago, in 1897, the British Navy ruled the oceans of the world. The sun never set upon the Union Jack; and British diplomacy, operating out of 10 Downing Street and Whitehall, by carefully chosen phrases, comprehended only by statesmen, maintained the precarious and delicate balance of power on which, for yet a short time, hung the peace of the world. Most diplomacy is bluff; but the difficulty lies in the risk that someone may "call it"–and who can know or tell? In BC 1000 a wise man said, "The lot is cast into the lap; but the whole disposing thereof is of the Lord." You never know until it happens; and then it is too late. From birth to death life is a constant hazard; and that is what makes it so interesting.

I was born in China in 1899, one year before the Boxer uprising. My birthplace was Kuling, a valley in the Lushan Mountains, which rise five thousand feet, between the Yangtze River at Kiukiang and the Poyang Lake at Nankangfu. The mountains are only thirty miles in length, and are not connected to other ranges. Southward the hills are low and covered with

---

1. My mother, Margaret Roys Stevenson, had in her possession, along with other materials from China, this history written and typed in 1988 by Arthur Duff, with an accompanying map of Kuling, which I've added in the front matter with the illustrations. Arthur Duff was the son of John Duff, who began the store in Kuling and later built a hotel there. He married Jeanie Woodbridge, Grace's younger sister.

APPENDIX C: THE HISTORY OF KULING, CHINA

pine trees. At Kiukiang there was a small British concession,[2] presided over by a consul and a tiny river gunboat.

My parents were missionaries, who had been retired because of malignant malaria. They decided to stay in China and seek means of support locally, an almost impossible assignment since foreigners were restricted by the concessions.

At that junction [1897], the Lushan Mountains were used by both missionaries and British traders at Kiukiang, as a summer resort to escape the intolerable heat. Among those using temporary accommodation was an English missionary named Edward S. Little, an extraordinary character and sinologue. The fact that he was a missionary of Christianity did not interfere with his natural friendliness and ability to establish common ground with Chinese of any social level, from the humblest farmer or coolie to the richest, ranking officials. He could reside in a temple, where the priests burned incense, and chanted their prayers to the huge idols. That didn't bother him at all. He ate their vegetarian diet, and never embarrassed them by introducing meat or eggs. I am sure that if there had been Rotary Clubs in those early times, he would have had them singing songs as full members. After all, did not the Apostle Paul address the Epicureans and the Stoics on Mars Hill at Athens?

Mr. Edward S. Little was of the calibre of Cecil Rhodes of Africa. Even as foreigners and their Chinese converts were being murdered by the hundreds in North China, Mr. Little was empire-building in his small way, and his way was patterned to the spiritual injunction of Christ, "Be ye wise as serpents and harmless as doves." Machiavelli would have been green with envy.

Well knowing that the priests in the larger temples would never be bribed or tricked into any act of disloyalty against their own people, and that they would risk decapitation if they succumbed to temptation, E.S. Little climbed higher into the mountains, following ancient tracks or wood-cutters' trails.

There had once been over two thousand temples or monasteries on Lushan. Most had been destroyed beyond repair by the Tai Ping rebels in 1850–60. These rebels were the fanatic followers of a convert to the Baptist Mission in Hong Kong. Hung by name, he was a half-crazed scholar who

---

2. A concession, which several foreign countries had in China during this period, means a strip of land conceded to an alien government for its economic use, usually with the privileges of self-government and extra-territoriality.

had failed the imperial Examinations. He became obsessed with the idea that he was the younger brother of Jesus Christ, now charged by Jehovah with the destruction of idolatry in China, following in the footsteps of Joshua and the children of Israel. He gathered a rabble and marched north, slaughtering the intelligentsia and the priests as they went. They captured Nanking and threatened Shanghai, but feared the foreigners. They were eventually to be crushed by General Charles (Chinese) Gordon[3] and his mercenaries.

By the year 1900 some temples had been repaired and their vegetable gardens planted by four priests, renegades, fugitives from justice posed as priests, one in this instance an army deserter. The temple ruin occupied by this man appealed to Reverend Little, perched as it was on a knoll overlooking a beautiful valley. The character of the occupant was a man after Mr. Little's own heart, what I describe as "the old man," "unregenerate" in holy writ. The British Empire was built largely through missionaries, was it not? Bible and Sword, an unholy alliance.

In those days there was little travel except by traders with local connections and references. A lone wanderer, other than an itinerant priest or a showman with his trained goat, sheep, small dog, and monkey, was immediately suspect: he could get accommodation nowhere and would soon be taken for interrogation. His best explanation would be that he had to flee from creditors. His best haven of refuge (as an alternative to literally rotting in a filthy and vermin-infested jail) would be to offer his services, for food only, to an army unit or to some large temple.

A northerner from the Peking area, immediately identifiable by his dialect, was taken to be an army deserter; and that they were scum and criminals was taken for granted and feared. A temple might accept them and would offer the best prospects: work hard, beg for old clothing from the priests, study a little of the ritual and chants, then one day disappear as an itinerant living on charity, moving north toward home.

The man E.S. Little befriended had left the army, lodged himself in a temple in the foothills of Kuling; then cutting wood on the mountain for the priests, he had discovered this remote ruin which was easily repaired in part and settled in. There was an abundance of good firewood to be cut and he lived a fairly good life by carrying it downhill to market. He cultivated a

---

3. Major-General Charles George Gordon, CB (28 January 1833–26 January 1885), also known as Chinese Gordon, Gordon Pasha, and Gordon of Khartoum, was a British Army officer and administrator.

APPENDIX C: THE HISTORY OF KULING, CHINA

small patch of vegetables, safe from the destructive wild pig which favored the lower valleys. His life was simple: he invested his surplus earnings in Chinese rice-wine and his spare time (during the hurricane season on that hilltop) in peaceful, idyllic slumber, protected by a savage mountain cur, half wolf, that he had stolen as a puppy from the temple, its ferocity exceeded only by its absolute devotion to its master.

In China temple lands were owned by the public, were undeeded and not saleable. E. S. Little knew all that. He also knew all about "Fung-shui" (the spirits of the winds and waters) which enjoy exclusive rights to all "high Places" and are easily offended by any intrusion upon their sacred domain. This ancient ruin may have been built in their honor. But the Chinese could always offer some trade-off, possibly the lovely valley below with its many streams of clear water, meadows, abundant wildflowers? Yes, that would do nicely, since it appeared to be completely uninhabited except for a massive ruin at the far end, possibly owned by that monastery which had not been reoccupied.

The treaties with China restricted foreigners to their "concessions" for both commerce and residence; but missionaries were exempted from these restrictions. E.S. Little was a missionary. He spent time and cultivated this "priest." And, when the man took to his wine, Little explored the valley and selected a knoll for himself, later to be known as Little's Hill. It was clothed in pine forest and, nestled against the mountains, was a sheltered hollow which would accommodate a large bungalow and that indispensable English tradition of which Wimbledon still stands as an indestructible monument, with Big Ben, Westminster Abbey, and the Houses of Parliament, when almost all else is gone. You guessed it: a tennis court.

Computers were not yet heard of; but enough had been fed into Reverend Little's brain to produce results which were to reverberate far beyond the limits of that little valley in the Lushan Mountains, hundreds of miles up the muddy Yangtze River and thousands of miles from Peking and Whitehall. It was to provide me with a place of birth and a basis for a "claim" against the present government of China, concerning which I have recently received a communication from the Foreign Office in London, but the old ruin on the top of the hill, still swept by the fog and mist, remains undisturbed to this day, knowing nothing of the significant role it played in the lives of so many people and in relations between the great nations.

Reverend Little had now gained the "priest's" confidence and made friends with the wolf-dog, in which he recognized another untameable, kindred spirit. He returned to his mission in Kiukiang, to carry on his duties as a missionary to the heathen and to ponder ideas which the bracing coolness of the mountain air had engendered, with thoughts of those ill missionaries and their infants and young children in the humid heat of summer in the Yangtze Valley. Yes, he would try.

When a missionary wished to acquire a property in China, he must first make his deal with the owner, examine his title documents and verify them as best he might. This must all be done in strictest privacy or popular opposition would quicky intimidate the owner and frustrate the transaction. Once the purchase was made and the money paid, the owner would take himself off, disappear for a time until resentment had died down. The buyer must then take his deed to the British Consulate, to be recorded as British property, and inform the Chinese authorities accordingly. Mr. Little drew up his plans with all these factors in mind. There were two kinds of "title" deeds in China: white deeds and red deeds. The former were unregistered, had not paid taxes, and had no validity in court. The red deed was one which had been duly registered, paid taxes, and was legal. For temple property no deed was made; temples were built on public land, were not transferable and could not be used for any other purpose. If the temple buildings were destroyed, the area became known as "miao chang" or temple grounds, like a common in England or a park in America.

Mr. Little now knew he could buy out the "priest." He could create a white deed for the property and a storm of opposition from the countryside and all classes of Chinese on principle. He knew further that the entire temple fraternity would unite in protests. This opposition could not be entirely ignored; it was dangerous to missionaries and to himself. He was also aware that the British Consul could frustrate the entire plan by flatly refusing to register the deed. But he was determined to see it though, regardless of any consequences.

First he carefully measured the approximate boundaries of the temple ruin and walled gardens as they had stood before the arrival of the Taipings in 1855. Then he piled stones to mark the corners. Meanwhile he proposed to the "priest" a transaction in which his only role was to sign his name on the white deed and leave for Shanghai by steamer, there to find refuge in the foreign settlement as a guest of Mr. Little, who owned a "country estate" there. The financial arrangements, which would make him independent for life, involved payment of Mexican silver dollars one hundred only. [China had borrowed silver from Mexico, in Mexican silver dollars which went into circulation and became the only currency: "Mex. $"]

Mr. Little then set his Chinese teacher and writer to study "white deeds" of foothill lands, poor, inexpensive and readily available to any Chinese with money and lacking good sense. He obtained a supply of the parchment used locally for such documents and copied the format for deeds dating back to antiquity. The teacher was a Shanghai man and could not have cared less about local opinion. He drew up a deed, using assumed names of previous owners and gave a name to the "priest," who could not remember his clan name, having run away from home to join the army while still in his early teens. (A Chinese saying has it: "That as good metal is not used to make nails, so a good son does not become a soldier"–"Hao t'ieh puh da ding; hao err puh tan ping.")

The deed was soon made, signed and approved by Mr. Little. The teacher left for Shanghai; and the "priest" was packed in a piano box recently arrived from Shanghai for the mission and shipped as such on the same steamer with the teacher, with the knowledge and consent of the captain of the British ship.

Giving time for them to arrive safely, Mr. Little then sent his ignorant garden coolie, a native of the Kuling foothills, with a handful of coins and dollars to the "Land Office" in the city, with a transfer form in the name of Lee The Lee, a genuine Chinese name, with a local address. No foreigner was mentioned, no mission rights to purchase property, no details of the "temple site." The coolie was briefed to answer no questions. He was merely a message boy. His instructions were to register the transfer, pay the taxes and obtain the "red chop" on the deed, and pay the transfer fees.

There are two kinds of foothill lands on any mountain in China: "chia san" and "yeh san," domestic mountain or wild mountain, the same word as applied to animals: wild or domesticated. The domesticated runs up to the limits of cultivation or of bamboo groves; beyond that is the wild land, which cannot be deeded or transferred. Anyone building there is a squatter on public land and has no title rights. Foothills land is cheap.

The land office merely looked at the forms and deed, collected the money and signed and stamped the deed with the "red chop." Remote land somewhere in the mountains for which there was no red deed registered? Why worry? The money is more interesting. Little now had a genuine red deed, registered and in order, for his temple site.

APPENDIX C: THE HISTORY OF KULING, CHINA

The next move was the point at which the "feathers hit the fan," as he told me in 1935 in Shanghai (when I leased his Chinese style house for one year; it was situated in an exquisite garden). I heard the complete story direct from him at that time, just as I have related it.

The Consul was quite unsuspecting and casually glanced at it whilst continuing to talk about other matters of interest. He was an accomplished Chinese scholar and, as his eyes ran over the deed, he caught his breath: "Little," he said, "you are mad. Surely you do not expect me to register this with the Chinese government? Land on the very top of a mountain, a temple ruin, you say. What Chinese will believe that I do not know the Chinese regulations? It is ludicrous, impossible." Said Little, "Register it, and notify them. I am prepared to fight this one all the way to London and in Parliament if necessary."

"Do you know, Little, that the Kiukiang Chinese are intensely antiforeign. They might burn our mission to the ground. I would fear for my consulate and the concession, were it not for the gunboat I can see from where I sit. The Chinese know its six-inch gun could knock the Tao-Tai's yamen[4] off its foundations in less than ten minutes. That is our only protection. The Empress Dowager [even then plotting with the Boxers for the Boxer Uprising and massacre of all foreigners] will order everyone in the Land Office executed for this." (She did.) Little persisted and said he would immediately cable London and the British Minister in Peking if the Consul refused. So the Consul finally agreed but warned Little to take precautions for himself and his mission compound.

The uproar which ensued must have shaken both the consul and Little. The leaders of the various societies met and killed a chicken on the city wall, using the blood to seal a death pact against the alienation of Lushan Mountains to foreigners. The Tao Tai sent his personal secretary to warn Little to remain indoors and posted a military guard at the mission gate. The secretary pled with Little to abandon the claim in the interest of friendship and for his own safety. Little responded by pointing to a brand new Winchester six-shooter on a rack in the corner and promising to shoot

---

4. In China Tao-Tai is an official at the head of the civil and military affairs of a circuit, which consists of two or more fu, or territorial departments called also, by foreigners, intendant of circuit. Foreign consuls and commissioners associated with taotais as superintendents of trade at the treaty ports are ranked with the taotai. *Webster's Revised Unabridged Dictionary,* published 1913 by C&G Merriam Co, 180. A yamen was, during the Chinese empire, the office or the official residence of a public functionary, as a mandarin; also any department of the public service.

APPENDIX C: THE HISTORY OF KULING, CHINA

intruders as fast as they came in the gate. All registered British property was under extra-territorial protection and would be defended as such. The secretary finally withdrew, shaking his head.

The case went to Peking and finally to London and was resolved when the Chinese Minister in London sought a loan from Britain. An astute member of Parliament, a friend of E.S. Little, attached a "rider" to cover the Kuling property, subject to negotiation to eliminate questions of "feng-shui." Little finally agreed to cancellation of the mountaintop site in exchange for the large valley below, reserving to himself only the knoll he had selected at the outset. He turned over the balance to a board of trustees consisting of members of the various missionary societies. This was the Kuling Estate into which I was born November 14, 1899, and where my parents spent their lives.

When the European War broke out in 1914, Kuling was already a thriving resort for missionaries. Some three hundred bungalows had been built, and the summer community numbered possibly fifteen hundred missionaries of many denominations. The valley, bought by E.S. Little and registered as his personal property both with the Chinese government and the British Foreign Office, had an elected council, an employed Estate Manager, a force of watchmen (police), who regally patrolled the valley to prevent looting and theft, and a public works department which built and repaired roads and bridges. They also constructed a trail up the mountain from the Kiukiang side. The valley had been surveyed and divided into building lots. These were sold to missionaries and foreign businessmen at prices established by the council. Actually, they could not purchase the land, which was on lease from the Chinese government to E.S. Little for 99 years. The owners of the lots were called landrenters.

In 1911 the Manchu regime in China was overthrown in a "revolution" of a bloodless sort. Actually the Chinese respect the Manchus, and there was little real resentment, since all were of the "yellow race." The revolution of 1911 was more like an American presidential election. No Manchus were slaughtered; they simply recognized the inevitable; they packed up and left. There had been virtually no intermarriage with Chinese (prohibited by law under the Manchu dynasties). Under the old Empress Dowager Tsu Shi, a concubine of the last of the great emperors, corruption and vice in government had reached intolerable proportions, and the last successor to the throne, Puh Yih, was a dolt, a puppet of the Japanese in Manchuria.

APPENDIX C: THE HISTORY OF KULING, CHINA

By 1914 any semblance of resentment against foreigners in the Kuling area had evaporated, since it derived enormous economic benefits from the foreign settlement. E.S. Little had no hesitation in returning the old "priest" from Shanghai to his Kuling residence, later transferring him to the service of the Estate Manager, a fine, old retired English gentleman. He became a muleteer, in charge fo the Manager's mule, on which he rode on tours of the valley, which was two miles in length, one in breadth, and involved climbing constantly to different levels and down again, too much for the heart and legs of an old man. Far from being the object of hatred, the "priest" now found himself something of a hero. E.S. Little was regarded as a tycoon; minstrels composed ballads in his honor, recounting how for one hundred dollars he had bought a whole mountain. I can recall one which started with the sounding of a small gong:

> "Tang-tang-tang-Li-The-Li mai Li Shan,
> Do show chien, wan tung pan," etc.
> (Little bought Lushan Mountain for how much?
> Ten thousand coppers.)

He was cheered. I can remember the "priest" and often talked with him. He still drank quarts of rice wine, enough to have killed any other man, but he survived and finally fell victim to a pickling process rather than a disease.

When I talked with Mr. Little, I omitted to ask him what happened to the "priest's" dog. I know that it was left to guard the temple site, since the priest could not take it with him. It had always found its own meat diet by hunting small animals. It probably continued to do so and continued to guard the ruin, now his lair. He may have fallen victim to a wolf pack (not common on those mountains) or more likely to a leopard, who regards dogs as a delicacy, much sought after. Mountain temples lock their dogs inside at night. I like to think he joined some pack and survived.

E.S. Little retired to New Zealand, where he ended his days on his plantation at Keri-Keri, growing passion fruit for juice, a not too popular product, and Chinese "yang tao" (strange peach) which he was the first to discover and to cultivate and named Kiwi fruit, now a multi-million dollar crop worldwide, for which he receives no credit in the year of Grace 1987 (*National Geographic*, May edition).[5]

5. Vietmeyer, "The Captivating Kiwifruit."

The Duff family were the first to settle at Kuling, and quickly became the principal agent there, and the supplier of practically everything from roofing to lumber, groceries to dairy products from their own herd of cattle. The Duffs had to do the butchering of beef in the summer season and maintained an ice house with ice collected in the winter. The Duff house was always filled to capacity in summer with ill people who arrived to escape death in the heat of the plains of the Yangtze Valley. The Duffs were forced into starting a hotel. A hospital followed by mission subscription, a church, library, etc. The Duffs built Kuling over a period of forty years. John L. Duff is buried there.

A TRIP TO KULING BY JULIA WILSON, HILLCREST GRADUATE 1921, FROM THE 1920-21 ANNUAL.[6]

Early in the morning of one of the warmest days in June we started on our trip to Kuling. Not a breath of wind was stirring, nor anything else for that matter.

We took the steamer at Hsiakuan [Shia Kwan] where we were surrounded, before the boat started, by a good many coolies eager to carry our baggage for us. When we came aboard about seven o'clock or a bit earlier we took our things into a cabin where one of us had to sit and watch them so that our interested fellow passengers might not become too interested and help themselves. After a little one of the servants came and took charge.

When the servant had come we were free to go out on deck and amuse ourselves as we pleased. We went out and read and slept and watched the different scenes which were to be seen on our way. In whatever thing we did we were always watched by a good many pairs of curious eyes anxious to see what the "foreign devils" were going to do next.

Among the many things which we saw on our way, the most common or nearly the most common sight was the many house boats. Some of them had families of beggars on them, others had people who were a good deal better off, some were larger, some smaller, some with sails on, some without them, all sailing up and down the river in a way that seemed aimless, but I suppose they had some aim in view. All along the banks of the river and inland for miles around, we could see the rice fields with little villages dotted here and there each with their groups of dogs and children.

6. Hillcrest Annual, 77–79.

APPENDIX C: THE HISTORY OF KULING, CHINA

On the bank of the river so near you could almost say on the river were numerous little huts barely high enough for a man to stand in. These were often surrounded by miles of very tall reed grass which the Chinese burn instead of wood or coal in many places.

Oftentimes when we were nearing towns, large or small, we would meet a man in a sampan, with a long stick driving a very large group of ducks which seemed too many for one man to drive, but he seemed to be succeeding. This was the way in which he drives his pigs to market, only they weren't pigs, they were ducks.

Another common scene on the river was a raft of poles about 100 by 160 feet. On this you would often see a hut or two with a whole family living in them.

One scene that one would not like to miss, whether it was his first or his twentieth trip, was the Little Orphan Island. It stands out in the center of the river like a big sentinel with a little temple on the top as a lookout.

As we drew near to Kiukiang we saw, a few hours before we got there, several ranges of mountains in the distance looking more like mirage than a range of mountains and the ones that we were traveling to in order to get away from the heat of the plains.

We watch eagerly as we start to round a point in the bank of the river which hides Kiukiang. As we round it we see the pagoda which assures us that we have reached a stopping point on our way. We draw up to the hulk and even in the flurry of getting off we realize that however warm Nanking was when we left we have reached a place that is infinitely hotter. We give our things into the hands of some of the Estate-house coolies and make our way to the Rest House, commonly called the Pest House, because of the nights spent there by unlucky people who happen to be the victims of a slow-moving boat. The nights are hot and besides being hot there is a continual popping of firecrackers and the yelling of peddlers.

Early in the morning we pack up and buy our tickets for the cooling car ride across the plain to Lien Hwa Dong, called by many people "Lay Me Down," because it is the place where we either get out of the car and into the chairs or out of the chairs and into the car.

At this place there is quite a good-looking foreign house in the upstairs of which there is a room for eating lunch and several rooms for resting. Here it is that we put the light things that we are carrying while Daddy or, if he isn't along, Mama orders the chairs for the trip up the mountain.

APPENDIX C: THE HISTORY OF KULING, CHINA

We get into our chairs and start up sometimes in groups and sometimes singly and go through the lovely mountain passes and see the beautiful sights on the way. There are a good many tea houses by the roadside at nearly all of which the chair coolies set down your chair, sometimes with a bang and sometimes they have pity on you and set you down with more care.

On the way up the mountain one sees on one side a precipice or else a very steep slope with a stream down below looking clear and cool, while in some places the waters fall over the rocks with a clear white fall. In some places, across the valley from the road we go up, the side of the mountain rises in a sheer cliff with trees and flowers growing in the chinks between the rocks. In other places we go right under a very large rock which looks as if it would fall over any minute. The bamboos grow in places looking as if they would have nothing at all to do with the other trees either in color or in position. One would find many kinds of flowers, some with names and some nameless. Down in the valley one sees the fields in their garb of summer green, with little white villages scattered here and there with the dark trees by them, while the river flows along alike a muddy yellow ribbon through the fields on its way to the sea.

We keep going up and down till if the day is cloudy we have clouds above, below, and all around us. In turning a corner of the mountain we suddenly, when we are least suspecting it, find that we can see the Gap end of Kuling. Then it is only a matter of minutes before we are at our home in Kuling, comfortable and cool once more.

Bibliography

"American Firms at Nanyang Exposition" in "Expositions and Conventions" in "China" in "International Meetings." 233. A google book on line.

"Albaugh, Miss Ida McKay, RN," article in phcmontreat.org/bios/Bios-Missionaries-China-1900-1920-PCUS.htm

Aubere, Jewell H. "A Reminiscence of Abraham Lincoln: A Conversation with Speaker Cannon." *The World's Work* 13, no. 4 (Feb. 1907) 8528–30.

Aurobindo, Sri. "The Assassination of Prince Ito." *Sri Aurobindo Birth Century Library.* Vol. 2.

Balmer, Randall and John R. Fitzmier. *The Presbyterians.* Westport: Praegar, 1994.

Beaver, R. Pierce. *American Protestant Women in World Missions: History of the First Feminist Movement in America.* Rev. ed. Grand Rapids: W.B. Eerdmans, 1980.

Bishop, Eunice Smith. *Family Letters from China, 1901–1950.* Brookfield, CT: DTP&M Services, 1991.

"Bishop Lewis." *The Christian Advocate* (New York) 96, no. 35 (Sept. 1, 1921) 1089, 1091–92. [Additional tributes to Bishop Wilson S. Lewis appear at pp. 1099–1101.]

Buck, Pearl. *My Several Worlds: A Personal Record.* New York: John Day, 1954.

Chao, Yuen Ren, *Autobiography: First 30 Years, 1892–1921,* Book I of Vol. 15, Chapter Six of *The Complete Works of Yuen Ren Chao.* Ithaca: Spoken Language Services, 1975. Peking: The Commercial Press, 2007.

"The Chefoo School at Lushan," article at Kulingamericanschool.com/chefoo-school-in-lushan.html

China Inland Mission and the Chefoo Schools Association Papers. In Mundus: *Gateway to Missionary Collections in the United Kingdom.* mundus.ac.uk/cats/4/904.htm

Crook, Winnie May. "A Word of Appreciation." [on Nanking memorial hospital and Miss Iva Hynds] *Woman's Missionary Friend* 50, no. 11 (Nov. 1918) 430.

"David J. Carver Professorship in medicine" in Johns Hopkins University webpage. http://webapps.jhu.edu/namedprofessorships/professorshipdetail.cfm?professorshipID=120

Downing, David. *The Jack of Spies.* New York: Soho, 2014.

Duanwu or "Dragon Boat Festival." https://en.wikipedia.org/wiki/Dragon_Boat_Festival

Duff, Arthur. "The History of Kuling." Unpublished, 1988.

BIBLIOGRAPHY

"Egbert Hayes," article in *China Missionaries Project*. Cgu.edu/oralhistory/china_missionaries_project.htm

Erh, Deke, and Tess Johnston, eds. *Hallowed Halls: Protestant Colleges in Old China*. Hong Kong: Old China Hand Press, 1998.

Espey, John J. *Minor Heresies, Major Departures: A China Mission Boyhood*. Berkeley: University of California Press, 1994.

"Francis Wilson Price" article in Shenandoah Presbytery's Mission Heritage. shenpres.org/mission-heritage.

"Ginling College." Article in Library.yale.edu/div/colleges/descriptions.htm,#ginling

Gordon, Samuel Dickey. *Quiet Talks on Power*. Chicago: Fleming H. Revell, 2007. [First published 1900]

———. *Quiet Talks on Prayer*. Chicago: Fleming H. Revell, 1951. [First published 1904]

Hersey, John. *The Call*. New York: Penguin, 1985.

Hillcrest School. *Purple and Gold* annuals for 1916 and 1920–21. Nanking, China. Article by Wilson, Julia, "A Trip to Kuling," In the 1920–21 annual, 77–79.

Hunter, Jane. *The Gospel of Gentility: American Women Missionaries in Turn-of-Century China*. New Haven: Yale University Press, 1984.

Johnston, Annie Fellows. *The Legend of the Bleeding Heart*. 1900 version: The Literature Network: www.online-literature.com/annie-johnston/4021

Kessler, Lawrence D. *The Jiangyin Mission Station: An American Missionary Community in China:1895–1951*. Chapel Hill: University of North Carolina Press, 1996.

Ketler, Isaac Conrad. *The Tragedy of Paotingfu: An Authentic Story of the . . . Missionaries Who Suffered Martyrdom*. New York: Fleming H. Revell, 1902.

Kingsley, Charles. "The Lido River," poem from *The Water Babies: A Fairy Tale for a Land Baby*. London: MacMillan, 1963.

"The Korea," Pacific Mail Steamship Co. http://eresources.nlb.gov.sg/newspapers/Digitised/Article/straitstimes19120423.2.8.1.aspx

*Lodwick, Kathleen L., comp. *The Chinese Recorder Index: A Guide to Christian Missions in Asia, 1867–1941*. 2 vols. Wilmington, Del.: Scholarly Resources, 1986. (Abbreviated: CRI; references are to vol. 1.)

"Lucy Gaynor." in "Quakers in China" in "Quakers in the World." quakersintheworld.org/quakers-in-action/308

"Lucy Gaynor," article in Northwestern University "Contribution to War Efforts: wardrounds.northwestern.edu/2013/04/medicine-surgery-and-military-conflicts-northwesterns-contribution-to-war-efforts/

"Major-General Charles George Gordon, CB" in https://en.wikipedia.org/wiki/Charles_George_Gordon

Mallory, Lieut. Charles K., U.S.N. "The Pacific Mail Steamship Korea." *Journal of the American Society of Naval Engineers* 14, no. 2 (May 1902) 378–395. (http://onlinelibrary.wiley.com/doi/10.1111/j.1559-3584.1902.tb01326.x/abstract)

MacInnes, Donald E. "James Whitford Bashford, 1848–1919." In *Biographical Dictionary of Chinese Christianity*. http://www.bdcconline.net/en/stories/b/bashford-james-whitford.php

McDowell, John Hugh. *History of the McDowells, Erwins, Irwins and Connections*. Memphis: C. B. Johnston, 1918.

Mellin Food Company. *The Mellin's Food Method of Percentage Feeding*. Boston: The Company, 1908.

BIBLIOGRAPHY

"Mid-Autumn Festival," in *Travel China Guide*. http://www.travelchinaguide.com/essential/holidays/mid-autumn.htm

Myers, Philip Van Ness. *A General History for Colleges and High Schools*. Boston: Ginn, 1897.

Nanking Cook Book, The. An Enlargement and Revision of the American Red Cross Book of Recipes for the Use of Chinese Foodstuffs. Nanking: Woman's Auxiliary of the University of Nanking, 1924.

Presbyterian Heritage Center, Biographical Index of Missionaries in China 1900–1920. Presbyterian Church of U.S. phcmontreat.org/bios/Bios-Missionaries-China-1900-1920-PCUS.htm.

Pound, Ezra. *ABC of Reading*. New York: New Directions, 1987.

Protestant Missionaries in China in *The Directory and Chronicle for China, Japan, Coria, Indochina, & Straits*. Google Book on line, 1043.

Pruitt, Ida. *A Daughter of Han: The Autobiography of a Chinese Working Woman From the Story Told by Ning Lao T'ai-T'ai*. Stanford: Stanford University Press, 1967. (An earlier edition: New Haven: Yale University Press, 1945)

"Quakers-in-action," www.quakersintheworld.org/quakers-in-action/308.

Riggs, Grace. *China Memoir about Grace and Her Husband Charles Riggs, missionaries in China*. Section on the Communist take-over in 1949. Unpublished, 67.

Russell, Wallace B., M.D., mentioned in *Methodist Episcopal Church. Board of Foreign Missions*, a Google book on line and *The Christian Advocate* 1910. https://books.google.com/books?id=36c6AQAAMAAJ&pg=PA1442&lpg=PA1442&dq=Wallace+B.+Russell+%2B+++Nanking+China&source=bl&ots=w4dMwOr3bg&sig=hVgS6X506bzcuqO1YtevgJE2c7A&hl=en&sa=X&ved=0ahUKEwj_jOSPktbQAhVCw4MKHfQbCbUQ6AEIHjAB#v=onepage&q=Wallace%20B.%20Russell%20%2B%20%20%20Nanking%20China&f=false

Sego, Mary A., "Clarence H. Robertson Papers" in Archives and Special Collections, Purdue University Libraries. http://www4.lib.purdue.edu/archon/index.php?p=collections/findingaid&id=562&q=philosophy+born+of+struggle

Service, Grace. *Golden Inches: The China Memoir of Grace Service*. Edited by John S. Service. Berkeley: University of California Press, 1989.

Showalter, Anthony J., "Leaning on the Everlasting Arms." music; lyrics by Showalter and Elisha Hoffman. 1887. https://en.wikipedia.org/wiki/Leaning_on_the_Everlasting_Arms

"Smythe, Margaret (Mardie)." Article in Cgu.edu/oralhistory/china_missionaries_project.htm

Spence, Jonathan D. *The Search for Modern China*. 2nd Edition. New York: W.W. Norton, 1999.

Spurling, Hilary. *Pearl Buck in China: Journey to the Good Earth*. New York: Simon & Schuster, 2010.

"S.S. China" in The Atlantic Transport Line. http://www.atlantictransportline.us/content/60China.htm

"The Third Plague Pandemic." Article in Wikipedia. http://en.wikipedia.org/wiki/Third_plague_pandemic

Vietmeyer, Noel D. "The Captivating Kiwifruit," *National Geographic* 171, no. 5 (May 1987), 682–88.

Union Seminary Magazine, Vol 67, Minutes General Assembly, 1866.

The University of Nanking Magazine. Nanking: University of Nanking, May, 1910.

BIBLIOGRAPHY

Waller, Nancy Thomson. *My Nanking Home, 1918–1937: A Very Personal Memoir.* Cherry Valley, N.Y.: Willow Hill, 2010.

"William P. Fenn, 90, Protestant Missionary." (*New York Times* obituary, 25 April 1993) http://www.nytimes.com/1993/04/25/obituaries/william-p-fenn-90-protestant-missionary.html

"William Seeley Lewis." (in *Notable Deaths* section) *Annals of Iowa* Third Series 14, no. 2 (Oct. 1923) 158.

Williams, Lilian C. *Yesterdays in China.* Newburyport, Mass.: Newburyport, 1956.

Woodbridge, Samuel Isett. *Fifty Years in China.* Richmond: Presbyterian Committee of Publication, 1919.

"Wright, Harold Bell" article. https://en.wikipedia.org/wiki/Harold_Bell_Wright

"Yuan-shan Djang (Chang Yuan-shen)." In: Powell, M.C., ed. *Who's Who in China.* 3rd ed. Shanghai: The China Weekly Review, 1925. P. 80. https://en.wikisource.org/wiki/Who%27s_Who_in_China_(3rd_edition)/Chang_Yuan-shan

"Yuen Ren Chao" article at http://en.wikipedia.org/Yuen_Ren_Chao.

General Index

Abraham (patriarch), 36
Africa, 6, 142
Agassiz, Alexander Emmanuel Rodolphe, 109n9
Agassiz Association. Watch Guard Branch/Society, 28n54, 41n114, 60n14, 76n88, 92n46, 109, 115n32
Alaska (steamship), 8
Albaugh, Ida McKay, 86
Alchine, Miss (Shanghai friend), 78
Alcott, Louisa May. *Little Women*, 118n7
Allison, Andrew, 87n22
Allison, Ella Gates Ward, 87
amah (nursemaid), 12, 118n3, 123, 125, 127
America. *See* United States.
American Advent Mission Society, 48n150
American Board of Commissioners for Foreign Missions, 9n16, 43, 103, 115n31
American Episcopal Mission, 26n43
American Protestant Association, 111n17
Amocat Trading (firm), 104
Anglican Church, 73n74
Ann Arbor (Mich.), 3, 17, 25
Anti-Opium League, 93n1
athletics, 44, 46, 62n27, 104n39. *See also* ball games.

Augusta Female Seminary (Staunton, Va.), 4
"Auld Lang Syne" (song), 140
Aurobindo, Sri. *Assassination of Prince Ito* (play), 92
automobiles, 12, 151

Babylon (sermon topic), 97
Bailie, Joseph, 43n123, 68n50, 95
Baldwin, Caleb Cecil, 115
Baldwin, Harriet F., 115
ball games, 22, 41, 104
baptism(s), 88–89, 105
Baptists, Northern, 6n3, 34n77, 76n87, 80n112, 142
Baptists, Southern, 10, 35n83, 71n64, 102n32, 108n4
Barakat, Edith Riggs, 31n66, 40n113, 90n33, 122, 123, 125, 126, 137
barber(s), 30
Barclay, Florence Louisa. *The Rosary*, 62
Barrie, Mrs. Howard G., 61, 62
Bashford, James Whitford, 48n149, 67, 120
Bashford, Mahala Jane Field, 120
bats, 62n26
Beales, Fred, 5, 34, 35
Beales, Harriet (Hatty). *See* Higgins-Schmidt, Harriet.
Beaver, Robert Pierce, 67n45
Beebe, Josette Hilda. *See* Dennis, Josette.

157

GENERAL INDEX

Beebe, Margaret Hyde. *See* Niles, Margaret.
Beebe, Robert Case (Rob), 27n46, 29, 31, 40, 48, 93
Beebe, Rose B. Lobenstine, 27n46, 37, 109
Beebe family, 5, 27, 46, 56n186, 104
Beh Gih Goh (hill), 30n59, 68
Berkin (Burkin), John, 61n20, 89
Berkin, Leila L. Doolittle, 61n20, 89
Berkin family, 61
Bible & Bible study, 23, 24, 25n33, 26, 33, 39, 45, 48, 49, 51, 54, 60, 62, 63, 64, 68, 70, 81n119
Bible Teachers Training School, 35n79
Bible translations, 13, 22n26, 68n46
bicycle(s), 12, 31, 70, 75, 76, 77, 99, 105
bi-polar disease, 2, 3, 82n120
Bishop, Eunice Elizabeth Smith, 9n16
Bishop, Luella, 87, 96
Bishop family, 116
Blackstone, Barbara (daughter of J.H.), 25n33
Blackstone, Barbara Treman, 25n33, 43, 46, 48, 49, 52n168, 56, 59, 65, 69, 78, 86, 102, 105
Blackstone, Eleanor, 25n33
Blackstone, James Harry, 25n33, 28, 43, 46, 47, 49, 52, 55, 56, 59, 66, 70, 71, 75, 77, 78, 81
Blackstone, James Harry, Jr., 25n33
Blackstone, William (son of J.H.), 25n33, 66
Blackstone, William Eugene, 25n33, 66, 70, 71, 73, 97
Blackstone family, 6, 25, 26, 42–59 *passim*, 67, 70, 71, 72, 78n101, 81, 92, 93, 105, 116
boats, 13, 31, 50n158, 55, 59n10, 64, 73, 75, 59, 150, 151
Bowen, Arthur John, 81, 93n1, 99n22
Bowen, Mrs. Arthur John, 81n116, 99n22
Bowen, Arthur John (son), 99n22
Bowen family, 93
Boxer Rebellion, 6, 7, 81n119, 125, 127, 141, 147
Bradbury, William Batchelder, 89n30

Britain, 21n20, 54n177, 90n35, 141, 143, 144, 145, 147–48
Brockman, Fletcher Sims, 35–36n84, 58n1, 81n115, 87, 89
Brockman, Mary Buford Clark, 58, 87, 89
Brockman family, 35
Brown, Charlotte Thompson, 102
Brown, Francis Augustus, 77, 102n32
Brownie cameras, 65n36
Bryn Mawr College, 57n190
Buck, John Lossing, 4, 124, 126
Buck, Pearl Sydenstricker, 4, 9, 76n90, 109n7, 118n4, 122–25, 126
  Good Earth, The, 125
  Sons, 124
Buddhism, 22n26, 50n158
Buford (ship), 67
Bullock, Amasa Archibald, 25, 49, 71, 87, 88
Bullock, Anson Burlingame, 25n36, 91, 94, 116, 121
Bullock, Frank, 25n36, 102, 103
Bullock, Ruth, 25n36, 48, 49, 88, 94, 101, 102, 103
Bullock family, 34, 52, 94, 105, 110, 116
Bull's Head (mountain), 37
Bulow (ship), 21
Burkin. *See* Berkin.
Butchart, Harvey, 104n40
Butchart, James, 104
Butchart, James Baird, 104n40
Butchart, Nellie Daugherty, 104
Butler, Esther H., 81

cablegram(s), 19n10, 33n73, 93n2
California, University of (Berkeley), 38n97
Calling of Dan Matthews, The (Wright), 20
calomel, 101, 120n13
Cameron (W. Va.), 1
cancer, 17n4, 89n29, 90n36
carriages, 12, 31, 41–42, 60, 75, 77, 102, 116, 120
Carver, David June, 22, 24, 26–37 *passim*, 40, 44, 45, 46, 48, 49, 55, 69, 137, 139, 140

GENERAL INDEX

Carver, Hally Council, 140
Cashmere Bouquet soap, 116
castor oil, 101
Catholic Church, 6, 77, 81n115, 111n17
Chang Hsuin (general), 97n13, 99n24
Chang-Y-Chun (general), 78n97
Changchow, 138
    Ch'i Shan School, 139, 140
Changshu, 138
Chao, Yuen Ren, 22n25, 25n35, 129, 137–40
Charles, Mr. (physics teacher; Nanking), 22n25, 139
Chen (Chin), Mr./Prof. (Nanking visitor), 36, 40, 50, 72, 75
Chen Chuen Shang (Cheng Chun-sheng), 4, 9, 13
Cheyenne (Wyo.), 18
Chiang Kai-Shek, 11
Chiangli, 35n81
Chicago (Ill.), 18
China, 4–12, 21n20, 27n48, 46, 55n181, 58n1, 62n27, 67n46, 76n90, 91n37, 106n48, 122–26, 127, 142, 143, 144, 145, 147–48
China (ship), 18
China Continuation Committee, 22n23, 36n84, 89n28
China Inland Mission (CIM), 12, 39n102, 61n16, 62n21, 76n87, 87n24, 89n28, 89n32, 91n38, 112n20
China Sunday School Union, 120n12
Chinese Christian Advocate, 28n54
Chinese Christian Intelligencer, The, 4, 9, 13
Chinese language, 4, 5, 13, 22n26, 23, 24, 64, 70, 72n66, 81n119, 90n34, 124, 137–38, 140. *See also under* Roys, Harvey Curtis.
Chinese Medical Missionary Association, 27n46
Chinese Scientific and Industrial Magazine, 38n97
Chinese Scientific Magazine, The, 38n97
Chinkiang, 3, 4, 7, 31, 39n102, 51n162, 59, 109, 115, 118

Chiuchiang. *See* Kiukiang.
Christian Endeavor in China, 6n3, 22n23, 90n33, 106n48
Christian Endeavor Sundays, 25n33
Christian Literature Society, 6n3
Christmas, 56, 57, 81, 91, 92, 105, 116, 121
Church Missionary Society, 46n141, 108n5, 114n29
church services, 28, 30, 32–40 *passim*, 44, 45, 48, 49, 52, 58, 62, 71, 72, 73, 76, 80, 81, 84, 86, 88, 92, 95, 97, 103, 104, 105, 106, 110, 114, 115, 119, 120, 127. *See also* communion services.
CIM. *See* China Inland Mission.
Cincinnati (Ohio), 111n16
cinema, 29
circumcision, 101
Cixi, Empress of China, 6, 7, 140, 147, 148
Clinton, Jacob Mancil, 20
clothing. *See* dress.
Clough (Cluff), Emma S., 89
Coldwater (Mich.), 18
Colorado (ship), 8
Columbia (S.C.), 3
communication(s), 4, 18–19n10
communion services, 32, 58, 110
Communism & Communists, 11, 12, 125, 128
concessions, 142, 144, 147
Confucianism, 66, 124
Confucius, 27n48, 43, 124, 127
Cook, Frederick Albert, 92n47
cookbook, Nanking, 41n114, 48n150, 56n185, 57n190, 69n54, 81n116, 102n33, 114n27
cooking & baking, 62, 63, 80. *See also* food.
cooks (servants), 12, 32, 75, 108n4, 125, 127
Cooper, E. J., 89n32
Cooper, Margaret Palmer, 89
Crawford, Oliver C., 71
croquet, 34, 35, 38

159

GENERAL INDEX

Da Djung Ting (bell temple), 68
Da sz fu (servant), 80
dancing, 35, 47n146, 130
David, King of Israel, 81
Davidson, Dorothy Williams, 21n20, 28n52, 29n57, 118n7
Davidson College, 106n48
Davis, Alice (daughter of J.W.), 30n58, 79
Davis, Alice I. Schmucker, 30n58
Davis, John (son of J.W.), 30n58
Davis, John Wright, 30, 43, 45, 49, 50, 51, 53, 54n175, 55, 56, 65, 67, 68, 71, 79, 87n22
Davis family, 30
deeds (documents), 145–47
Dennis, Herbert E., 27n46
Dennis, Josette Hilda Beebe, 27n46, 92, 93, 101, 109n9
Derry, Miss (Kuling friend), 97
Desire of Ages, The (White), 20
Dexter, Mrs. (Kuling widow), 34
Ding Ming-wong, 65
diphtheria, 126
Disciples of Christ, 5, 6n3, 54n178, 68n50, 81n115, 94n4
divorce, 27n49
Djang Yuan-shan, 49, 140
Djao Dzeng Wei, 45
Djo, Mr. (University of Nanking faculty), 80
Djo Sein Sen, 80
dolls, 92, 112, 116
dominoes, 35, 36, 75
Dong (tailor), 107
donkeys, 26, 29n57, 72
Donovan, Mr. (Nanking friend), 92
Dragon Boat Festival (*Duanwu*), 28
dress (clothing), 26, 92, 95, 112
Drum Tower (*Gu Lou*), 30, 68, 116
Drummond, Emma Frances Lane, 26n38
Drummond, W. J., 26n38, 77
Drummond family, 26, 28, 43
Dubois, Théodore. *The Seven Last Words of Christ*, 110
DuBose, Elizabeth Capers Zemp, 88
DuBose, Hampden Coit, 88n26
DuBose, Palmer Clisby, 88

Duff, J. Arthur, 22n21, 63n30, 141, 144, 147, 149
Duff, Jeanie Woodrow Woodbridge (Jean), 12, 22, 36n85, 41n114, 60n14, 63n30, 84, 89, 95, 97, 105, 107, 108, 112, 115, 117, 118, 119, 127, 141n1
Duff, John L., 86, 141n1, 142, 150
Duff, Margaret Ostler, 86, 142
Duff family, 8, 61n18, 63, 150
Dzeng Wen Djen Gung, 50n158

Easter, 69, 94, 108
eclipse (lunar), 112
Eddy, George Sherwood, 111
  Pilgrimage of Ideas, 111n17
Edith (American friend), 51
Educational Association of China, 28n54, 38n97, 94n4
Egbert, Dennis, 25, 50, 52, 69, 72, 119–20
Egbert, Hazel, 72, 119–20
electricity, 5, 54, 71, 99n25, 102
Elliott, Henrietta Rose Spitzer, 62
Elliott, Thomas Maxwell, 62n25
Emerald Grotto, 37, 39, 62, 97
English (academic subject), 23, 24, 28, 29, 139
English language, 8, 13, 22n26, 23, 125, 138, 139
Epworth League, 114
Evangelical Association of North America, 103n38
Evangelistic Association, 90n33
Evans, H. F., 41n114, 74n80, 84, 85, 102, 103, 106, 108
Evans, Mrs. H. F., 41n114, 113
Evans, Mary L., 41n114
Evans, Philip, 41n114
Evans family, 41, 74, 84, 92, 114
Ewing, John, 111n17
Exner, Max Joseph, 62

famine, 21n20, 67, 68n50, 125
Fayan Wenyi, 116n37
Fearon, Dora Christian, 35
Fenn, Courtenay Hughes, 81
Fenn, William Purviance, 81n119

finances/salaries/money, 79, 81, 86, 102n34, 145–46. *See also under* Roys, Harvey Curtis.
fireworks, 30
floods, 75, 76, 125
flowers, 24n29, 87, 94, 152
Fong, Dr. (Kuling guest), 36
Foochow
    Hwa Nan Women's College, 68n46
    Medical Mission Hospital, 115n31
    Union Theological Seminary, 68n46
food, 8, 12, 32, 39, 70, 75, 79, 93, 94, 95, 96, 97, 103, 108, 124, 125, 128, 140, 142
Foreign Christian Mission, 94n4, 104n40
"42" (game), 36
France, 21n20
Franklin, Benjamin. *Autobiography*, 139
Fredericksburg (Va.), 4
French language, 3, 4
Fryer, John, 38, 41
Fukien Christian University (Fuzhou, Fujian), 112n20
Fung-shui (spirits), 144, 148

Gain, Theodore, S.J., 77
games, 21, 37, 84, 108. *See also* athletics; ball games; croquet; dominoes; "42"; golf; tennis.
Gao (pastor in Nanking), 81n116
gardening, 69, 94, 95
Garrett, Frank, 90, 107n3
Garrett, Lawrence, 90n33
Garrett, Margaret ("Mardie"). *See* Smythe, Margaret.
Garrett, Verna, 90n33
Garrett family, 107
Gaunt, Thomas, 108
Gaunt, Mrs. Thomas, 108
Gaynor, Lucy Alice, 83, 99n22
General Electric Company, 54n177
"Gentle Jesus, Meek and Mild" (hymn), 89, 105
German language, 4, 76n88, 139
Germany & Germans, 4, 21n20, 54n177, 73n72, 111n17
Gilbert, Alvin W., 76, 103n36, 129

Gilbert, Mrs. Alvin W., 76n88, 103, 113, 129
Gilbert, Alvin (son), 76n88
Gilbert, Edmund, 76n88
Gilbert, Jeanette, 76n88
Gilbert, Katherine, 76n88
Gilbert family, 121
Gill, John Monro Banister, 26, 28, 30, 31, 41, 42, 49, 59, 72, 75, 77, 78
Ginling College. *See under* Nanking.
Girl of the Limberlost, A (Stratton-Porter), 33, 34, 36n89
golf, 35
Gongping Ye (Ernie), 59n9, 69n51, 78n97, 137
Good Earth, The (Buck), 125
Gordon, Charles George, 143
Gordon, Samuel Dickey, 86, 90n33
    Quiet Talks on Power, 86n17, 89
    Quiet Talks on Prayer, 86
Gore, Abby, 18
Gore, Ella Roys, 18, 36, 41, 51
Gouv. Jaeschke (ship), 74
Gracey, Wilbur Tirrell, 26, 76n88, 77–78
Grand Rapids (Mich.), 4, 5, 17
Grant, J. S., 34, 76, 80, 81
Gray, Alfred V., 69n54
Gray, Minnie Moore, 69
Great Books as Life-Teachers (Hillis), 31
Great Britain. *See* Britain.
Great Republic (ship), 8
Grier, Henrietta B. Donaldson (Nettie), 86
Gu Lou. *See* Drum Tower.
Guangxi (province), 10

habit, 72, 90
Haden, Robert Allen, 79
Halley's comet, 19, 24, 25
Hallowe'en celebrations, 90, 113
Hamilton, Ernest Adolph, 114
"Hang Up the Baby's Stocking" (song), 91
Hangchow, 7, 57n190, 109
Hankin, Betsy Riggs, 122
Hanson, Perry Oliver, 94
Hant (Kuling friend), 121
Hanyang, 79

Harris, Lucy E., 84
Hart, Virgil C., 81n115
Harvard University, 109n9
Hasrees family, 114
Hawaii, 11
Hayes, Egbert M., 96, 119
Hayes, Eva F. Morris, 119
Hayes, John Newton, 96n10
Hayes, Mercie Melissa Briggs, 96n10
Hayes family, 104, 120
Helen (Coldwater, Mich. friend), 18, 29n56, 37, 39
Helm, Benjamin, 7
Henke (Heuke), Frederick Godorich, 95
Henke (Heuke), Selma Hirsch, 95
Hiawatha, The Song of (Longfellow), 118n7
Higgins-Schmidt, Harriet Beales (Hatty), 5, 18n5
Higgins-Schmidt, Helen, 18
Hillis, Newell Dwight. *Great Books as Life-Teachers*, 31
Hilster, Miss (Nanking friend), 42
Hiltner, Carrie K. Schultz, 102n33
Hiltner, Walter Garfield, 99n22, 102, 113
Hiltner family, 113
Hixsom, Miss (Nanking guest), 107
Hogan, Judith A. Stevenson (Judy), 1–3, 63n30, 71n64, 122, 123, 125, 127–28, 129
holidays (Chinese), 43, 45, 66. *See also* Dragon Boat Festival; Moon Festival; New Year's Day.
"Home, Sweet Home" (song), 140
Homer. *The Odyssey*, 118n7
Hong, Mr. & Mrs. (Nanking guests), 72
Hong Bin, 48
Hong Kong, 11, 91n37, 142
Hong Xinquan, 10
Honolulu (Hawaii), 19, 91n37
horseback riding, 28, 42, 44, 48, 52, 64, 65, 72, 73n72, 74, 113, 127
hospitals, 13, 64, 81n116, 83n2, 99n22, 125, 150
Houston, Matthew Hale, 7
Houston family, 58n3
Hsüan T'ung (Pu-Yi), Emperor, 76, 148

Huaian, 103n36
Hughes, Jennie Van Name, 64
Hummel, Anna May, 28–29n55, 54, 115
Hummel, June, 54n176, 115n35
Hummel, Mildred Stuart, 28, 35, 42, 46, 49, 54n176, 78n102, 86, 92, 103, 104, 112, 118
Hummel, William Frederick, 28, 31, 32, 33, 34, 35, 36, 39, 41, 42, 46, 49, 54n176, 67, 69, 70, 74, 75, 80
Hummel family, 92
Hung Hsiu-ch'üan, 142–43
hunting, 49, 50, 64, 105, 108, 117, 119, 127
Hutcheson, Allen Carrington, 99n22
Hyde, Miss (Kuling friend), 86, 97
hymns & hymn-singing, 20, 28, 32, 33, 34, 35, 39, 89, 105
Hynds, Iva M., 99, 100, 103

I.S.C. (International School in China), 103, 112, 113, 117, 118n3
"I Think When I Read That Sweet Story of Old" (hymn), 89
India, 9, 67n46, 111n17, 127
infanticide, 65n37, 123, 125, 127
Inslee, Elias Brown, 7
International Missionary Alliance, 89n28
Iowa, 18
Itō Hirobumi, Prince, 92n43

Jacksonville (Fla.), 56n185
Japan, 9, 11, 20, 21, 35n79, 67n46, 78n97, 89, 91n37, 92n43, 125, 148
Jardine Hulk (ship), 99
Jefferson, Charles Edward. *Things Fundamental*, 71
Jesus Christ, 10, 143
Jews, 27n48, 111n17
jinrikisha. *See* rickshaw.
Johns Hopkins University & Hospital, 22n25, 90n36, 93
Johnson, Miss E. C., 62n21
Johnson, Misses (Kuling friends), 62
Johnston, Annie Fellows, 131n1
Johnston, Sarah M. Black, 112

GENERAL INDEX

Jordan, Miss A. B., 97
Joshua (Israelite leader), 143

Kay, Mrs. Dr. (shipboard friend), 20
Kentucky, 8
Kerikeri (New Zealand), 149
Kessler, Lawrence D., 10, 35n80, 74n76, 95n6
Ketler, Isaac Conrad. *The Tragedy of Paotingfu*, 73
Kiang Tse, 75
Kiangnan Provincial College. *See under* Nanking.
Kiangsi (province), 141
Kiangsu (province), 7
Kiangyin, 35n80, 55n179, 87n22, 95n6
King, Margaret, 89
Kingsing (ship), 59, 60
Kingsley, Charles. *Water Babies. The Lido River* (poem), 139
Kiukiang, 31, 32, 39, 40, 60, 64n32, 97, 112, 141, 142, 145, 147, 148, 151
    Elizabeth Shelton Danforth Hospital, 64
    William Nast College, 60on12
kiwi (fruit), 8, 149
Kobe (Japan), 21
Korea, 35n79, 35n84, 58n1, 73n72, 87n24, 89, 92n43
Korea (ship), 90
Kostroma (Russia), 127
Kuang Hsü, Emperor, 140
Kuling, 6, 8, 13, 31, 32, 41n114, 56n185, 59, 61n18, 84, 86, 88, 97, 99, 111, 121, 125, 141–52
    CIM School (Hudson Taylor School), 12, 39, 62, 63
    Cradle Rock, 32, 33, 35
    Duff (J.L.) & Company, 32n71, 61n18, 63n30, 150
    Hankow Gorge, 63
    hotel, 32n71, 61n18, 63n30, 150
    Russian Valley, 33
    Water Falls, 37, 38, 111
Kung, Mr. (tutor), 124
Kupfer, Carl Frederick, 60on12
Kupfer, Lydia Krill, 60on12
Kupfer family, 60

Lacy, Emma Nind, 120
Lacy, William Henry, 120
Ladies Home Journal, 29
Langdon family, 33. *See also* Longden.
Lao Dai (rickshaw boy), 40, 75
Lao Tse, 127
LaQuen, Mr. (Kuling friend), 32, 33
Lasell, Ruth, 114
Lasell, Sidney L., 114
"Leaning on the Everlasting Arms" (hymn), 18n6
"Legend of the Bleeding Heart, The," 26, 131–36
Lemon, Mr. (Nanking decedent), 46
Levering, Joshua, 108
Lewis, Robert E., 91, 92n45, 93
Lewis, William Sealey, 48
Li Yüan-hung, 99n24
Lien Hwa Dong, 40, 111, 151
lightning, 120–21
Lincoln, Abraham, 139
Lindsay, Mabel Fishe, 62, 87
Lindsay, W. W., 62n21, 87n24
Lindsay family, 62
Linge, Miss (shipboard friend), 20
Little, Edward S., 8, 61n18, 141, 142, 143, 144–49
Little, Ella C. Davidson, 35n80, 87n22
Little, Lacy L., 35n80
Little family, 35, 38
Little Orphan Island, 151
Little Women (Alcott), 118n7
London Missionary Society, 79n103
Longden, Alice, 33n72, 37, 88, 93
Longden, Wilbur C., 33n72
Longden family, 33, 35, 36, 38, 59
Longfellow, Henry Wadsworth. *The Song of Hiawatha*, 118n7
Loong Wo (boat), 64
loquats (peepaws), 96
Los Angeles (Calif.), 99n22
love, 42, 59, 64, 65, 66, 127, 128
Lu, Mrs. T. T., 63n31
Lucas, Grace M., 41
Luke, Jemima T., 89n30
Lushan Mountains, 8, 141, 142, 147
Luther, Mr. (Nanking guest), 121

GENERAL INDEX

Lutheran Church, 73
Lyon, David Willard, 22

McAlister (Okla.), 1
McCloy, Charles Harold, 117n1
McCloy, Emma, 117n1
McCloy, William A. (Billy), 117
McDowell, Clotilda Lynn, 67
McDowell, William Fraser, 67
Machiavelli, Niccolò, 142
Machin. *See* Macklin.
McKee, Abby Porter Ketchum, 88n25
McKee, Augusta List, 88
McKee, Irwin William, 88n25
McKee, Samuel Clark, 88
McKee, Sydney, 88n25
McKee, William James, 88n25
Macklin, Alice, 113
Macklin (Machin), William Edward, 68, 81n115
Macklin family, 104
mail (postal service), 34, 37, 40, 41, 48, 51, 53, 55n183, 65, 77, 78, 86
malaria, 8, 142
Malone, George Howard, 48n150
Malone, Mrs. George Howard, 48n150
Malone, Mrs. H. W., 48n150
Malone family, 48
Manchuria, 55n181, 148
manic-depressive condition, 3, 47n146
Marble, Miss (Kuling friend), 112
Martin, Arthur Wesley, 28n53, 55n180
Martin, Mrs. Arthur Wesley, 28n53
Martin, Arthur (son), 28n53
Martin, Elizabeth, 28n53
Martin, Frances, 28n53
Martin, Mildred, 28n53
Martin family, 28, 29, 30, 31, 32, 55, 116
mathematics, 76n88, 104n40, 106n48, 138
measles, 94
Medical Missionary Society of China, 104n40
Meigs, Mrs. (Nanking missionary), 94n4, 119n7
Meigs, F. E., 94n4
Meigs family, 94

Mellin's Baby Food, 90
Mencius (Mêng-tzǔ), 124
Mendenhall, Mrs. (Kuling resident), 36
mental health/illness, 2–3, 82n120, 129–30. *See also under* Roys, Grace Woodrow Woodbridge.
Methodist Episcopal Church, 5, 6n3, 28n53, 28n55, 48n149, 55n180, 64n32, 67n45, 68n48, 81n115, 87n23, 91n38, 94n3, 97n12, 111n16, 112n20, 120n12
    Woman's Foreign Missionary Society, 67n46
Methodist Episcopal Church, South, 5, 6n3, 47n146
Methodists (unspecified), 12, 28n54, 32, 36, 52, 54n178, 60n12, 64n32, 68n46, 95, 115
Mexico, 145–46
Miao (teacher), 138
Michigan, 25n31, 57n189, 96n10, 119
Michigan, University of (Ann Arbor), 3, 4, 17n2, 19, 33, 35n81, 64n32, 119n10, 120
milk, 8, 63n31, 90n35
Millward, Jennie Fitzgerald, 92n44, 115n31
Millward, Martha Ann, 92n44, 117
Millward, Mary Frances, 92
Millward, William, 92n44, 115n31
Millward family, 115
missionaries, 4, 6–13, 26n42, 61n18, 67n45, 77n95, 81n115, 90n34, 123, 125–27, 128, 142, 143, 144, 148
    Chinese attitudes towards, 7, 13, 63n31, 77n95, 123, 142, 147
    relation with Chinese, 12, 27n48, 36n88, 72, 105, 124, 125–27, 128
Missionary Review of the World, 86n17
Mississippi, 47n147
Moffett, Cara Lena (Carrie), 87
Moffett, Kate Hall Rodd, 87n22
Moffett, Lacy Irvine, 87n22
Molland, Miss (Kuling friend), 87
Molland, Charles Edwin, 87n23
Molland, Lily Webb, 87

money. *See* finances.
Moon Festival, 40, 42
Mooney, Annie Elizabeth Wilkinson, 48n147, 79
Mooney, James Potter, 79
Morgan, Lorenzo Seymour, 58n2
Morgan, Ruth Bennett, 58
Moscow (Russia), 127
moths, 33n74, 36, 37
Muir, Gertrude M., 91
Murray, Andrew. *With Christ in the School of Prayer*, 18
music, 19, 29, 37, 41, 42, 45, 70. *See also* organ; piano; singing *and under* Roys, Grace Woodrow Woodbridge.
Myers, Philip Van Ness. *A General History* . . . , 139–40

Nagasaki (Japan), 21
Nanchang, 96n10, 141
Nankang Pass, 33, 36, 38
Nanking, 5, 11, 13, 21n20, 22, 25, 26n44, 31, 35n79, 40, 57n189, 66n42, 80, 97n13, 99n24, 143
    Adeline Smith Home & School, 6n3, 68n48, 91 101n28
    American Friends Mission, 81n115
    Beggars Caves, 37, 42
    Bible Teachers Training School for Women, 88n26
    Disciples Mission, 81n115
    Disciples of Christ (Christian) College, 54n178, 94n4
    Drum Tower Hospital, 58n3
    Examination Halls, 44
    Feng Rweng Men (gate), 25n34, 50n158
    Foreign Hospital, 101, 102n33
    Ginling College, 5–6, 12
    Han Si Meng (ruins), 50, 55, 69
    Hillcrest School, 12, 21n20, 27n46, 28n53, 29n57, 38n101, 41n114, 47n147, 54n174, 54n178, 60n11, 60n14, 67n43, 76n88, 90n33, 92n46, 94n4, 95n7, 104n40, 105n44, 106n48, 107n1, 107n3, 109n9, 114n27, 115, 118n3, 118n7
    Hu Bei Zhai School, 26, 69, 77
    Hwa Yuan, 70
    Kiangnan Provincial College, 5, 22n25, 26, 31n63, 36n88, 40, 70, 72n66, 75, 76, 80, 120, 137–40
    Ladies Missionary Society, 45, 67, 104, 114
    Lotus Lake (Hswein Wu Hu), 25, 50, 108n4
    Methodist Episcopal Mission, 81n115, 118
    Ming tombs, 26, 69, 70
    Mission Catholique, 81n115
    Philander Smith Hospital, 27n46
    Presbyterian Mission, 81n115
    Presbyterian School, 56, 81
    Quakerage, 48, 81
    Qingliangshan Park, 116
    San Pai Lau (restaurant), 96
    San Sen Low, 75
    Shia Kwan (West Gate; district), 24n29, 29, 30, 31, 41, 42, 43, 44, 46, 50n158, 51n162, 66, 67, 75, 77, 99, 105, 150
    Sing Djai ko (YMCA night school), 45
    South Gate, 69, 77
    Spirit Valley (temple), 49, 72
    Suqian Ren Ji Hospital, 58n3
    Tai Ping Lu (Hua Pai Lou), 78
    Tai Ping Men, 50n158, 69, 80
    Theological Seminary, 30n58, 65n38, 68n46, 71n61, 87n22, 106n48, 115
    Union Language School, 88n26, 90, 115, 120
    University, 5, 6, 21n20, 23, 27, 28n53, 28n54, 28n55, 29, 36n88, 40, 41, 44, 45, 46, 54n178, 55n180, 68n50, 74n77, 78, 80, 88n26, 92, 93n1, 94n4, 95n5, 97n15, 99n22, 104n39, 122, 128
    YMCA, 22n24, 81n115, 106n48, 110, 117
    Yuch'ang Hsiang Tailors, 138

GENERAL INDEX

Nanking, Rape of (1937), 78n97, 99n22
Nanking Association, 12, 25, 48, 55, 59, 67, 70, 71, 96, 110, 121
Nanyang Industrial Exposition (1910), 5, 6, 24, 27, 30, 31, 42, 44, 45, 46, 53, 54n177, 104n39
Nashville (Tenn.), 22n25, 139
National Clock Co., 114
Nebraska, 18
Nevada, 18
New Orleans (ship), 31, 78
New Year's Day (Chinese), 40n113, 59n8, 61
New York City, 8
New Zealand, 149
Niles, Frank Sergeant, 109
Niles, Margaret Hyde Beebe, 27n46, 109, 113
Ningpo. Trinity College, 46n141
Norman (Oklahoma), 1, 3, 128
    Central State Mental Hospital, 2
North Carolina, 35n80
North China Union Language School (Peking), 25n35, 28n54, 106n48, 140

Odyssey, The (Homer), 118n7
oil (fuel), 71n65, 99
Oklahoma, University of (Norman), 1, 3, 129
Olympic Games, 62n27
opium, 21n20
Opium Wars, 21n20
Oregon, 126
Oregonian (ship), 8
organ, 26n45, 35, 76, 140

Pacific Mail Steamship Company, 19n10, 90n37
Pacific Ocean, 4, 19
Palmer, Margaret. *See* Cooper, Margaret.
Palo Alto (Calif.), 63n30
Panama, 8
patience, 52, 114
Patterson, Anne Houston (Annie), 58
Paul, the Apostle, 142
Paxton, John Wardlaw, 118
Paxton, Una Edith Hall, 118n5

peanuts, 63
peepaws (loquats), 96
Peking, 35n81, 96n10, 143, 147, 148
    Union Medical College, 96n10
Perkins, Henry P., 103
Peter, Eleanor Elizabeth Whipple, 97n16, 108
Peter, Jane, 97
Peter, William Wesley, 97n16, 108, 113
Peters, Miss (Nanking friend), 68, 110
Peters, Mrs. (Nanking friend), 103, 113
Peters family, 113
Pettus, Sarah Lydia DeForest, 25n35, 70, 140
Pettus, William Bacon, 25, 33, 140
Pettus family, 36
Philippines, 67n46
philosophy (academic subject), 22n25
photography, 65n36
physics (academic subject), 1, 4, 5, 22n25, 32, 122, 129, 139
piano, 2, 26, 27, 37, 44, 60n11, 76n89, 140
picnics, 30, 33, 36, 37, 39, 41, 62, 70, 97, 99
pigtails. *See* queues.
Pilgrimage of Ideas (Eddy), 111n17
Pittsburgh (Penn.), 111n17
plague, 8, 55n181
pneumonia, 116
Pound, Ezra. *ABC of Reading*, 109n9
Poyang Lake, 33, 141
prayer, 23, 30, 40, 49, 51, 52, 55, 62, 63, 64, 65, 69, 73, 74, 114, 121
prayer meetings, 45, 70, 104, 107, 115, 118
Presbyterian Board of Foreign Missions, 7
Presbyterians (unspecified), 1, 5, 7, 12, 22n23, 54n178, 81n115, 106n48
Presbyterians, Northern, 6n3, 25n36, 26n38, 29n57, 49n155, 50n157, 61n20, 69n54, 71n61, 87n23, 89n28, 93n1, 96n10, 102n33
Presbyterians, Southern, 3, 4, 7–8, 30n58, 35n80, 47n146, 47n147, 48n147, 58n2, 58n3, 79n104, 79n108, 87n22, 88n26, 103n36, 118n5
Preston, Miss (Nanking resident), 105

166

GENERAL INDEX

Price, Francis Wilson (Frank), 106n48, 118n7
Price, Julian, 106n48
Price, Philip Francis, 106
Price family, 108
Pruitt, Ida. *A Daughter of Han*, 122
psychology (academic subject), 22n25
Pu-Yi, Emperor. *See* Hsüan T'ung.
Purple Gold Mountain (Tzu Ging Shan), 28, 29n57, 68n50, 72n67

Quakers, 81n115, 81n116, 83n2
queues, 10, 26n42, 77, 78, 81
Quiet Talks on Power (Gordon), 86n17, 89
Quiet Talks on Prayer (Gordon), 86

rabbits, 2
Rachel (Nanking friend), 113
railroad. *See* trains.
Randolph-Macon College (Ashland, Va.), 118n4
rheumatic fever, 2
Rhodes, Cecil John, 142
Ribble, Margaret Elaine Stevenson, 1, 2–3
Ricci, Matteo, S.J., 81n115
Richmond College (Richmond, Va.), 22n25
rickshaw(s), 12, 20, 27, 40, 42, 63, 68, 72, 73, 113, 116, 125, 127
Riggs, Charles, 122, 126
Riggs, Edith Clara. *See* Barakat, Edith.
Roberts, Isaacher Jacox, 10
Robertson, Clarence Hovey, 140
Rosary, The (Barclay), 62
Ross (Rosse), John, 93
Rotary Clubs, 142
Round Table (legends), 118n7
Rowe, Caroline, 60n11
Rowe, David N., 60n11
Rowe, Harry (son of H.F.), 60n11
Rowe, Harry Fleming, 60n11, 77, 108
Rowe, Louise, 60n11
Rowe, Maggie Nelson, 60, 101, 104, 108
Rowe family, 60, 63
Roys, David, 3

Roys, Emmeline Beales, 4, 5, 17, 18, 33, 34, 35, 36, 37
Roys, Grace Woodbridge (Gracie), 1, 2, 98n19, 117, 121n15, 129
Roys, Grace Woodrow Woodbridge, *passim*
  character & temper, 3, 56, 60, 61, 66, 107, 128, 129
  childhood, 51n162
  Chinese name, 29
  mental health & illnesses, 2–3, 5, 13, 23n27, 30n58, 43n125, 46n144, 47–55, 59, 74n82, 82n120, 114n28, 128, 129–30
  miscarriage, 61n19, 73n71, 74n78
  as musician, 2, 26n45, 27, 44, 76
  pessary, 101, 102, 103, 104, 106
  pictures, 41, 65n36
  pregnancies, 70, 72, 74, 79n106, 83–84, 98, 99, 117, 120
  sexuality, 3, 47n146
  "Songs for Children" (paper), 113, 117, 118n3
  as teacher, 3, 5, 6n3, 12, 39, 62n24, 101n28, 116, 129
Roys, Graham, 4, 5, 18n5, 30, 33, 35, 36, 37, 41, 43, 45, 51, 53, 59, 62, 66, 71, 82
Roys, Harvey Curtis, *passim*
  character & temper, 49n152, 58, 59, 60, 62, 66
  Chinese language study, 5, 24, 25, 32, 41, 65, 79, 80, 83
  clothing, 26, 95
  education, 4, 17n2, 33
  faith & religion, 18, 19, 23, 33, 35, 46, 48, 49, 52, 55, 59, 65, 72
  finances & pay, 53, 65, 80
  handiness, 31n61, 71n65, 75, 76, 99, 119
  as missionary, 4, 5, 67, 70
  as photographer, 65, 75
  reading, 19, 20, 21, 32, 33, 34, 37, 38, 43, 62, 70, 71, 74, 86n17, 88, 89
  as teacher, 1, 3, 5, 23, 25, 26, 28, 29, 30, 32, 40, 41, 44, 45, 55, 58, 59, 65, 66, 67, 69, 70, 122, 129, 137

Roys, Harvey Curtis, Jr., 1, 2, 3, 98n19, 117n2, 120
Roys, Margaret Elizabeth (Margaret Louise). *See* Stevenson, Margaret Elizabeth
Roys, Richard Dennis, 2–3, 12, 50n160, 54n174, 65n36, 98–121 *passim*
Roys family data, 82
Russell, Anne. *See* Taylor, Anne.
Russell, Elizabeth Mai Hutchison, 70, 76
Russell, Wallace Boyd, 23, 27, 46, 55, 68, 70, 71, 78
Russell family, 5, 48, 55, 56, 58n4, 71, 81
Russia, 92n43, 111n17, 127–28

Sabbath observance, 18, 19, 20. *See also* church services.
St. Petersburg (Russia), 127
salaries. *See* finances.
Sampson, John Russell, 57n190
San Francisco (Calif.), 5, 8, 18n10, 91n37
Sarah (Kuling friend), 121
Sarvis, David L. (Davie), 56n185, 94, 121
Sarvis, Guy Walter, 56n185, 89
Sarvis, Mary Alice, 56
Sarvis, Pearl Maude Taylor, 56n185, 87, 89
Sarvis family, 90, 121
scarlet fever, 1, 2, 117n2
Scott, Thomas Arnold, 73
Searle, Mr. (Nanking guest), 119
sedan chairs, 13, 60, 63, 111n15, 125, 151–52
selfishness, 59, 60n15, 61, 107
servants, 12, 22n26, 23, 32, 51n162, 69, 91, 102, 109, 119, 125, 126, 127, 150. *See also* cooks.
Settlemeyer, Charles Spurgeon, 54n178, 94n4
Settlemeyer, Charles William, 54n178
Settlemeyer, Edna Kurz, 54n178, 70, 94n4
Settlemeyer, George Kurz, 54n178
Settlemeyer family, 54, 55
Seven Last Words of Christ, The (Dubois), 110
Seventh Day Adventists, 20n13
Shakespeare, William

Merchant of Venice, The, 118
Midsummer Night's Dream, A, 119n7
Shanghai, 5, 6, 8, 12, 13, 21n20, 22, 26, 30, 36n84, 38n97, 40, 41, 51, 56, 57, 58, 62n21, 65, 66, 73, 74, 77, 78, 79, 86n16, 87n23, 87n24, 89n28, 90, 91n37, 91n38, 93n1, 96, 98, 100, 103n38, 105, 106, 107, 108n4, 109n7, 111n16, 112n20, 114n29, 119, 127, 138, 143, 145, 146, 147, 149
American School, 12
Holy Trinity Cathedral (Anglican), 46n141
Lincoln House, 78
Union Church, 58
YMCA school, 79
Shao Sao (servant), 117
Shaw, Ella Cecelia, 6n3, 68n48, 91n38, 91n41
Shaw, Ima, 91
Shen (Changchow teacher), 139
Shields, Ella Randolph Page, 47n147, 108
Shields, Evy, 48n147
Shields, Randolph Tucker (1877–1958), 47, 48, 95
Shields, Randolph Tucker (1910–1997), 48n147
Shields family, 48
Shih-Ch'un (student), 138
Shih Li Pu, 97
Shih Mei Yu. *See* Stone, Mary.
Shoo Pau (servant), 101
Showalter, Anthony Johnson, 18n6
Sichuan (province), 81n116
Sinchang, 106n48
singing, 19, 35, 36, 92, 95. *See also* hymns.
"Sir Gareth of Orkney" (play), 109
Sloan, Thomas Dwight, 54, 99, 100, 101, 102, 104, 105, 108, 114, 120
smallpox, 114
Smith, Edward Huntington, 8–9
Smith, Grace Wilbur Thomas, 8
Smythe, Lewis, 90n33
Smythe, Margaret Garrett (Mardie), 90n33
Snell, John Abner, 47

GENERAL INDEX

snow, 55, 62, 94, 104, 118, 119
social gospel, 111n17
Society for the Diffusion of Christian and General Knowledge among the Chinese, 104n40
Sons (Buck), 124
Soochow, 13, 47, 48, 50, 51, 52, 53, 54, 55, 57, 74, 79, 87n22, 88n26, 91, 96n10, 104, 138
    Big Pagoda, 79
    Elizabeth Blake Hospital, 47n146, 79n104
    Haden House, 56
    Tish-Ying-I-yueiu, 74
    University, 79
South Carolina, 48n147, 57n189, 88n26
sports. *See* athletics.
sprue (disease), 118n4
Spurling, Hilary. *Pearl Buck in China*, 122, 126, 127
Stalin, Joseph, 128
Stevenson, Judith A. *See* Hogan, Judith.
Stevenson, Margaret Elaine. *See* Ribble, Margaret.
Stevenson, Margaret Elizabeth Roys, 1, 2–3, 12, 25n33, 33n74, 35n83, 41n114, 42n120, 46n143, 47n146, 47n147, 49n152, 56n185, 61n19, 64n32, 65n37, 74n80, 79n106, 82n120, 83n1, 84–121 *passim*, 129, 130, 141n1
Stevenson, William Robert, 1, 42n120, 111n17
Stewart, Anna May White, 88, 89
Stewart, William Ramsey, 88n26, 89
Stewart family, 35n79, 89
Stone, Mary (Shih Mei Yu), 64, 86
Story of the Other Wise Man, The (Van Dyke), 105
Stowe, Everett M., 112
Stratton-Porter, Gene. *A Girl of the Limberlost*, 33, 34, 36n89
strawberries, 69, 71, 95, 96
Strobel and Wilkin Company, 92n47
Stuart, Alcy Orma, 28n54, 34, 35, 39
Stuart, Anna May, 28n54, 34, 35, 39
Stuart, David Todd, 8n11

Stuart, George Arthur, 28n54, 74
Stuart, George Golden, 28, 34, 35, 38, 41
Stuart, John Leighton, 7n11
Stuart, John Linton, 7
Stuart, Mildred. *See* Hummel, Mildred.
Stuart, Vera Alice, 28n54, 34
Stuart, Warren Houston, 7–8n11
Stuart family, 32, 33, 34, 35, 36, 37, 41, 48, 51, 57, 67, 69, 78
Student Volunteer Movement, 4
Sun Yat-Sen, 10–11, 99n24
Sun Yat-Sen Revolution, 10, 11, 26n42, 26n44, 27n47, 31n66, 34n77, 60n11, 76–78, 79, 80, 83n2, 125
Swenson, Gladys Virginia, 76, 77, 97
Swenson, H., 28
Swenson, K. Moll, 29n55, 76n87, 97n14
swimming, 32, 33, 34, 35, 37, 38, 39, 72, 73, 74, 85, 111
SYC (Student Y in China), 44
Sydenstricker, Absalom, 58n3
Sydenstricker, Caroline Stulting (Carie), 118n4, 123, 124
Sydenstricker, Pearl. *See* Buck, Pearl.
Sydenstricker family, 4, 9, 109n7, 118

Taft, Marcus Lorenso, 111
Taft, William Howard, 111n16
Tai Chin Gong Miao, 74
Tai-Dzu, Emperor, 30n59
Tai Ping rebellion, 10, 142–43
Taoism, 22n26, 74n76
Taylor, Anne Russell Sampson, 57, 98n17, 109
Taylor, James Hudson, 39n102
Taylor, Richard Vipon, 57n190, 98
tea(s), 12, 29, 30, 32, 35, 36, 37, 38, 42, 43, 52, 55, 62, 63n31, 67, 68, 69, 70, 74, 76, 81, 89, 92, 95, 96, 97, 104, 110, 112, 113, 127, 128
teething, 47n147, 94, 95, 96, 98, 102, 106, 107, 108, 109, 110, 111, 114, 118, 120
telegraph & telegrams, 7, 19n10, 39
telephone, 71n65
Temple of the Clouds, 37

tennis, 6, 12, 23, 25, 27, 28, 29, 30, 33, 34, 35, 37, 38, 41, 44, 45, 52, 69, 71, 73n72, 74, 76, 95, 108, 127, 144
Thanksgiving Day celebrations, 52, 79, 103, 115
"There's a Song in the Air" (hymn), 89, 105
Things Fundamental (Jefferson), 71
Tientsin. YMCA, 140
tiffin, 12, 44, 57, 70, 78, 119
Tilly (Kuling friend), 121
Ting (teacher), 138
Ting Meng-Yu (teacher), 138
toilet training, 93, 97, 103, 105, 108, 110
Tokyo (Japan), 20
Tom (Kuling friend), 121
Tootell, George Thomas, 96
Tragedy of Paotingfu, The (Ketler), 73
trains, 5, 8, 10, 11, 13, 18, 24n29, 31, 47, 51n162, 55n183, 59n10, 75, 79, 80, 91n37, 120, 138
translation(s), 22n26. *See also* Bible translations.
travel, 143
Tsingtau, 73–74, 108
    Pension Luther, 73
typhus, 83n2
Tzu Ging Shan. *See* Purple Gold Mountain.
Tz'u Hsi, Empress. *See* Cixi.

Union of Congregationalists and Presbyterians, 106n48
United States, 8, 9, 10, 21n20, 31n66, 54n177, 90, 111n17, 126, 128, 129, 139
United States Navy, 1

vaccinations, 55
Van Dyke, Henry Jackson. *The Story of the Other Wise Man*, 105
Vaughan, Helen, 99
violin, 37
Virginia, 7, 106n48
Virginia, University of (Charlottesville), 57n190

Walker, Alfred James, 46
Waller, Nancy Thomson, 123, 125
    My Nanking Home, 122
Walley, John, 64n32
Walley, Louise M., 64
Wang Amah, 123
Watch Guard Society. *See* Agassiz Association.
water supply, 71n65
Weber, Carl Maria von. *Seymour* (hymn tune), 89n31
Webster's Collegiate Dictionary, 139
Weldon, Mr. & Mrs. (Kuling friends), 86
Wesley, Charles, 89n31
Westbrook, Mrs. C. Hart, 101
Wharton, Mr. (Kuling friend), 32, 34
White, Ellen Gould Harmon. *The Desire of Ages*, 20
White, Laura M., 6n3, 101, 103
White, Wilbert Webster, 35, 36, 88n26, 89
White Lily Club, 109n9
Whitmore, Frank Beach, 22, 23, 24, 26, 29, 31, 68, 69, 71
whooping cough, 110
Wilkinson, Annie Elizabeth. *See* Mooney, Annie.
Wilkinson, Annie Narcissa Barr, 48n147, 52, 53
Wilkinson, Gretchen, 48n147, 58, 79
Wilkinson, James Richard (1860–1935), 48n147, 49, 50, 52, 53, 54, 55, 74, 91
Wilkinson, James Richard (1892–1955), 48n147, 79
Wilkinson, Martha Rose, 48n147, 79
Wilkinson family, 56, 79
Williams, Charles L. Loos, 109n9
Williams, Dorothy. *See* Davidson, Dorothy.
Williams, Edward Thrasher, 109n9
Williams, John Elias, 29n57, 50n157, 64
Williams, Lilian Cora Caldwell, 21n20, 29n57, 50, 63n31, 68n50, 75n84
    Yesterdays in China, 50n157
Williams, Mary, 21n20, 29n57
Williams, Richard, 21n20, 29n57

Williams, Walter, 21n20, 29n57
Wilson, Franklin, 38n101
Wilson, Janet Woodrow, 60n13, 90n36
Wilson, Joseph Ruggles, 60n13
Wilson, Julia, 38n101, 40n109, 150–52
Wilson, Mary Rowley, 38n101, 95n7, 101, 108, 151
Wilson, Mitchel, 38
Wilson, Robert Orr, 38n101
Wilson, Thomas Woodrow, 3, 60n13, 90n36
Wilson, Wilbur F., 38n101, 95, 101n29, 108, 115n34, 151
Wilson family, 52, 115
With Christ in the School of Prayer (Murray), 18
women, 6, 67n45, 128
Women's Messenger, 6n3
Women's Work, 6n3
wood (fuel), 63, 143, 151
Woodbridge, Casper Ligon, 32
Woodbridge, Charles Jahleel (Charlie), 12, 22n21, 41n114, 60, 84, 85, 89, 97, 105, 107, 108, 115, 118, 119, 127
Woodbridge, Grace Woodrow. *See* Roys, Grace Woodrow Woodbridge.
Woodbridge, Jeanie Wilson Woodrow, 3–4, 37, 40, 47, 50, 51, 53, 54, 55, 57, 60n13, 79n106, 89, 90, 93, 128
Woodbridge, Jeanie Woodrow. *See* Duff, Jeanie.
Woodbridge, John Sylvester, 38, 39, 44, 51, 57, 61, 85, 89
Woodbridge, Louise (Charlotte Louise), 32, 36n85, 37, 39, 44, 48, 51, 52, 53, 57, 58, 69, 70, 78, 85n14, 114
Woodbridge, Mamie, 27
Woodbridge, Samuel Isett (1857–1926), 3–4, 9, 13, 22n26, 27n48, 31n60, 36n85, 37n95, 40n111, 41, 42n120, 43, 45, 47, 51, 54n175, 55, 57, 70, 73, 77n95, 88–89, 90, 93, 96, 98, 100, 105, 106, 115, 116, 119, 124, 128
Woodbridge, Samuel Isett (1886–1973), 27, 33
Woodbridge, Woodrow Wilson, 60
Woodbridge family, 30n58, 32, 34, 35, 36, 37, 38, 39, 51n163, 63n30, 99n21
Woodrow, James, 8, 60n13, 109n9
World War I, 11, 148
World War II, 128
World's Work, 139
Wright, Harold Bell. *The Calling of Dan Matthews*, 20
Wu-chang, 79
Wyoming, 18

Yan Lein Lin (Yang Lein Len), 79
Yang, Grace, 85, 88
Yangchow. *See* Hangchow.
Yangtze River, 3, 8, 13, 22n22, 33n75, 59n10, 75n86, 99n24, 138, 141, 150–51
Yates, Miss (Nanking friend), 103
Yates, Ellen Peck Baskerville, 103n36
Yates, Orville Ford, 103n36
Yellow Sea (Yang-tse-kiang), 22
YMCA, 4, 5, 20, 22n23, 22n25, 25n35, 28n54, 29n57, 31, 35n79, 35–36n84, 37, 38n101, 58n1, 61, 62n25, 62n27, 65n38, 67n45, 79n103, 81n115, 87, 88n25, 91n40, 95n7, 96n10, 97n16, 104n39, 111n17, 117n1
Yokohama (Japan), 3, 8, 20
Yuan Shika, 11
Yuen Ren Chao. *See* Chao, Yuen Ren.
YWCA, 1, 85n10, 97

Zhang Dong Zhai, 59
Zhu Yuanzhang, Emperor, 78n97

Scripture Index

Deuteronomy
33:25 — 17

II Chronicles
16:9 — 89

Job
1:22 — 113

Psalms
1 — 90
19 — 81
91 — 81
103 — 89

Proverbs
23:7 — 81

Matthew
10:16 — 142

John
32

Acts
17:18ff — 142

I & II Corinthians
72

I Corinthians
13:7 — 59

Hebrews
1 — 64

I John
4:18a — 59

Revelation
72

Job — 49, 53

www.ingramcontent.com/pod-product-compliance
Lightning Source LLC
Chambersburg PA
CBHW062037220426
43662CB00010B/1537